SHADOWS
ACROSS THE
SAHARA

Other titles by the same author

The Lost Camels of Tartary

SHADOWS
ACROSS THE
SAHARA

TRAVELS WITH CAMELS FROM
LAKE CHAD TO TRIPOLI

John Hare

CONSTABLE · LONDON

Constable & Robinson Ltd
3 The Lanchesters
162 Fulham Palace Road
London W6 9ER
www.constablerobinson.com

First published in the UK by Constable,
an imprint of Constable & Robinson Ltd 2003

A copy of the British Library Cataloguing in Publication Data
is available from the British Library

ISBN 1-84119-626-6

Printed and bound in the EU

To: HV – for inspiration
Pips – for support
Kate – for everything

(*Top*) Hans Vischer, 1906 (*Bottom*) John Hare, 2001

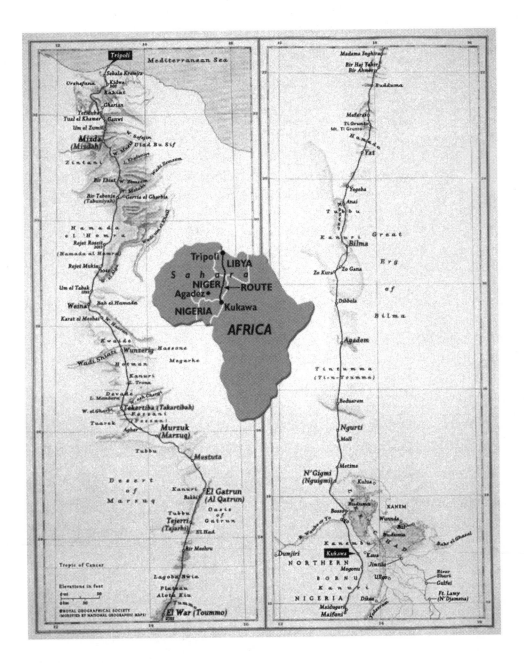

The Great Camel Highway

followed by Vischer in 1906 and Hare in 2001

Do what thy manhood bids thee do, from
    none but self expect applause;
He noblest lives and noblest dies who makes
    and keeps his self-made laws.

All other Life is Living death, a world where
    none but phantoms dwell,
A breath, a wind, a sound, a voice, a tinkling
    of the camel bell.

—   —   —

Wend now thy way with brow serene, fear
    not thy humble tale to tell:
The whispers of the Desert-wind; the Tinkling
    of the camel's bell.

The Kasidah
Richard Burton

Contents

Illustrations

Percy, one of our stalwart team of twenty-five camels
Crossing the river Yobe — the border between Nigeria and Niger
Argali and Ehom skinning a goat, Ngigimi (Niger)
Professor doctoring Argali using Chinese 'needles', Ngigimi (Niger)
Jasper and Johnny plotting the route, Tintumma plateau (Niger)
Sunset in the Sahara
Crossing the Great Erg of Bilma (Niger)
Bilma oasis (Niger)
Cones of salt at Bilma (Niger)
Johnny 'operates' on Jasper's eye
Ancient man's rock art at Yat (Niger)

Dead camel on the treacherous road north of Tummo (Libya)
A Fortnum & Mason hamper arrived (Libya) to brighten Christmas 2001
The old fort Murzuk (Libya)
Mestuta, an uninhabited oasis full of desert jinns (Libya)
Ibrahim Kwaidi (Libya), grandson of Vischer's friend Sheikh Ahmed
Shikou, our Tuareg guide in Libya
A camel's footprint after travelling nearly 2,000 miles
A sheepskin boot for a sore camel's foot
Lake Um el Mar, north of Tekertiba (Libya)
Shadows across the Sahara
The last stretch of the road to Misda (Libya)
Journey's end — Misda (Libya)

* All photographs taken by the author

1

It was a very simple sketch of a forsaken camel. As I stared at it, I was instantly transported back to the bleak, harsh and utterly demanding landscape of the Hamada el Homra, 'the red wilderness' of Libya. The mighty sheet of rock strewn with sharp stones that stretches as a plateau to the north for 180 miles and from the east to west for 360. Treeless, without water or vegetation, swept relentlessly by a bitterly cold north-east wind, it was the last big challenge that lay in front of us before we reached Mizda in northern Libya. It was the final effort on our three-and-a-half-month journey with camels across the Sahara, the Hamada el Homra, a desert described as 'the first in terms of difficulty among all the deserts in the Sahara . . . where shouts and laughter cease and the human voice is drowned.'

The camel is clearly past caring that its companions are leaving it behind. It stands there, a solitary forlorn figure awaiting an inevitable death. The sketch entitled 'Sick camel left behind alone in the Hamada' was drawn by Hanns Vischer, in 1906. He described the scene as follows:

> In crossing the Hamada, one of our camels went sick and had to be abandoned; I cannot think of anything more pathetic than the picture of that animal as it stood motionless looking after the caravan, growing smaller and smaller until it was a mere speck, and was finally lost to sight behind the sky-line.

On 25 January 2002, nearly one hundred years later, we too had a camel in the 'red wilderness' that was utterly exhausted by the 1,500 mile trek. I willed him to continue. I knew that when we escaped the icy grip of the Hamada, we might manage to coax him forward. If the camel reached the well at Tabonia, we would be surrounded by lush vegetation where he could eat, rest and possibly recover. But here, in this pitiless desert, with five days hard slog ahead of us before we reached the edge of the plateau's escarpment, the situation was hopeless.

We had fashioned boots to help him overcome the problem of cracked and swollen feet, first from a sheepskin, which in a day was cut to pieces by razor-sharp stones, then from the stout inner tube of a truck tyre. This kept him going for two more days, but then utter fatigue took hold. He would go no further. I hated doing it, but I knew that now there was no alternative. So we released the poor creature that had served us so well, to an inevitable end.

When Hanns Vischer undertook the journey nearly a hundred years ago, he related that he lost over thirty camels. But Vischer had travelled with a substantial number, and we had a mere twenty-five.

Yet his little sketch, shown to me by his son on a glorious spring day in an apartment overlooking Regent's Park, moved me greatly. Just as the discovery of Hanns Vischer's book over twenty-five years earlier had persuaded me to resolve to try, one day, to undertake the journey that Vischer had made in 1906. I loved his book, with its tale of encounters with terrible desert tracts where no water could be found for days and where oases were few and far between. It gripped me with a wonderful sense of the amazing capacity of a camel to survive in the toughest of surroundings and on the longest of journeys. It told of hostile tribes and marauding Tuareg, all related with a modesty that understates the staggering achievement of bringing freed slaves and stranded pilgrims from Tripoli along an ancient camel road back to the safety of their homes in Nigeria.

It will be of no surprise to those who have lived in northern Nigeria, that the favoured slaves were Hausa, the men for their skill and intelligence, the women for their looks. The road Vischer followed, the Tripoli-Murzuk highway to Borno, carried, and still carries, a great deal of salt from the Niger oasis town of Bilma. But it was, up until the end of the nineteenth century, essentially a slave route and by the late 1850s over two-thirds of the value of the merchandise carried by the caravans plying the road was made up of slaves.

In the nineteenth century every European who travelled this blood-stained road recorded his horror at the thousands of human bones with which it was strewn. They were mostly those of young women and girls, and were particularly numerous around the wells, showing how often the last desperate attempt to reach water had led to death from exhaustion. Only the most robust survived the desert march and these were little better than living skeletons when they reached Murzuk in central Libya. Here they were rested and fattened for the Tripoli market where prime slaves were sold, according to the explorer Major Dixon Denham, at a profit of 500 per cent. Merchants could afford to lose 80 per cent of their human cargo on the journey and still return a profit. Hence the proliferation of human skeletons. Today, the sides of the road are still strewn with bones, the sun-bleached bones of camels. But it remains one of the three great trans-Saharan camel routes, and must be numbered among the oldest highways in the world.

On the road there are long waterless stretches which caravans cross at their peril. But there is a greater certainty of finding water and grazing where they are expected, and in the face of this compelling circumstance neither war nor blackmail nor colonial imperialism has forced the toiling caravans permanently to forsake this desert highway. Instead of slaves, caravans today take camels into Libya to satisfy a Libyan predilection for camel meat. So the camel road has endured in spite of the advent of the internal combustion engine.

This old trade route across the Sahara from Tripoli to Lake Chad – a route strewn with vestiges of Roman Imperial traffic – had not been traversed by a European prior to Vischer since 1892. Hornemann had crossed in 1800 to Borno, and died. His companion, Frendenburg, died at Murzuk, the capital of the fertile Fezzan in the middle of Libya, and there Ritchie also died twenty years later. In 1822–3, Denham, Clapperton and Oudney crossed the Sahara and Oudney died. Then nothing was attempted until Richardson set out in 1845, and again, with Barth and Overweg, in 1850. The journey or the Niger climate killed Richardson and Overweg after the crossing. Vogel was the next victim: he met Barth, but was later killed, and Beurmann who went to enquire about him was murdered too; but Barth survived, and left an account of his travels and discoveries that many rate as travel journals of the highest calibre. A Miss Tinne was treacherously assassinated by the Tuareg in Murzuk in 1869; and the German explorer, Nachtigal was chased out of the Tibesti area in the same year. Barry expired after passing through Murzuk to Ghat in 1877. It is not an encouraging history. Hanns Vischer was repeatedly warned by the Turkish authorities, who at that time ruled what is now Libya, that he would certainly be murdered, and everyone else seemed to be of the same opinion. Many of the names of those earlier travellers are still remembered, but Vischer, who in 1909 was considered by the

Illustrated London News to be an explorer on a par with Shackleton, is a forgotten hero. And it was partly to restore his memory that I wanted to undertake the journey. For while those other explorers of Vischer's era and earlier are still honoured, the name of Sir Hanns Vischer and his many and varied achievements, have largely been forgotten. Another compelling motivation was to publicize my own personal crusade to save that unique and highly endangered species, the wild Bactrian camel of China and Mongolia. The Sahara and Gobi deserts are separated by culture, religion and a huge distance, but the camel, whether carrying one hump or two, links them.

So who was Hanns Vischer? Born in Basle in 1876, Vischer was by birth a Swiss citizen, but his family's strong evangelical convictions inspired him to become a missionary with the Church Missionary Society in Hausaland. After two years he was disenchanted with CMS educational attitudes towards Africans and decided to become a British citizen and enter the Colonial Administrative Service. After a few years serving in the administration, Vischer made an application to transfer to the Education Department and he there developed a system whereby northern Nigerians were educated within their own culture. As he outlined, the teacher 'must not weaken the finer traditions in the heritage of his pupils by superimposing a system of education unrelated to their past.' In other words, northerners were to be educated with due regard to their religion and cultural background and not within the culture of an alien race.

This was a novel and highly controversial concept at the time, but its huge success in the north led Vischer to high office in educational affairs with the government in Britain and to a knighthood. His mud house, *Gidan dan Hausa,* stands in Kano city to this day. Well cared for and recently restored, it symbolizes the affection which the northern Nigerian held and still holds for a man who it was said, if you dressed him appropriately, 'could pass for a native in five countries.' It is strikingly apparent from just reading his book, that he instinctively followed the wise words of an old Jesuit priest: 'It is wonderful how much good a man can do in the world if he does not want to take the credit of it.'

On his desert journey, Hanns Vischer mingled in his caravan the most combustible materials he could possibly have collected. There were the Mecca pilgrims, who insisted on being escorted back to their homes in northern Nigeria; the freed slaves, who were to be his armed escort but who more often themselves needed escorting; turbulent and treacherous Tubbus from Niger, and haughty Arab camel drivers, who regarded black men as dirt and Christians as reliable fuel for hell fire. There was old Alhaji Abdu who had been a corporal under Gordon at Khartoum; 'and had seen much fighting in many lands since he had been taken as a young slave from Borno to Upper Egypt some sixty years before.' 'I have served under Gordon Pasha,' he said. 'Now it is your duty to look after me and take me and my wife back to Borno.'

There was the aged woman Fatima and her son Alhaji Zaid: 'The old dame's courage and her son's loyalty and knowledge of the desert practically saved the entire caravan', indeed, she was an uncanny old witch and 'kept the men in a holy fear.' When she 'swung her long hard stick round the heads of her entourage' she rose to majesty: 'Stronger and better men might have trembled at the sight of the long thin figure, the narrow face with the hair died red, and the easy flow of language which seemed to wither the listeners like a fire, and made itself heard above the greatest noise' and there was Hauwa, a gigantic Bagirmi woman, who had the gift of prophecy, and who would go into frantic convulsions when the spirit seized her, making the most unearthly noises. She needed four men to hold her until she had delivered her revelation, but her prophetic gift, by means of a tacit understanding with Vischer, took a beneficial tone of encouragement as soon as cheerful revelations were found to bring a corresponding reward of tea and sugar. When the guide and the Tubbu camel drivers, who joined the caravan at Murzuk, plotted an attack with Tuaregs that included a quite incidental killing of Vischer, her prophetic convulsions proved to be invaluable:

> Then Hauwa, the good great prophetess, came stoutly to the fore, and rose to the occasion with a colossal visitation from the nether world. Even Marabut Senussi [the guide] shook with fear when the enormous woman, with cries like the bellowing of a bull, announced to the world that Satan had taken possession of her. With many 'Allah Akbar,' 'Allah Kerim,' friends and husbands carried the writhing form to a tent, where the cries redoubled, and it took the combined strength of the escort and the pilgrims to hold the great creature down. It seemed as if all the spirits in hell tore at the body . . . Presently one emerged from the tent and asked me to come, for the devil had called me several times by name. I went and beheld a most uncommon spectacle. On the ground, stretched out at full length lay Hauwa, with rolling eyes, foaming at the mouth and growling like a huge angry cat. Husband and friends sat or knelt on her chest, arms and legs, holding on like apes in a thunderstorm, as the twitching and writhing body tried to throw them off. One of the men beat a drum, and the whole awestruck congregation bent and swayed to the rhythmic sound . . . Hauwa called me, and this is what she said, or rather howled in broken sentences: You are a Nasarani (a Christian); you are a man of God, no harm will come to you or any one. Don't eat anything these Tubbus give you, and don't sleep or put the rifle from your hand . . . The night fell, and the camp had regained its old cheerful aspect. A large dinner was prepared, and of course I did not fail to send much sugar and tea to Hauwa. The drums were brought out as of old, and careless of Tuaregs and Tubbus the men, Bagirmi, pilgrims and all, danced till late into the night. Hauwa had accomplished more with her prophecies than a thousand threats or promises on my part could have done.

Vischer found that 'the responsibility of looking after my little family often spoilt the pleasures of the gloriously free desert life.'

The Arabs and the Africans were perpetually on the verge of shooting each other. He had little idea too of the tempers of his 'black ladies' when he set out. Nothing could equal their language when roused, and it took very little provocation to rouse them.

> Fights among the black sisters were of almost daily occurrence. No march was too long, no road too trying — so soon as they arrived in camp, they were ready for the fray. The sticks were chosen by their husbands, and they took care to provide heavy ones; 'it clears the blood,' they said. Then, in the stillness of the desert night, when the tired camp sought a few hours' sleep, one could hear high-pitched voices singing out a string of unsavoury epithets, followed by a regular tattoo of heavy, well placed blows, gradually growing fainter as the thick muscles tired and 'the blood cooled down.' The next morning all ill-feeling had vanished, and the various incidents and points of the combat were discussed amidst roars of laughter for the rest of the day . . . It is a characteristic of the African that he usually ends by seeing the humorous side of the situation, and this, in spite of all his faults, makes him the delightful travelling companion that he is . . . I have seen old men hanging round their horse's necks, or falling off their camels, over a joke they had heard perhaps twenty minutes before.

Vischer, his adventurous journey, his turbulent travelling companions and his infectious enthusiasms, were my great inspiration. On leave in England from serving as an administrative officer in Kukawa, he had persuaded the British Colonial Office to allow him to return to his post overland, instead of by sea to Lagos and thence up country to Borno. He had travelled from Tripoli in Libya to Kukawa on the shores of Lake Chad, the then capital of the Kanuri empire of Borno in northern Nigeria. Having achieved his goals after a highly successful and exciting journey, Vischer became restless. The desert sirens called him back and he asked his boss in the Northern Nigerian Political Service if he could make the south—

north journey. On 19 September 1907 he received this curt but not unsurprising reply.

> Dear Vischer,
> Yours of yesterday . . .
> This is one of the many matters on which I disagree with you. I have reported on you that you are for the first time now on trial as an administrative officer and that I prefer my staff to do the work they are paid for, rather than seek personal kudos or geographical advancement in foreign territory. I am Resident [Provincial Commissioner in the Nigeria Political service] before a Fellow of the Royal Geographical Society. If you are bent on the journey, you should resign and make room for a man who is satisfied with his job. Plain speaking but I like to run my own show . . .
> Yours sincerely,
> W.P.Hewby

Nearly one hundred years later I, too, wanted to run my own show and complete the journey that Vischer had been prevented from undertaking.

Many people today find it difficult to understand a deeply felt emotional tie with northern Nigeria. They see Nigeria as a corrupt country, permeated with bandits and drugs, a country that squandered its potential oil wealth on short term gain and whose capital, Lagos, is one of the worst cities in the world. But I spent my youth in the north, and in remote and inaccessible districts enjoyed some of the happiest and most productive years of my life. I got to know the Hausa and the settled and nomadic Fulani peoples. I thought of the north as a separate and diverse culture, light years removed from the sin cities of the south, and so it was.

But the past is another country and I realize this only too well.

'That is the land of lost content – I see it shining plain. The happy highways where I went, and cannot come again.'

The desert camel road that led to the north was different. This was not a highway that I had trodden. The Kanuri people, who inhabit Borno, were not known to me, and yet I felt, even after an absence of nearly forty years, that I could once again re-engage with northern Nigerian bush life and travel. But what of Niger, that vast, sparsely populated country that straddles the Sahara, and what would the reaction be from Qadhafi's Libya? They presented bigger problems and I knew that, if funds permitted, a reconnaissance trip to both these countries was indispensable.

The British ambassador in Tripoli had forwarded my south–north camel travel request to the Libyan authorities. After an anxious wait of six months, I was told that permission had been unexpectedly granted. It seemed to me important that I immediately followed this up, and so in the spring of 2001 I set off for Tripoli.

Libyan government security had directed me to make all the administrative arrangements with a Mustafa Tarhuni of a tourist company called, Sukra Travel. Mustafa quite clearly had a hot line to people in power and so, as instructed, I visited him in his shabby office in the back streets of Tripoli with the British embassy's second secretary, Bridget Brind.

'I will do anything you want me to,' Mustafa said in perfect English. 'Absolutely anything. If you want to hire camels, I can find them for you. Tents, equipment of any description, all this can be made available.' As he spoke, I could see the dollar signs revolving in the whites of his eyes.

Richard Dalton, the British ambassador, warned me that Libya could be expensive for a foreigner. 'If you have prepared a budget,' he advised me with a smile, 'I suggest you double it.'

I mentioned invitations and visas to enter the country, a problem in Libya, and the wily Mustafa assured me, rubbing his hands together in anticipation, that there would be absolutely 'no prob-lem', both for me and for the people who would be travelling with me. Richard Dalton warned me to distance myself from the embassy in this respect. 'If you appear to be too closely attached to the Foreign Office, the Libyan authorities might suspect that you have an ulterior motive.'

But I didn't have to keep my distance at the Nigerian embassy. To my delight, I discovered that the Nigerian ambassador to Libya, Lawan Gana Guba, was a Kanuri from Borno. He was young, vibrant and full of enthusiasm.

'How I wish I could come with you,' he said enthusiastically. 'Maybe I will come. Will you take me?'

'Of course I will. I'll sign you up now.'

He laughed. 'Are you going to Maiduguri before you set off?'

'Yes.'

'Then see the Governor, he's a good man, and see the Shehu, he should be told what you are going to do. You should also visit Professor Kari Tijjani at the Trans-Saharan Centre. He'll be very interested in your plans, in spite of the fact that you were an administrative officer and he was once the biggest Marxist in Nigeria.'

When I had assured him Libyan security had cleared the journey, his response was, 'That's excellent. It means that Qadhafi is aware of what you are planning to do.'

'Really?'

'Yes, if security has approved it, he must be aware.'

The ambassador walked out of the embassy to see me off and sent me away with his personal driver. I left him feeling that I had unwittingly discovered a significant supporter.

In Libya I had also hoped to obtain additional funding especially after what the British ambassador had said. But in spite of being invited to attend a party at the embassy given for the British business community, I had drawn a complete blank. The few British companies operating in Libya were, not surprisingly, in no mood to support a 1,500-mile camel hike across Saharan sands or a struggling wild Bactrian camel in China. Most were struggling themselves to survive. My one material success was in obtaining from a friendly Australian oilman a set of small scale maps which covered, in detail, our proposed camel route through southern Libya, and before I left Bridget Brind inadvertently did me a very good turn. It was through her that I met a jolly and loquacious English-speaking taxi driver called Ahmed Qadhafi.

I explained to Ahmed that I was intending to retrace, in reverse, the journey a British citizen had made from Tripoli to Kukawa a hundred years ago.

'I am particularly keen to see the Jew's Gate that leads out of the old walled city,' I said. 'I would also like to see Bumeliana, the place where traveller Vischer first camped with his camels and freed slaves amidst the Bumeliana date palms.'

'It's not a problem,' said Ahmed cheerfully. 'I know Bumeliana, but I am not exactly sure where the Jew's Gate is. I have a friend who is an historian who lives in the old city. He will help us.'

Car horn tooting, Ahmed whisked me off into the old city to find his friend. He lived in a tall, narrow nineteenth-century house which opened onto a large empty space, and was fortunately at home when we called. He was short, with a dark goatee beard and was dressed in a voluminous light blue robe. A matching turban was tied jauntily around his head. Like Ahmed, his acute sense of humour was not far from the surface. When he had listened carefully to his friend's question, he let out a great peal of laughter.

'The Jewish quarter. The Jew's Gate. You are there.' He flung open his arms and grinned at us revealing a set of sparkling gold-capped teeth.

'This is it. It's not called by that name any more, but this is most definitely it.'

'But there's nothing here,' I said. 'It's an empty space.'

'Precisely. All the Jews were kicked out of here in the 1970s. Their houses were razed to the ground. Only their synagogue remains.'

He pointed to the one remaining, large and dilapidated building

that was securely boarded up. I walked over to the old synagogue. Its
roof had almost disappeared but by peering through a gap between
two wooden planks, I could just make out that it had once been a
place of worship.

'And the gate?'

'Come, I'll take you through it.'

We walked through what had obviously been a gate in the old city
wall. Part of the wall had disappeared but the gate was still intact. As
I walked into the busy street outside, bustling with people and
traffic, I gasped out loud in amazement. Vischer had positioned little
sketches as visual headings at the beginning of each chapter of his
book. The first chapter begins with a pen sketch of the Jew's Gate. To
my great satisfaction, I discovered that if one positioned oneself
correctly and avoided the traffic and the tarmac, the view was
exactly the same as the one that Vischer had sketched. For some
reason, I felt immensely happy.

We drove on to Bumeliana, which is about five miles from the old
city and has been retained as an open space. Some of the date palms
are still there, just as described by Vischer, but I immediately realized that I would not be able to bring camels here. Lorries and cars
buzzed around Vischer's old campsite on four sides. It was a mar-
ooned oasis, surrounded by the horrors of our time and engulfed by
traffic fumes and pollution. The date palms were drooping in obvious distress. Bumeliana was definitely not camel country in 2001.

But the discovery at the gate had made me curiously elated. I felt
that I had been nudged, ever so gently, in the right direction and it
could be no bad thing that it was a Qadhafi who had given me the
nudge. I still needed to reconnoitre Niger and Nigeria, but funds
were low. Then Vischer himself came to my rescue. A chance
encounter led me to the Bradshaw Foundation which sponsors the
exploration of primitive rock art sites. It happened that Vischer had
paused to sketch some in Niger and so the Foundation promised me
$3,000 in return for news of any new rock art I might discover on

my journey for their website. I was delighted. The essential ground-work could now continue.

They did me another favour by introducing me to Sidi Moham-med Illes, Tuareg chief and tourist entrepreneur, who happened to be staying in London with Charlie Rappoport, his French business partner.

Charlie, plump, amiable, in his late thirties and dressed in an old tee-shirt and shorts, padded off on bare feet into the kitchen. On the back of the tee-shirt, the words, 'Fear Woman, Live Long' were emblazoned in large, bright green characters and on the front, underneath a foaming glass of Guinness was inscribed the slogan, 'Guinness for Power.' I smiled. This must be the Frenchman, Charlie Rappoport. The tour operator with a West African background who had made his home in Ireland. The tee-shirt said it all.

Sidi was seated, cross-legged, in the middle of the sitting-room floor, a deep blue turban draped over his ankle length, off-white, travel-stained Tuareg gown. In front of him was a huge bowl of couscous.

'It took me a year to get a visa to visit London,' Sidi exclaimed, shovelling a brimming spoonful of couscous into his mouth. 'Can you imagine? It won't take you a year to get a visa to visit Niger.' He wiped his mouth with the back of his hand. 'And when I finally get here, I find that all the streets are full of slave people. I don't understand you English. Why do you let them in? I've never seen anything like it. You must all be crazy.'

I sensed that this was Sidi's first visit to London. He was thin, with a shock of greying black hair, restless eyes and a lop-sided grin under a deep blue turban. He hadn't shaved for at least four days. I grasped an out-stretched hand and squatted down in front of him.

'*Kana lafiya?*' I asked, greeting Sidi in Hausa.

'Ah, you speak Hausa. Good. My English is bad, isn't it, Charlie?'

Sidi gave me a roguish grin. 'Not that I really like speaking Hausa. It's a slave language.'

My eyes opened wide in amazement. I had never heard anyone speak like this before.

'Understand, Mister John, that I am a full-blooded Tuareg. My grandfather was a powerful chief, long before the French stole our country. He was a slave raider, who plundered caravans and oases all the way along the road that you are hoping to follow. His fame spread all over the Sahara. He was famous, greatly feared and very successful.' Sidi prodded himself in the chest with his spoon. 'Look at his useless grandson. See for yourself how low our proud family has descended. What am I? Nothing but an agent for tourists, pocketing their money so that they can enjoy themselves in the sun. What a comedown for the head of a warrior family. My grandfather would disown me.'

Sidi lowered his head and dropped the spoon which clattered to the floor. He could, quite clearly, have been offered a lead in many an amateur theatrical production. But this was someone who had been recommended as a man of his word, who would attempt to strike a hard bargain but who, once it was struck, would honour it, a man who would not let me down. Nevertheless, I could not help wondering how far I could trust this maverick Tuareg chief who in his youth had fought in Algeria as a freedom fighter and who clearly regarded the majority of Britain's immigrant population as slaves.

Sidi cut in on my thoughts. 'So you want to cross the Sahara with camels?'

'That's right.'

'And you want to travel along the old camel route from Nigeria to Tripoli?'

'Correct.'

Sidi leant backwards on the outstretched palms of his hands. He stared directly at me for the first time.

'Why?'

'Because I do,' I replied.

He laughed out loud at this inconsequential reply. 'And you want me to find you camels that are strong enough to undertake the journey?'

'Yes.'

He sat up and with a sudden, ostentatious gesture, tied his turban tightly around his head.

'You realize that this journey will be very tough, not only on the camels but also on you. No foreigner has followed the road for a very long time.'

'I know,' I replied. 'I think that the last foreigner who travelled the road in 1906 was British. Two of his sons, both in their eighties, are alive and living in England. He was called Hanns Vischer.'

'Hanns Vis-ch-er.' Sidi pronounced the name slowly. 'Hanns Vis-ch-er,' he repeated. 'Was he a spy?'

'No,' I replied emphatically. 'His nickname was *dan Hausa*, son of the Hausa.'

'You mean son of the slave,' muttered Sidi, giving me a sideways look.

It was not too difficult to follow the working of Sidi's mind. Having summed me up and concluded that, although I might be slightly crazy, I appeared to be firmly resolved to make the journey, his thoughts turned abruptly towards practical matters. Such as money and what he could make out of me.

'A camel will cost you £300, that's the price of a baggage camel,' he paused for effect. 'A good riding camel will cost almost £200 more.'

'I will need sixteen baggage and nine riding camels, twenty-five camels in all.'

'Do you still want to make the journey?' Sidi asked with a laugh.

'Naturally.'

Sidi pushed aside the bowl of couscous and looked me straight in the eye. 'That's a lot of money,' he said.

'I'm listening.'

'Then you have to add on to that the price of my Tuaregs who will come with you, the prices of guides who will not be cheap, the price of ropes and saddles, the price of grass and food . . .' his voice tailed off. 'Do you still want to go?'

'Yes.'

'Well in that case, we had better sit down in Agadez and have a detailed discussion. Can you come soon to Agadez? We can go off together and look at camels. You can meet some of the Tuaregs who will be coming with you. We can finalize everything.'

'Yes.'

'When?'

'In August.' I was giving myself three short months to find a lot more money.

Sidi jumped up from the floor with surprising alacrity. He grasped my hand and shook it vigorously. 'We will welcome you,' he cried. 'We will make you feel at home.'

Charlie stood in the background a half smile on his face. Although he could not understand the Hausa, he had heard and seen enough to realize that Sidi had ensnared me.

'I have a fax,' Sidi said. 'And a telephone. They hardly ever work but I have them. Let me know as soon as possible when you will be coming. If you can't get hold of me, Charlie will know where I am.'

I left the house and stepped into the bright May sunlight with Sidi's, '*Salut, mon grand voyageur*' ringing in my ears.

I met Sidi three months later in very different circumstances. He was stretched out on colourful cushions, surrounded by courtiers in a mud-walled compound in Agadez, the ancient town bordering the fringe of the Sahara in Niger. He was shaded from a blazing, midday sun by grass mats thrown casually over wooden poles. It was a far cry from London. This was Sidi the Tuareg chief, turbaned, assured and the leader of his clan. It was hot, very hot, and Roddy, my brother-in-law, who had accompanied me on the recce trip was perspiring profusely. A distinguished music critic and journalist, with no experience of West Africa, Roddy had pitched himself headlong into the sub Sahara. He adjusted effortlessly.

'Welcome, Mister camel man,' cried Sidi, rising slowly from the pile of leather cushions. 'Did your plane arrive in Niamey on time?'

'Yes, and it enabled me to find the time to get hold of a set of small scale maps which cover the whole of the journey from Kukawa to Gatrun.'

Sidi gave a half smile and raised an eyebrow.

'You are fortunate. Allah is looking after you. Those maps are not easy to obtain. The government thinks that they could be useful to spies.'

I didn't tell Sidi that an introduction from a friendly professor in Maiduguri University had enabled me to get hold of the maps. Nor did I tell him that it was not until I had pored over them that I realized just what we were attempting to do. In some places the straggling line of the road broke up into a series of dots, in others the line clung to tiny outcrops of rocks. The lines of sand dunes were uncertain as they shifted constantly. In southern Niger, before and after reaching the oasis of Bilma, the route was surrounded by an interminable expanse of desert. In northern Niger, where the route was over rock and stone, there appeared to be no vegetation of any sort and very few wells. I had to summon up reserves of courage when I studied them. We were embarking on a very tough journey, and the maps spelt that out explicitly.

'And how do you like Agadez?' asked Sidi.

To my great relief, Agadez had changed surprisingly little from when I first visited it over thirty years before. Mysterious tribesmen in black turbans and gowns still walked the narrow streets, swords dangling from their sides, daggers thrust through their belts. Donkeys and goats still outnumbered motorized vehicles. The medieval mosque with its quaint mud tower spiked with wooden sticks was intact. The old French colonial fort, now a hostelry, continued to hire out iron beds and sweaty mud huts to travellers, and it was still insufferably hot. Agadez remained what it had been for centuries, a desert frontier town, where one filled up goatskins with water and sacks with dates, flour, sugar and other essentials before attempting a desert crossing.

Sidi offered us sweetened green tea. He was in an expansive mood.

'This is Argali,' he said, pointing to a light-coloured somewhat portly man of about forty-five with a huge shock of curly black hair who hovered in the background. 'He is my brother. And this is Ehom, another brother.'

Ehom was tall, very black and slim. However close the relationship was with their mutual father, their mothers were definitely of a different hue.

'They will be coming with you on the expedition. They are both very reliable and very efficient. They know the desert.'

The two men showed no emotion whatsoever. Their eyes never left me. I sensed that they were taking stock, summing me up and wondering if they could cope with me for many weeks on a protracted journey across a hostile desert.

I had come to see Sidi to talk money, and for the next two days, with the help of Roddy, I wrestled with currency exchange, trying to convert millions of CFA (Niger) francs to French francs through UK pounds to US dollars. We bargained for ropes, saddles, daily rates of pay, fees for the Tuaregs' return journey and, of course, for camels. It was hot, sweaty and distinctly uncongenial work, conducted on the floor in Sidi's stifling mud house. The only other piece of furniture in the room was a wooden table strewn with papers and supporting the fax machine which didn't work. Mosquitoes buzzed around us and flies paddled through our sweat which dripped from both of us in a steady stream. In between frustrated slaps to try to exterminate our tormentors, Roddy drew up tables of currency exchange. My mind leapt backwards and forwards from French francs, to Niger francs, to pounds and eventually landed in an unclear and unformed heap amidst a pile of mental dollars.

By the end of two days the protracted but necessary haggle came to an end. Roddy and I were both exhausted and my head throbbed. As a result of our agreement, I had placed a great deal on trust by giving Sidi a hefty advance to buy equipment and camels. I realized full well that as soon as my back was turned he could leap into his four-wheel-drive vehicle, stash the banknotes beside the loaded pistol, deftly stored in a box beside the hand brake, and disappear into desert sands – never to be seen or heard of again.

I had to trust someone and on balance, Sidi seemed a suitable repository for trust. I placed a large pile of US dollars in Sidi's outstretched hands, muttered a little prayer and hoped for the best.

The agreement reached with Sidi was that he would sell me twenty-five camels from prime stock in the Air mountains to the north of Agadez. The camels of Air are prized because of their ability to cope with stony ground, and we were certainly going to encounter plenty of that. Sidi promised that the camels would meet us on an agreed date in October at the town of Ngigimi in southern Niger. The camels would be walked there and I calculated that, even before we started on our 1,500-mile journey, my camels would have already covered 400 miles.

However, he adamantly refused to take the camels across the border into Nigeria and, in spite of my pleas, he wouldn't be budged. He didn't want to encounter what he called 'Nigerian mischief'. This meant, that if I was authentically to follow Vischer's trail, I would have to hire camels in Nigeria for the ten-day trek from Kukawa to Ngigimi.

Sidi also agreed to allow his Tuareg brothers to accompany me to Gatrun in southern Libya – but no further.

'My influence does not extend northwards from Gatrun,' he said.

Ngigimi to Gatrun was a good stretch, a 1,000-mile journey, but it left me with further problems. How would I travel on to Tripoli from Gatrun? And with whom? The British ambassador in Libya had hinted that the Libyans would be waiting for my arrival like rapacious vultures. What if camels died en route or were too weak to continue the journey? How would I replace these camels? Would I have a dollar left in my money bag to buy or hire anything? These somewhat depressing thoughts were abruptly broken when Sidi placed a hand on my shoulder.

'Would you like to visit the Libyan consul general? It could be useful to have Libyan support for your expedition in Niger. It will also help me to get the necessary Libyan *laissez-passer* documents for Argali, Ehom and any other people that accompany you.'

I thought this seemed a sensible suggestion as we were to reach the Libyan border by crossing Niger, and so on the third day, Sidi drove Roddy and me to the outskirts of Agadez and the office of the Libyan consul general.

At first, our welcome was very stiff. Salem Ali Mugber could not comprehend what I wanted, why I had come to see him and what I was attempting to do. But when, after half an hour of meticulous translation, he eventually understood that I had already received permission from Libyan security to make the journey and to cross the international border between Niger and Libya at Tummo, his whole demeanour changed. The hitherto solemn face of the portly little man broke into a huge smile of welcome, he took me by the hand, led me into his palatial office and offered me tea. He then called out to a gatekeeper in Arabic and moments later an elderly man with finely chiselled, noble features was escorted in.

'This is Colonel Qadhafi's uncle,' said the consul general. 'I thought you might be interested to meet him.'

I shook hands, we beamed at each other and there was a further line by line explanation of my intended journey. Behind him stood another much younger man who turned out to be a Hausa called Dahiru Gambo from Kano. He was en route to Tripoli to translate

Qadhafi's famous *Little Green Book* into Hausa. He had heard of Vischer, knew Vischer's Kano house and was delighted to meet up with someone who was attempting to take camels across the desert in Vischer's footsteps. So there was general bonhomie all round.

That evening, the consul general drove Roddy and me out into the desert. After a convivial stroll on which we discussed everything from Taleban turbulence to Libyan logistics, we squatted down on folded legs to eat a picnic with our fingers, a sumptuous meal of couscous, rice and mutton off coloured cloths spread over the sand. As we ate, we watched the sun set majestically over the lights of Agadez. The meeting had been a great success. I felt that if I needed a Libyan ally in Niger, there was one to hand.

Before we finally left Agadez, I was introduced to another of Sidi's brothers. This one was a closer blood relation than either Argali or Ehom. He was, as Sidi said, 'same mother, same father'. He was called Haidara and I instinctively liked him. Small and neatly dressed, he appeared calm and very perceptive. There was a dignity about him that Sidi lacked. Much later, in very different and extremely difficult circumstances, I was to benefit greatly from the inherent wisdom of Haidara.

We now headed south for Nigeria and, after deftly avoiding the grasping outstretched hands of Nigerian border customs officials, we reached the town of Daura. It was here that a good friend, Mamman Daura, a successful business man and an acute and highly respected northern Nigerian political guru, had allowed us use of his house and, more importantly, his car and driver. The loan of his car, in the capable hands of driver Haruna, was a very generous gesture. Our ultimate destination was Kukawa in Borno, over 500 miles to the east. But first we had to cross the bandit plagued roads of the north.

2

We were dreamers dreaming greatly in the man-stifled town,
We yearned beyond the sky-line where the strange roads go down.

As quoted by Vischer

Borno is a state and an emirate in northern Nigeria, situated to the west and south-west of Lake Chad. It is also the home territory of the Kanuri tribe. The Hausa have a proverb about the Kanuri which is far from complimentary and which neatly encapsulates an ancient animosity. It runs: 'See a snake, see a Kanuri. Kill the Kanuri.'

But Borno is also a term that for over 500 years described an empire that shifted its centre of authority from the east of the lake, to the sandy, thorn-strewn marches to the west. Even at its lowest ebb, its frontiers extended far beyond the northern and eastern boundaries of the modern state. The Borno empire reached its apogee under Mai Idris Alauma during the sixteenth century, who was able to pacify disparate tribal groups and stabilize the central government. Later, the ruling dynasty of the Seyfuwa was replaced by that of the remarkable al-Kanemi, and his successors governed the empire of Borno until 1893. During all these years the economic base of the empire was the trans-Saharan slave trade which was controlled by the state. Slavery had been practised in the area around Lake Chad since times immemorial, and the earliest written sources, dating from the ninth century, speak of rulers enslaving their own people or neighbouring tribes and selling them to North Africa by way of the desert highway.

The present capital, Maiduguri, is presided over by a state governor, a provincial government and the traditional ruler of Borno, the Shehu. Both Vischer and our expedition team heard the Kanuri language spoken in Tejerri in southern Libya and in Bilma in Niger, 500 miles to the north. Bilma was described by Vischer as clearly falling under the authority of the Shehu. In Murzuk in central Libya the current Shehu still owns property. All these lingering relics bear witness to the extent of the Borno empire, and the former authority of the Shehu of Borno.

In 1906, the capital of Borno was Kukawa, where Vischer worked, and where we planned to set out on our expedition. However, Kukawa was in Vischer's day a ghost town. Thirteen years earlier it had been attacked and overthrown by Rabih Fadl Allah, a Sudanese adventurer who had embarked on a career of bloody conquest which engulfed parts of Sudan and the Lake Chad basin, and brought him directly into armed conflict with Borno. In December, 1893, Rabih attacked Kukawa in an attempt to wrest power from Shehu Hashim. For three days, Kukawa was pillaged and burnt by Rabih's soldiers. When the explorer Boyd Alexander, who made the first accurate survey of Lake Chad, visited the town at the turn of the century, he noted that the northern part of the town where the old Shehu's palace once stood had been demolished and 'one passes through about a mile of the town where the houses are all in ruins.' Over 3,000 skulls were piled in a heap in the market. Nine hundred and fifty horses were seized and 3,800 people were taken as slaves. The loot included 1,000 ivory tusks, 30,000 sheep and goats, 1,000 camels and over 1,000 head of cattle.

The Shehu escaped to the north on rafts across the Komadugu Yobe river, which we were to cross in similar fashion over a century later. His baggage, animals, slaves and women all fell into the hands of Rabih's soldiers. Kukawa never recovered from this total destruction.

Rabih was killed by French colonial troops in 1900, and his territory divided between the British and German governments. When Sir Frederick Lugard (later Lord Lugard), the Governor of Northern Nigeria, visited the town in 1904, he wrote to his wife: 'As I strolled out for a few minutes after sunset I came on a human skull and bones, for they lie scattered still among the mealie stalks and the crops which have grown from the blood of the dead.'

Shehu Hashim was described as a man 'whose intelligent and open face was lit by a gentle but piercing gaze.' But the current Shehu Umar, leaves a very different impression.

Today the shell of a huge unfinished mosque stands, swathed in a sheath of grey concrete, outside the present Shehu's palace in Maiduguri. The design is magnificent, the current state of the building depressing. The vast concrete base, awash with plastic bags, rusting tins and broken wooden scaffolding, sends out an unmistakable signal that no work is currently in progress. In design and grandeur it outshines the Shehu's palace of brick and mud, but dilapidated and neglected, it speaks not of Allah but of the imperfections of man.

An animated crowd of Kanuri youth surrounded Roddy and me as we arrived to pay our respects to Shehu Umar. They jostled us, plied us with questions, and exuded a faint air of menace. The vast space in front of the palace and the mosque seemed to be full of similar youth dressed in flowing blue or white gowns; buying, selling, scrapping, squabbling or kicking footballs. They all appeared to be under twenty-five and there was not a girl in sight. Was this a cross-section of the unemployed or unemployable of Maiduguri? I asked myself. Having forced our way through the mob, we were swept through the palace gates and up some unsteady stairs to the Shehu's audience chamber. We were then waved by door-keepers towards high-backed ornate wooden chairs positioned at haphazard intervals around a long wooden table. As I pulled mine out to sit down, it toppled backwards with a crash and just as I stooped to retrieve it, the Shehu's retainers entered the room. These impassive and impressively tall bodyguards were all dressed in the traditional *balta-balta* uniform of white cloth, smocked with four red and four green motives, which has not changed since Rabih's day. They were followed by Umar Ibn Abubakar Jarbay, Shehu of Borno.

In contrast to his retinue, the Shehu was small and neatly dressed in a white gown and turban. As he sat down, stiff and unsmiling, I was struck by his eyes. They were glazed and distant, and appeared incapable of focusing on me or anything. He motioned to me to speak and I told him in somewhat stilted Hausa what we were attempting to do. The Shehu sat impassively, without uttering a word and I could not fathom whether he was listening to me or not. I tried to tweak his attention by referring to the extent of the Borno empire in the past, how its influence in the desert had stretched as far as Murzuk in Libya. Not once did the Shehu utter. I came uneasily to the end of my account.

The Shehu slowly turned his head towards me. His dull, unseeing eyes gave away no sign of emotion, or even of life. At last he spoke.

'Will you be taking a doctor?' he asked in a soft, querulous voice.

'No,' I replied. 'We have no plans to do that.'

'What a pity,' he said and promptly got up and left the room, closely followed by his bodyguard.

'May your life be prolonged. May you live for ever,' they cried out as Umar Ibn Abubakar Jarbay, the Shehu of Borno disappeared.

Little has changed. When Major Denham met the Shehu in

Kukawa in March 1823 the Shehu spoke not a word. Denham described him as 'seated in a sort of cage of cane or wood . . . Our glimpse was but a faint one, through the lattice work of his pavilion . . . in front of [him] was an extempore declaimer shouting forth praises of his master with his pedigree.'

We travelled on to Kukawa, now a crumbling township containing few hints of its earlier glory and its former size. The mud walls that surrounded the town have long since disappeared. Alhaji Masta, who used to live there, and who had come with us from Maiduguri, affirmed that one hundred years ago the walls encompassed the houses of two hundred thousand people. Its current appearance belies its turbulent history. When we arrived Alhaji Masta supervised our dealings with a cheerful man swathed in a dark blue robe who introduced himself as Abubakar, Chairman of the Local Authority.

'He is responsible for finding the thirteen camels that you want to take with you to Ngigimi,' said Alhaji Masta. 'He is reliable. Give him the date and they will be ready for you.'

I mentioned 13 October, almost two months away.

'No problem,' said Abubakar convincingly. 'They will be here.'

'And what's the price of hiring a camel for the seven-day journey to Ngigimi?' I enquired.

'Oh, I have no idea,' replied Abubakar disconcertingly, at the same time breaking into loud laughter.

'Can't we agree a price now?'

'No. That's not possible.'

I pressed them for a figure – any figure. Alhaji Masta whispered that they could not give me an answer now because they had not discussed it with the camel-owners. It was an unusual request. People did not travel with camels these days. Good camels will be difficult to get hold of and we would need reliable herdsmen. I had an uneasy feeling that Alhaji Masta's cut was going to be substantial.

'You will have to look out for bandits,' said Abubakar, grasping my hand firmly as I turned to leave. 'They're giving us a great deal of trouble.'

'Bandits?'

'Yes, they come from Chad, cross over the lake and steal our livestock. They burn our outlying buildings and terrorize our women. They're like a plague of locusts. '

'Are they armed?'

Alhaji Masta roared with laughter. 'Yes, they are, and not with spears or bows and arrows. They all carry AKs. You'll need an armed escort and you'd better ask the Governor to give you one. Look out for them, because they shoot first and ask questions later.'

When we later paid our respects to the Governor of Borno, I brought up the subject of these Chadian highwaymen. He promised me a Nigeria Police escort to accompany our camel caravan to the Niger border. But the escort never materialized.

Before leaving Kukawa we were taken by Alhaji Masta to see the tombs of former Shehus. A mud building with a tin roof covered three fairly insubstantial graves. That was all. Nothing memorable. Just a faint clue to the huge importance of Kukawa, over a hundred years ago.

Our estimable, quiet and supremely efficient driver landed us safely back in Daura. We had covered over five thousand miles including visits to Kaduna, Zaria and Kano as well as to Maiduguri and Kukawa.

In Kano, my old friend and northern political maverick, Sule Kumo, introduced me to the Galadiman Kano, a senior official in the emir of Kano's household, so that the Emir could be informed of our journey. He also took us to see Hanns Vischer's old house. This ninety-year-old mud building was – in stark contrast to the grievously over-populated, traffic clogged, dilapidated Kano city – clean, freshly painted and restored to its former glory. In his own house, I saw that Sule still retained the scowling portrait of Ayatollah

Khomeini, which loomed menacingly over the visitor as he entered the front door.

'Ah,' he said to me, 'when you have completed your camel journey to Tripoli, we will employ you as an adviser to my project for a trans-Sahara railway which will give northern Nigeria an outlet to the sea. We will no longer have to rely on the unreliable Yorubas in the south – who hate us anyway – and at long last we will be able to establish our own independent country.'

I was delighted to discover that Sule with his free-thinking political views and religious enthusiasms remained quite unchanged.

A hired car took us to the Nigeria/Niger border crossing at Jibiya. There, customs officials squatted like scruffy uniformed vultures, beadily eyeing unsuspecting itinerants to see what could be extracted as a 'dash.' Driver Hammadu pressed banknotes into the hands of one of them which ensured that the substantial barrier was lifted.

Southern Niger townships have none of the romantic allure of Agadez. They are squalid, grasping and mean and the state of the roads mirrors the state of the towns. The back streets are unsafe, the people sullen. Hammadu and his lugubrious assistant, Ali, were not exactly bundles of fun. They continually exchanged whispered asides and the rotund, unsmiling Hammadu belched loudly, hawked voraciously and spat accurately, with a frequency that became wearisome. But he had one asset. When we were stopped at roadblocks, he informed the custodians that he was driving the car of the Chief of Muriya. I had no idea who the Chief of Muriya was or where he resided, but his name certainly commanded respect. At every roadblock, we were waved deferentially on towards Niamey. No questions, no comments. The writ of the Chief of Muriya runs large in southern Niger.

Two days later in Niamey, amid the splendour of a setting sun and with plump fruit bats flying unswervingly over our heads, I walked

with Roddy along the banks of a rain-swollen river Niger. We reflected on how our whirlwind West African ride had been a success.
Camels had been organized in both Nigeria and Niger and small
scale maps of the whole of our journey's route through Niger
obtained. Friendship and encouragement had been proffered,
enthusiasm kindled. The dream was materializing into substance and
a timetable had been fixed. I was conscious that my next priority was
to gather up my team.

*   *   *

The batting order was headed by seventy-seven-year-old Jasper
(Japper) Evans. A bush man of immense charm and resource, Japper
is an expert on camels. I felt he would be invaluable as the ad hoc
team vet, who would bring with him a life-long experience of
Africa. There was no other man of his age anywhere in the world
that I would have taken on the expedition. More importantly, we
got on. We had been together on a wild Bactrian camel survey in
China's Gobi desert in 1997, and from his ranching base in Kenya I
had frequently hired his camels to go walkabout in Kenya's north.

Yuan Guoying, the 'professor', a sexagenarian retired Chinese
professor of zoology, had been invaluable in obtaining permission
for me to enter the Lop Nur area of the Gobi desert. I wanted to
repay his kindness by offering him a chance to be the first Chinese
person to cross the Sahara on a camel.

A boulder pitched into untroubled waters sends out more than
ripples. The effect of September 11 2001 on our pre-expedition
plans, although minuscule in comparison with tragedies world-
wide, was none the less a reality. The *National Geographic* photographer withdrew and the organization itself which was supporting us
financially pressed hard for a twelve-month postponement. But on
that fateful date, my twenty-five camels were already striding pur-
posefully towards a rendezvous in Ngigimi and the professor, after
months of laborious wheedling and form-filling, had nearly obtained

all his visas and permissions to travel. Furthermore, I was conscious that the world might be even less safe in twelve months. I was determined to continue.

There were religious riots in Kano, pressures from Jasper's family, a strange telephone call from Sidi in Agadez, seeking a postponement of two weeks because of fighting in northern Niger — pre-expedition planning appeared to be suddenly falling apart. But meanwhile I had recruited Johnny Paterson who, with an impressive resolution to drop everything and come, helped to keep our expedition's actuarial scales in balance. Johnny, younger by thirty-plus years than the rest of us, had had long experience of driving trucks across Africa and Asia. He seemed highly organized, intelligent and confident. We badly needed his youth and energy, particularly as, unlike Vischer, who carried with him ten Winchester rifles, one Wespi, carbines, three revolvers, a pistol and nearly 2,000 rounds of ammunition, our caravan could not travel with guns. If we did, we would be a source of interest to would-be robbers, customs officials and Libyan and Niger security.

* * *

'No, I'm sorry. It's not possible.' The Libyan ambassador to the Republic of Kenya waggled an upturned index finger in front of me and shuffled uneasily in his office chair. He was large, well muscled and dressed in an open-necked cream silk shirt. He smiled at me. But it was a mechanical gesture, his dark eyes were cold and hard. I searched them for a hint of compassion.

'But the professor is a distinguished visitor from China, a vital member of our expedition team. All the other team members have been given visas to enter Libya. Surely . . .'

'The word "surely" does not feature in our system,' interrupted the ambassador in impeccable English. 'We follow our rule book and my instructions are quite clear. I have to refer his application to

Tripoli. Tomorrow is Friday and the embassy is closed, so please return on Tuesday.'

'But we fly to Lagos tomorrow. The tickets are booked.'

'I'm sorry, I cannot issue Professor Yuan Guoying with a visa to visit Libya. His name has not been cleared in advance and furthermore Sukra Travel has recently been removed from the embassy list of approved tourist agencies. They have, to use an English expression, been black-listed.'

Remembering Dr Mo Shelly, a softly spoken, somewhat nervous Libyan entrepreneur, who had mysteriously surfaced and helped me in London, I clutched at my last tenuous Libyan straw.

'Is it possible for you to telephone a number in the UK?' I asked.

The ambassador looked up at me, his eyes opened wide. 'In the UK? You want me to telephone the UK?'

'Yes.'

'It won't do you any good. I've already told you, the system does not allow me to issue a visa to the professor.'

'Please.'

'Will you pay for the call?'

'Yes.'

'Give me the number.'

He looked at me in annoyance as I searched in my bag for Dr Shelly's leaflet. I found it and scanned its extraordinary message, 'Cydamos Limited. We endeavour British Public to a glance and feel this historical and tural (sic) heritage. . .the have of culture.'

Dr Shelly answered the call. Abruptly, the ambassador rattled off a succession of questions in Arabic with the dramatic intensity of a machine gun. I visualized Mo Shelly reeling backwards under this verbal assault. The ambassador paused, and I studied the hard outline of his face as he listened impatiently to Dr Shelly's answers. Then his features softened and his body relaxed. He slumped back in his chair, the two men started laughing together and the ambassador burst into a loud and animated conversation.

'He is my brother,' he roared slamming down the receiver twenty minutes later. 'We're from the same clan. We're extended family brothers – blood brothers.' He slapped his right thigh. 'Oh, he's a good man, a very good man.'

'And the professor's visa, ambassador?' I asked tentatively.

'Oh, yes, the visa – no problem. That's no problem at all. Where's his passport?' I handed it to him. 'You can pick up the visa in an hour,' he paused, 'after you have paid for the telephone call.'

We shook hands. But it was over two hours later before we left the embassy. The custodian of the visa stamp had locked it in his safe and had disappeared off to the mosque. There was no duplicate key.

I had received an interesting lesson in the workings of both Libyan bureaucracy and the Libyan mind. It was to stand me in good stead.

We were flying to Nigeria via Kenya, to pick up Japper and to introduce the professor to both Africa and Kenyan wildlife. In this we were successful. There were elephant on Japper's ranch in Laikipia. The professor not only saw them, but he was able to christen his new video camera, on which he had invested a large chunk of his family's fortune, on an elephant with a flapping torn left ear and a sagging right tusk. Impala, waterbuck, giraffe, zebra, dik-dik, gazelles and oryx all came out of the bush to play spot the professor. 'Gooda, very gooda,' he shouted out in delight. It was a satisfied professorial expression that we were to hear many times in the future.

The journey from Lagos to Maiduguri was once more eased by my good friend Mamman Daura and evening found us ensconced in the palatial rest-house of Mamman's bank, where the welcome was friendly, the electricity was working and the buckets in the bath-room were full of water.

That evening, I took another uneasy look at the 1:200 000 scale maps of our route through Niger that I had picked up in Niamey. The absence of running water in the rest-house focused my mind. The maps caused me once again to pause and ponder. The track was frequently described as '*trace incertaine*', '*trace mal définie*' and there were water points which were highlighted '*eau douce abandonée.*' It was water that concerned me. Vischer had left a good record of the wells where he had obtained water. But that information was almost one hundred years old. Many of those wells might have been abandoned and they could have filled up with sand. There was no way to glean this from the map, or of obtaining reliable information on the ground. I mused on the description that Denham had made in 1823 and how he had dubbed the tracks as 'difficult and dangerous roads'. Later on during the expedition that telling phrase flitted in and out of my head with alarming frequency.

Next morning, Johnny, acting in his capacity as quartermaster-in-chief, set off on the pillion of a motor-bike taxi, to seek out stores, victuals and chattels. The professor busied himself with his Chinese diary which later in the expedition was to reach voluminous proportions, and Japper and I set off to meet Gisela Seidensticker-Brikay.

Gisela, a chain-smoking German scientist of indeterminate age, had lived and worked at the University of Maiduguri for many years. She had an encyclopedic knowledge of the Kanuri, their culture and their politics. My question to Gisela was simple.

'How and where do we cross the river Yobe?'

The Komadugu Yobe river, which at certain points forms the boundary between Nigeria and Niger, appeared on some maps to flow from west to east into Lake Chad. But Lake Chad had diminished to a twentieth of its size since Vischer's day, and I had no idea of the Yobe's width or depth. Gisela had canoed down the river in the early 1990s and knew it well but was no longer certain whether it reached the lake any more. 'You'll have to cross at Bisagama near the Nigerian customs post on the road to Bosso. The river there is neither wide nor deep. Can camels swim?' she asked, laughing hoarsely.

'Yes.'

'That's good.'

She smiled at us and blew out rings of smoke which expanded, elongated and broke up over our heads.

'The camels will cross the river in no time. But then unlike you, they won't have to deal with customs officials.'

On the evening of 24 October 2001, we were all bedded down in our sleeping bags in Alhaji Masta's carpet-strewn, mud-built, corrugated-iron-roofed go-down in Kukawa. I didn't realize at the time that this would be the last roof of any description that I was to sleep under for three and a half months.

We had all spent most of the previous day in Maiduguri market. When Boyd Alexander visited the market almost one hundred years earlier, he described a scene that can be replicated to this day.

> In the busy throng are to be seen the wandering Shuas standing by their tethered oxen which have brought in sacks of grain; the Fulani by his sheep and goats . . . the merchant with piled slabs of potash and dried fish . . . and the big balls of blue dye for the dyeing of cloth. Here come Hausas from many parts, some to buy the renowned cattle of Borno; others who are weavers and plaiters to sell their wares of cloth and straw, bernouses and hats, and little parchment boxes that contain blue chalk [antimony], beloved of the women for painting their eyes . . . And the shed is crowded where the barber plies his trade, rubbing on water and shaving the heads of his patrons who squat before him.

All of these things, and much more, can be bought today, and heads are still shaved. We bought sacks of macaroni, rice and spaghetti, our staples for the trip, together with onions, cabbages, tins of tomato puree and anything from asparagus to peas that might enliven an evening meal. Cabbages and onions keep in the heat, and the slimiest and blackest cabbage, when cut, will often contain a succulent green heart. We bought oranges, although these shrivelled rapidly and, at the professor's insistence, we acquired a box of apples. We felt that these would all too rapidly mush down, but were proved quite wrong – they lasted for nearly three weeks.

'We're going to need plenty of corned dog,' said Japper pointing to tins of canned beef that were piled high on a trader's wooden table. So they went into the sack alongside tins of sardines, pilchards and packets of sweet Marie and Nice biscuits. A Chinese kerosene cooker, wooden boxes to strap on the side of the 'kitchen' camel and countless other luxuries from garlic to tiny red hot pili-pili peppers had been added to our stores.

The invaluable wooden kitchen boxes had been devised by Japper to a design he had used for many years in the wilds of northern Kenya. He had come with the measurements and Johnny oversaw their construction by a clever carpenter in Maiduguri. Nine foot, four inches long, three foot, one inch wide and one and a half feet deep, they are constructed from plywood with a fitted wooden lid which when lifted out of both boxes and placed horizontally on the top, forms a table. Ropes which fit under each end of both the boxes are tied together on either side of a camel's hump. Provided they are evenly balanced, a strong, fit camel has no difficulty in carrying them when they are fully loaded.

Although I had ordered *salgas*, the skins of goats which are carefully cured to carry water so that it doesn't become tainted, these would not be available until we reached Ngigimi and had met up with Sidi and my camels. So we purchased plastic flat-sided four-gallon water containers to take with us on our travels with the hired camels. I later discovered that by far the best water container was the inner tube of a truck tyre, cut in half. Tied at both ends, this could be easily slung onto the side of a camel. It carried a considerable amount of water which remained sweet over a long period of time.

Many of the market stalls were covered with stickers in support of Osama bin Laden, but there was not the slightest antipathy to us as whites and our nationalities were quite irrelevant. Just outside the main market, where we had been taken to buy *kilishi*, delicious wafer-thin slices of peppered sun-dried meat, the stall-holder asked us to purchase an extra slice for his bin Laden Support Fund. This was said in jest, but there was a noticeable undercurrent of support for al'Qa'eda among the Maiduguri market fraternity. I asked him why he wasn't selling *kilishi* in the market-place. 'The health inspector chased us away,' he replied. 'He said that we attracted too many flies.'

I had brought with me a satellite telephone and a Magellan GPS (Global Positioning System) which could, I was informed, if coaxed with due consideration, dispatch an email as well as tell us, within a space of a few yards, exactly where we were. Both these concessions to the current age came with us against my better judgement, but on the insistence of our American sponsors, still jittery after September 11. I was originally sent two satellite phones and immediately returned one of them as being superfluous. Unfortunately, unknown to me at the time, one of the phones was packed with an instruction book in English and the other in Arabic. In my haste to rid myself of extraneous equipment, I returned the wrong booklet. As no member of the team read Arabic, including our herdsmen, we were taxed to a degree when we eventually brought the phone into operation. It was fortunate that Johnny was a master of the modern, but secretly I was glad that technology was not going to become too easy an option in times of crisis.

Additionally, these two items of twenty-first-century kit needed to be charged to enable them to operate. In order to allow me to do this, I had been sent two solar panel chargers, one of which could be strapped onto a camel. But we soon discovered that the vagaries of the camel and the arc of the sun made this method impractical. So, using one of the voluminous turbans that each of us carried, Japper volunteered to have the panel tied to his back while mounted on a camel. When the sun shifted in the sky, Japper adjusted the satellite phone charger. I suspect that this novel usage was a first for a Tuareg turban. Sartorially, the professor tied his Tuareg turban in a manner that made him appear like a walking wounded soldier with a serious head injury from the Great War, while Johnny appeared as a double for Peter O' Toole's impersonation of T.E. Lawrence. Goodness knows what I looked like.

Some people expressed surprise that we were not travelling with a back-up vehicle. Apart from the fact that it would have been useless in sand dune areas, I did not want to travel in this way. I wanted us to travel as near as possible to the way that travellers for centuries have crossed the Sahara.

Until man mastered the camel, Africans to the south of the Sahara had been totally cut off from the people who inhabited the coastline to the north. I wanted our expedition, to be completely reliant on the wonderful creature that had first enabled man to cross hitherto unconquerable barriers of sand, in some of the remotest and poten-tially most hostile areas of the world.

The camel's temperament is wholly at variance with popular belief. A camel is patient, tenacious and infinitely long-suffering. The impression held in the minds of people who have never worked with camels, is that they are vicious, that they kick, bite and spit, and that they have not the slightest empathy with the human race. Certainly, one can find camels that show all these negative qualities, but it is frequently as a result of a brutal and unsympathetic training and upbringing. Handled carefully and looked after with consideration, a camel will respond to an individual handler like a horse or a dog. And they are not stupid. Japper taught domestic Bactrian camels in China to recognize his own words of command in three weeks, commenting, 'They pick up English faster than foreigners.' It is an animal that can travel without water for over a week and can carry its own reserves of food, stored as fat, within its hump. Wild Bactrian camels in the Gobi desert, can go much longer than a week without water, but an animal laden with up to 100 kilos (300–350 pounds) of kit needs water at least every seven days. Travelling over firm, rock-free terrain, a camel will average two and a half to three miles an hour and can cover up to twenty-five miles a day. I have curled up with a camel at night to shelter from the wind, and Japper befriended a camel on a march in Kenya which sought him out wherever and whenever he could find him. But a word of warning. Tuaregs will tell you that, like some humans, a camel has two characters, one positive and the other negative. When you get up in the morning, you are never quite certain which character you will meet. In spite of their benign characteristics, it is as well to check.

When we reached Kukawa, the price of camel hire had blown up out of all proportion because of Sidi's two-week delay. The hired caravan had, with the herdsmen, been watered and fed while waiting for us to arrive. This all had to be paid for. The camel-owning Alhaji who had hired me the thirteen camels and three Arab herdsmen – Zachariya, Mohammed (1) and Mohammed (2) – was determined to extract the last inflated naira out of me. Both he and Alhaji Masta knew that this camel windfall was unlikely to be repeated. The haggle lasted for over an hour, but as the sun set the negotiations were at last concluded, if not quite to my satisfaction.

It had been a very hot day, and in the comparative evening cool, the inside of an arctic sleeping bag, that had been bought for the cold desert nights, was sticky and uncomfortable. But I soon became oblivious of discomfort, as I listened to the half-remembered, unchanging tenor of northern Nigerian village life that echoed all around me.Behind the mud wall of Alhaji Masta's compound there was a mosque. As the sun slowly disappeared, the faithful were called to prayer. I heard the rhythmic pounding of grain in a wooden mortar, accompanied by a soft song and a clap of hands as a young girl threw her pestle high into the air. A shrill-tongued voice rang out from a woman, no doubt bending over a clay cooking-pot. Her husband, newly back from the farm, grumbled a reply. A dim female shape passed beside our go-down, carrying a chicken under her arm

and some eggs. I smiled to myself at a scene that recalled an unen-
forceable law that was once passed, forbidding chickens to be carried by their legs. As Alhaji Masta's household settled to an evening
meal, conversation was conducted in whispers until the shrill cry of
a child punctuated the air. A drum beat. There was life and laughter.
But this was not a night to dance and the shouting and drumming
ceased as abruptly as it had begun. A dog began to bark, endlessly.
Another dog took up the chorus. As I lay silently perspiring, with
Kukawan mosquitoes buzzing greedily around my head, I re-read
Vischer's eve of departure words by the light of a torch: 'Presently
all became quiet, and nothing could be heard save the munching of
the camels . . . Behind me the moon shone above the black trees, in
front lay the camp and the loads all ready at last to start, and, farther
off, the white sand dunes, the desert, and the horizon, "where the
strange roads go down". Then happy like my black brothers, who
have never a care for the future, I lay down to sleep.'

*   *   *

'They look a little nervous but they are certainly used to load-
carrying.'

Japper and I were inspecting the hired camels as fingers of light
spread rapidly and unevenly across a grey early morning sky.

'See the marks on that one, where the ropes have rubbed and the
saddle sore has healed?'

Zachariya, a youth of about twenty with light-coloured skin and a
cheerful smile, came over to us.

'The camels are good, fit and strong,' he said to me in Hausa.
'They won't give us any trouble.'

'What are those strange rings?' I asked, pointing to one of the six-
inch diameter, metal rings tied above the nostrils of three of the
camels.

'They're only for decoration. We tie them on the lead camels. It
gives the other camels in the caravan a marker to follow.'

'They look like enlarged gun-sights.'

The crudely made wooden saddles that had been provided were built to be placed on top of load-carrying camels. This meant that none of us would be able to ride independent of the roped caravan. The saddles had long tails that curved upwards and were studded with metal. These somewhat phallic objects, served no practical function and were apparently purely for decoration.

Japper picked up one of the saddles and tested the strength of the ropes and nails which held its supporting struts together.

'Unless they are well padded on top, our backsides are going to suffer,' he observed prophetically.

I had anticipated that it would take up to three hours to load up, especially as our kit had to be packed carefully into hessian sacks that we had bought and had turned into camel carrier bags in Maiduguri. Unfortunately, the sacks had previously been filled with pungent pepper, and no sooner had we started to put our loads inside them, than we fell about coughing and sneezing. But, amazingly, all was ready by 8.30 a.m. and, with hasty farewells and a cheerful wave, our caravan finally set off, heading north out of Kukawa. The months of plotting and planning, the delays and disappointments, the pressures from America and individuals, all these frustrations evaporated. At long last we were on the road and a dream that I had held onto for more than a quarter of a century matured into reality.

I could not resist noting that Vischer's departure from Tripoli had been a lot less orderly and it had taken a whole extra day to reorganize scattered loads, frisky camels and rival camel drivers. Our frictions were to develop later, but for the moment we were drawing away from Kukawa, following a dusty winding track through the maize, guinea-corn and catch-crops of the farms that surround the ancient Borno capital. Cocks were crowing, people were stirring, and blue smoke from cooking fires spiralled upwards into an early morning haze. Greetings were shouted back and forth, and as we moved away from quickening human activity, the farm-land abruptly gave way to scrubby bush. I recognized the wild paw-paw, and the bitter-sweet yellow cherry, growing among acacia shrubs with their sharp white thorns, some as long as six inches, which could lame a horse if trodden on. A camel is the only animal able to feed on acacia by crunching it up in his seemingly cast-iron mouth.

Swaying rhythmically backwards and forwards on a camel, hour after hour, there is all the time in the world to think. As we set off, my thoughts travelled back to earlier days in West Africa, when I had crossed thousands of miles of bush on foot and horseback. It had once been the soul of life, and in those distant days I couldn't get enough of it. Every new tract of country was an exploration, every new village an adventure. As for discomforts, they vanished quickly enough. A long trek in furnace heat usually ended with a bath and a meal. Drowned like a rat in an hour's heavy rainstorm, one dried out before a roaring log fire and laughed at earlier misery. There were the joys of early mornings in rain-washed air, the tingle of evening cool when the sun had gone, and a recollection of all the incidents which the day had brought. I was roused from these rose-tinted memories when we rode past a cluster of myrrh trees that wafted an intoxicating scent. Japper said later that young Somali girls cut the branches, burn the resin and then stand in the perfumed smoke to make themselves smell sweet.

As for me, after an interval of many years, I was savouring that utterly liberating feeling of riding off into the vast empty space of Africa.

3

You cannot find a peril so great that the hope of reward will not be greater . . . Go forth, then, and . . . make your voyage straight-way.

Prince Henry the Navigator

'Do you have a permit to allow you to take these camels out of Nigeria and into Niger?'

The self-important official, with the torn khaki tunic, sagging belt, voluminous shorts, and a peaked cap at least three sizes too small for him, puffed himself up, rolled his eyes and stared at me. As the chief of customs and a non-northerner commanding the remote Komadugu Yobe river crossing near the tiny hamlet of Bisagama, he must have felt cut-off and isolated. I pictured him sitting lonely and aloof in a mud thatched hut, swilling his Star beer and entertaining nostalgic thoughts of lush green palm oil groves and a home in the steamy south. I sensed that, for him, Bisagama customs point must be a punishment posting. His one serious duty, according to a policeman to whom I had talked earlier, concerned guns. The high-waymen who cross over from Chad are flush with kalashnikovs and there is a lively cross border trade in weaponry. I suspected that illicit revenue might be filtering down into the customs officer's sticky hand. If so, the house in the steamy mangrove swamps could be larger than I imagined.

But we were very different. He had been called from his house to confront travellers, some of whom were white, who wanted to leave Nigeria with camels. Camels! What an opportunity. What a chance for aggrandisement. This was a real job for a senior officer in the customs service.

'All our papers are in order. We're carrying visas and invitations for Nigeria and Niger, certificates from the National Geographic Society, invitations from Libyan . . .' my voiced trailed away.

'But the camels, where are the permits for the camels?'

'You can't be serious, do we need camel permits?'

'No permits, no permission to cross the river. It is all written down in the rule book. Section 21, Paragraph 23 A – livestock can only be exported from Nigeria by land, sea, road or river,' he glanced at me meaningfully, 'if the relevant permits have been issued. Bring me your passports.'

I collected the team's passports and handed them over.

'Aha, British passports. Now that's a much bigger problem.'

'Why?'

'Because your country is full of cattle sickness. Mad cows with feet and mouth. We know all about it. You burn your cattle, millions of them, because they are sick. Don't think for a moment that we don't know about these things. And here is a Kenya passport. Kenya has rinderpest and east coast fever. Very serious notifiable diseases. And the owner of the passport is a farmer.' He shook his head from side to side. The peaked cap wobbled precariously. 'Your problems are enormous.'

'But how can any of this affect the camels that we hired in Nigeria just under one hundred miles away. What are you talking about? None of what you are saying makes sense.'

The little man, whose name I later learnt was Augustine Ekundayo, had hooked his thumbs into his sagging belt and was slowly patting his extended, beer-inflated stomach.

'Didn't you travel from England to Nigeria via Kenya?'

'Yes.'

'Then you could be carrying countless malignancies. They could be swarming all over your shoes, they could be attached to your trousers. You could be,' Augustine paused for effect, 'a contaminated source.'

'But what has all this got to do with our camels?' I persisted.

'The camels could have caught malignancies from your persons. They could take these contagions into Niger. Then Nigeria would be blamed, there would be an international incident. I would be made accountable and I would be dejobbed in a twinkling on account of these inconsiderate actions by your good self. This catastrophe would fall on my head and shoulders, but you would be the instigator. If I was dejobbed, I would return to my home in the south with a heart and intestines filled with misery. You would pitch me into a vale of tears.' He wagged a forefinger in front of my nose. 'Remind yourself of how I would have to face a tearful wife and twelve voracious children with my pockets filled with non-existent naira. Not a solitary penny.' Augustine was carried away by his own eloquence. 'No, you cannot travel across the river into Niger. This situation is very serious.'

He turned away and began to walk slowly back towards the village. As he did so, the Alhaji from whom we had hired the camels mysteriously appeared, somehow he must have jumped on a lorry and come to meet us at the river crossing. He went over to Augustine and for a few moments talked earnestly to him. Then he came over to me.

'You have seriously contravened the rule book,' he whispered, 'but for a consideration, he is prepared to waive the rules . . .'

I heard a shout. Augustine had turned and was striding towards me. He abruptly stopped, stood stock still and pointed at the professor who had set up his tripod and was taking a video of the river, the camels, the wooden boats and our loads sprawled all over the sandy shore.

'That is illegal,' he pronounced. 'No person is permitted to take photos on any Nigerian border. Seize that camera,' he called out to my erstwhile friend the policeman, who was sitting slumped against a tree dressed in a faded Nigeria Police jacket with a brightly coloured wrapper tied around his waist. He rose slowly to his feet.

'Professor, I called out, please put your camera away.' Beneath his large white plastic Chinese coolie hat, Professor Yuan Guoying was engrossed in his filming. He had no idea that he had become the centre of a controversy.

I turned to Augustine. I felt it was my turn to be eloquent. 'Please understand that this gentleman is a very high-ranking official from China. He's a very important guest of the Nigerian government. If anything happens to him there certainly will be a major international incident – and you will be held responsible. Dejobbed? They won't even wait to hear your explanation. You'll be put in prison. Incarcerated? Forget your tearful wife and twelve voracious children. You'll never see them again.'

I stared at him. I could see his resolve falter. He called off the policeman and turned to me, with a slack smile.

'Have you spoken to the knockhead?' I must have looked bemused because he continued, 'The knockhead, you know.' He bent forward and banged his head on the back of his hand. 'The Muslim, the Alhaji, the knockhead.'

'Yes.'

'Did you understand his message?'

'Yes.'

'Then you can cross.' He grinned at me. We had already wasted well over an hour, and my patience was wearing thin.

The loads were stacked into three wooden canoes while a group of laughing, jostling small boys stripped off and drove the reluctant camels into the river. The current was weak and the water wasn't deep. I suspect that the camels' feet only left the sandy bottom for a few minutes. The boys, waded, swam and slapped the water behind the camels to encourage them forward. We followed in the canoes and in a surprisingly short time we had crossed the Yobe and were lodged, with all our loads and camels, firmly in Niger. Alhaji sidled up to me. 'The customs officer needs a consideration for being so understanding,' he whispered. 'There is also the fee for the boatman who ferried your loads across. Then there are the boys who. . .'

I was tired of the wheedling whine of this slick Alhaji. I gave him some money which he immediately pronounced was too little. My patience had worn thin and I exploded. Alhaji remonstrated, and then waddled away muttering to himself.

We had taken three days to reach the river. During that time slack muscles had chafed and ached with the constant swaying movement of the camels. It had been hot during the day – over 105° Fahrenheit – and warm at nights, too warm for arctic sleeping bags, so we slept under the white cloths that Johnny had brought to shade us from the desert sun. Japper had been proved right about the saddles and our bottoms were sore. I felt that this pre-Ngigimi run with hired camels was, for all of us, a period of basic training and we had begun to settle into a rhythm and routine. It takes time. Detachment from the bustle of modern living and assimilation into a non-mechanical world does not come in twenty-four hours. We had discovered how to pack up in an orderly fashion, to handle ropes and how, under Johnny's wary eye, to load the wooden kitchen boxes.

We had found out that it was not a good idea to take an hour off for lunch. If we did, camels had to be unloaded and their loads tied back on again, a time-consuming exercise. We learnt that the best way for us to cook at the end of a tiring day was to leave it to the herdsmen and not to attempt to do it ourselves. What they ate, we ate and we followed this practice all the way until journey's end. As the great explorer Heinrich Barth commented 150 years earlier, 'It requires a good deal of labour to prepare it [food] well and this, of course, is a difficult matter for a European traveller, who has no female slave or partner to look after his meals.' Quite.

No sooner had we left Kukawa than we encountered an unrelenting and most persistent obstacle, a tiny grass burr, the *karengia, (Pennisetum distichum)* which covered the entire route to the river and would irritate us for over a hundred miles beyond. Barth attacked it with small pincers. Dr Oudney, who accompanied Denham and Clapperton, wrote that; 'the dogs lay down & cried and the foot travellers made great lamentations – they are really troublesome and fasten themselves like grappling irons . . .' Johnny, who had started out striding through the bush like a Heinrich Barth manqué, was left with irritants which lasted for days. Their extremely sharp little seed pods, detach easily from the burr head and burrow deep into one's skin. When you try to brush them off your trousers or legs, they burrow into your hands. If you scratch your head, they are soon in the hair and diving deep into your scalp. Persistent and tenacious, we carried some of them into Libya and we must have assisted them immeasurably in pushing their frontiers northwards. Strangely, we noticed that they did not attach themselves to the camels and put this down to the lie of the hair on a camel's leg.

Mohammed (2) had been low with fever on and off for most of the journey and when we crossed the river he vanished. I remembered how Vischer's Tubbus had done a bunk at certain intervals on his journey and drew some comfort from a shared experience. Augustine had delayed us for so long that we were forced to bed down near the river, much to the delight of savagely voracious mosquitoes who tested both the efficiency of our mosquito nets and the new anti-malaria prophylactic which I insisted that everyone swallowed each morning. We would have plenty to contend with and I didn't want fever to strike. I was particularly concerned about the professor whose blood had not been sucked by malarial mosquitoes in the past.

Our route took us towards Bosso, ten miles away, where there is a Niger customs post. No sooner had we arrived at Bosso than one of our camels unaccountably spooked. He ran round in circles trailing our loads, and when he had shaken them off, he headed west into the scrub at a tremendous pace. I had read that occasionally a camel can suddenly have a fit and take off, running on and on until it drops. Herdsmen are fearful of these bewitched animals which sometimes pass them at high speed, frothing at the mouth with a wild look in their eye. They consider them to be possessed by a malign spirit and make no attempt to stop them. The wretched animal gallops on and on, heedless of hours of daylight or darkness, not stopping to rest and ignoring any other camel. After travelling for several days in this crazed fashion it drops down dead.

While Zachariya set off to track the camel, we entered the concrete office block that served as the Niger customs post at Bosso. It was hot and the soldiers who sat outside were sprawled flat out under a large acacia tree. One of them eyed us suspiciously as we passed. The others were fast asleep. The customs office was managed by an extraordinary individual, smartly dressed in khaki uniform and seemingly commanding respect from his two officials who hovered in attendance dressed in turbans and long flowing gowns. The commandant was noteworthy in that he seemed unable to remember what he had done five minutes beforehand. He took Japper's passport and I watched as he placed it carefully in the drawer of his desk. Then he asked Jasper for his passport.

'It's in your drawer,' Japper said politely.

'Oh, yes,' said the official absentmindedly. He opened the drawer and took it out.

He held the professor's passport upside down and nodded sagely. 'Chinese,' he intoned after long consideration. All this accrued to our advantage as Japper had not got a valid visa for Niger, the one vital piece of documentation that we were not carrying. The official became muddled. He stared hard at the professor's visa and began to question him about China.

'China is good, very good,' said the professor with a smile as he handed over a badge with an emblem of the Chinese flag linked to that of Russia. The other two officials held out their hands. The professor parted with two more badges.

Amid all this jollity, we received permission to proceed, our documents were duly stamped, and with handshakes all round we walked out of the benign atmosphere of the Niger customs post at Bosso and into the blazing sunshine. One hour later, Zachariya returned. He said that he had searched and questioned many people but he had not found the missing camel. As it had taken off unloaded, we decided to press on with our hired caravan, minus one camel, and adjust our loads accordingly.

Our route took us close to the former coastline of Lake Chad, once the sixth largest lake in the world. One hundred years ago, Vischer described how he had passed by the reed-grown swamps of the lake after leaving Ngigimi, in Niger, but he could not have done that today. During the last fifty years, the lake has dried up and retreated, until now it is only one-twentieth of the size that Vischer would have known. In 1823, Denham placed the shore at ten miles from Kukawa, now it is nearer thirty; but even in those days, the Bahr el-Ghazal overflow river system to the north-east was totally dry and full of the bones of great fish. A man told Denham that in his grandfather's lifetime, it was a day's journey to cross the Bahr el-Ghazal.

The lake-bed is flat and shallow, and even in the relatively high water levels of the 1950s, the lake was no more than fifteen feet deep. Vogel, writing home in 1854, gave a graphic description of how quickly the Lake Chad waters can advance or retreat:

A few days ago, I went on horseback to Gurno, a town nineteen English miles south-southwest of here [Kukawa], which, about thirty days ago, had been nearly entirely gulped up by water. I found most houses still almost completely submerged in the floods. The water had risen about twenty feet within three days! Since the Kanenbu villages close by had not suffered from the floods I can but explain this remarkable occurrence with a depression in this place (which would also explain why such an unusual water level could remain for thirty days without having decreased even one foot) – a rare incident where earthquakes are unknown and which is hundreds of miles distant from any volcanoes!

Historically, Lake Chad received most of its water from rains that fell annually from June to August. But at the end of the 1960s, the sub-Saharan region experienced a series of devastating droughts. As the rains increasingly failed, local people became more dependent on Lake Chad as a source of water. In the 1970s, irrigation schemes were initiated and these too, no doubt, contributed to the lake's shrinkage. Then the rains failed again and the lake's level fell to a point when no further irrigation could take place.

The lake's decline and the years of drought and unreliable rainfall have had an enormous impact on the nine million farmers, fishermen and herdsmen who border the lake and depend on it for their livelihood.

When a situation becomes extreme, human beings fight to survive. One hundred and fifty years previously, Vogel found that: 'People here find it more convenient to raid the neighbouring lands than to farm and to catch a good number of slaves – mostly children between nine and twelve years old – to barter them with Tubbu and Arab merchants . . . In this kind of trade, a slave boy of about ten years is worth five dollars, a girl of same age will go for about seven dollars.'

Between Kukawa and Bosso we became aware of the first clear signals that the desert is advancing south. We noticed declining vegetation, and overgrazing that has degraded the area. More dramatically, new sand dunes were forming, and spreading irreversibly through the scrub. This was on land littered with tiny white shells, left over from a period when the waters of Lake Chad would have covered our track.

There has also been a substantial and irreversible effect on wildlife. Boyd Alexander mentions frequently seeing kob, gazelle and large herds of hartebeest. Near the western shoreline of the lake he saw hippo, rhino and herds of elephant over 400 strong. Hanns Vischer recounts sighting large herds of gazelle and Denham mentions lion outside the walls of Kukawa, leopards, jackals, civet cats, ostriches and giraffes.

Denham wrote on 12 March 1823:

> The lake . . . abounds with fish and water fowl of all descriptions . . . guinea fowl abound in the neighbourhood of the still water, and were our stock of powder more abundant we should supply our table plentifully. Gazelles are to be found in numbers and Mr. Clapperton is very successful, the flesh is a coarse sort of venison which I love not – nor do I the sport of killing them, to succeed it is necessary to lurk about the low trees for hours and catching them asleep, gives you the only chance of getting near enough to have a shot. I cannot think this gives the animal a fair chance. – I have shot but one and its soft black dying eye, which possesses an indescribable brilliancy seemed to look so reproachfully at me that I repented of the deed and vowed to sin no more.

As for elephants:

> The first night we saw forty-seven elephants feeding . . . at first they appeared to treat our approach with great contempt, yet after a little they moved off, raising up their ears most violently which till then laid flat on their shoulders, giving a roar that shook the ground under us, one was an immense fellow seventeen or eighteen feet high . . . one of the Negroes cast a spear at him

which striking him just under the tail seemed to give him about as much pain as when we prick our finger with a pin. The huge beast threw up his trunk and with a roar, cast from it such a volume of sand that unprepared as I was for such an event, nearly blinded me.

Thirty-one years later Vogel still commented on the 'unbelievable numbers of elephants and hippopotamuses' at the lake. He also complained about its mosquitoes and white ants 'which are like cock robins and mice in size'.

Apart from a few hares and four herds of duiker that numbered no more than twelve, and which understandably bolted when they saw us, we saw no other wildlife at all. The combined effect of over-population, drought and the disappearance of their habitat, has ensured that all the animals seen by those earlier explorers have tragically disappeared forever. However the mosquitoes, flies and white ants remain, and are as voracious as they were one hundred years ago.

That evening, we reached the borehole near the village of Kabe-laou. Here hundreds of the great horned Borno cattle were being watered, along with sheep, goats and over 200 camels. While we were watering our camels, the market headman approached me with an open palm. He was fishing for money, but a joke in Hausa headed him off with guffaws of laughter. When I talked to a grey-bearded cattle-owner, he lamented that raiders from Chad were causing a great deal of trouble. The bandits were stealing livestock and burning houses.

'The government does nothing about our situation,' he said. 'We are fighting a miniature war and we're on our own. Take care,' the sage added, 'the bandits will see you as an easy target. Most of them are former lake dwellers who used to be fishermen and lived on islands in the lake. Now the lake has dried up and the islands have disappeared. So they've taken to crime. The trouble is that they know every inch of the area – much better than we do.'

These bandits are the Bunduma or, as they call themselves, the Yedina. Their varied ancestors, some of whom were kinsmen of the Tubbu, established themselves on Lake Chad over the centuries, as fugitives from more powerful neighbours. There they learnt to make canoes from bundles of small reeds and so were able to enjoy both security and mobility. Barth dubbed them the 'famous pirates of Tsad.' They constantly raided the Kanuri lakeside villages and because of their aquatic lifestyle, the Kanuri found them impossible to conquer. Everyone feared the Bunduma and they prevented many of the earlier explorers from venturing onto the lake. In spite of the dramatic shrinkage of the water, they appear to have reverted to their old tradition.

Denham, on 12 March 1823, recorded in his journal:

> It is said you may go for forty days to the east and there are islands inhabited by people who live by plundering on the main land & then escape in canoes. These islanders visit the spot where I was [near Kabelaou] and sometimes . . . carry off with them bullocks in abundance, sack a village and bear away the inhabitants; yet nothing is done to crush them.

Plus ça change.

Sidi had warned me only to bring enough money for our immediate needs. I carried £900 and US$ 2,000 in leather pouches around my neck. Other than that, we had little worth stealing, apart from the camels and our cameras.

We camped two miles north of the borehole in a fold in the hills. Next morning, before we set off, the professor had disappeared to photograph the rising sun. He stood silhouetted on the skyline, bending over his tripod.

'Call him back,' said Zachariya anxiously. 'The bandits may see him. They will think that his tripod is a gun. It's too dangerous for him to do that.' Ever since he had been told about the Lake Chad bandits the professor had been urging me to carry firearms. ' The British government insisted that Barth carried guns and Hanns took guns as well,' he said. 'You should insist that we carry them, too.'

Japper overheard him on one occasion and commented, 'It's all right for the old prof because in China they wouldn't ask too many questions if he shot a Muslim bandit. They'd mostly likely end up giving him a medal. You should tell him that in Africa the authorities wouldn't ask questions either. The only difference is that they wouldn't congratulate us – they'd shoot us.'

To my great relief, Sidi was waiting for us when we reached Ngigimi. The journey from Kukawa with the hired camels had taken five days. He had with him my twenty-five camels, four Tuareg herdsmen, a Tubbu guide and a French journalist called Anna-Marie. The Tuaregs and the camels had been trekking from Agadez for over a month and had already covered almost 450 miles, a sobering thought when I reflected that there were 1,500 more miles in front of us.

Anna-Marie's name had been given to me by the *National Geographic* photographer as someone who could help us obtain camels to take us northwards from Gatrun in Libya, after Sidi's contract had expired. A blonde, mop-haired French girl in her late twenties, with a decided passion for Niger, deserts, and I suspect, Tuaregs, she was an exotic species in grey wind-blown Ngigimi, both alluring and bizarre.

'How do you get the funds to roam all over the desert? How do you stay alive?' I asked her.

'I am secretly investigating slavery in West Africa and the shipment of slaves to France,' she whispered clutching my arm. 'My magazine pays me to do this.'

'On a four-year assignment?'

'Yes, I am an undercover journalist,' she put a finger to her lips, 'but you mustn't tell the Tuaregs. My work is secret.'

'What do they think you're doing?'

She shrugged and gave a hoarse laugh, 'Enjoying myself, I suppose.'

Anna-Marie may have thought of herself as someone who worked undercover, but she made no attempt to hide her contradictory and bubbly personality.

'You are my slave,' she said later that evening as she stood, arms and legs akimbo, over a sheepishly grinning Sidi. She shook her floppy mane of hair, turned to me with a grin and said, 'Everybody thinks that Tuareg males are mysterious, the unspoilt masters of the desert. But when you get to know them, they're not so special, they're just like other men.'

After this brief introduction I decided that I was not going to rely on Anna-Marie for any assistance, either in Gatrun or anywhere else. Her sparky temperament was too volatile to be relied on. Anna-Marie reminded me of another blonde Tuareg admirer who, some years earlier, I had sat next to at a dinner for desert eccentrics. She had steadfastly refused to eat anything except fruit during the lavish four-course meal. We had been engaging in animated and informative chatter when she suddenly turned and, looking at me very earnestly, said, 'The clock has struck.'

'Really?'

'Yes, I never talk to anyone after nine o'clock at night.'

And not another word did she utter either to me, or to the gentleman who sat on her right.

I had already met Argali and Ehom, Sidi's two Tuareg brothers recruited in Agadez. The other two, Adam and Asalik, were Buzus, the descendants of Tuareg slaves.

Argali, tall, rotund, light-skinned and generally cheerful, sported underneath his long flowing turban his magnificent mop of fuzzy hair which he preened meticulously every day, either seated on the ground or on his moving camel. But he also had a volatile nature. At times, in contradiction of Denham's observation that Tuareg males don't sing because they consider singing effeminate, he would sing his way across the Sahara – a plaintive song, an endless, repetitive, tuneless rumination. If he couldn't sing, he chattered, imitating the follies of women in a high-pitched falsetto, cracking joke after joke and bursting into laughter at his own wit. But when a different muse settled on Argali's shoulder, he could become morose and sullen, his songs would fade away and he would not talk to anyone. All the Tuaregs were meticulous observers of Islam and prayed at the designated times of day. The rigorous obligations of Ramadan fell due during our trip, but were postponed by our herdsmen until after they had returned home – a ruling which is allowed by the Faith. Argali, however, appeared to have his own method of praying. At the end of his morning and evening prayers, he would spit to his right and then to his left, at the same time snapping his fingers in a dramatic gesture. 'It's all nonsense,' said Asalik dryly to me one day. 'It's Argali's version of Islam and no one else's.'

On another occasion, Argali convinced himself that Abba, our guide, was not leading us along the correct track. So without informing any of us, he set out to follow a different route. Concerned that we had lost him, Asalik set out to find out where he was. Three miles later we spotted him on the horizon, squatting beside his camel near the route that we were following. He had proved a point, but the rest of the team was not amused. Argali also had a dietary quirk although not as extreme as that of my blonde dinner companion. Most unusually for an African, he refused during the whole journey, to eat anything out of a tin. However, to us foreigners, Argali was courteous, friendly and ever willing to help. One cold windy night, with eyes half-closed, I crawled out of my sleeping bag for a pee. The requirement was urgent and I stumbled into the near distance for relief among our scattered loads. No sooner had proceedings commenced, than I discovered to my horror that the loads concealed Argali who, much to my embarrassment, reared up beside me before the operation was complete. Had I been a yard or two to the left a major Anglo/Tuareg diplomatic incident would have ensued. He accepted my apology with good grace.

In complete contrast, Ehom, designated by Sidi as the '*chef d'expédition*' was very dark, silent and anxious to avoid conflict with anyone. He never complained, his honesty was transparent and his judgement was sound. Though occasionally indecisive, I couldn't have had a better leader and his calm assessment of difficult situations was a considerable help.

Little Adam was cheerful and energetic, always whistling to keep up flagging spirits and constantly running up and down the camel caravan to steady or adjust loads. Swathed in a khaki turban, Adam was a peacemaker, who struggled hard on a number of occasions to lower the temperature when the short-fused Abba exploded into uncontrolled anger. Adam was skilled with ropes and knots and was a master at constructing the complicated rope netting that has to be fashioned when carrying large amounts of grass as forage for the camels. As he said to me, 'You will only get a pretty Tuareg girl for a wife if you know how to tie knots. Otherwise she won't look at you.'

Asalik was the enigma of the team. Darker than Ehom and always dressed in black, his intelligent eyes stared out from above the folds of a jet black turban which covered his nose and mouth. Asalik was an observer and a man of very few words. He was self-sufficient and self-contained, watching the strange foreigners intently and occasionally commenting to me in a soft voice when he felt that I should do something either with the camels or with one of the team. 'I was sent on this trip to protect you,' he said to me one day. 'I am here to ensure that nothing is stolen and that you come to no harm.' By the end of the trip I greatly valued the imperturbable Asalik. If there was one member of the expedition with whom I would re-cross the Sahara, it would be Asalik.

Vischer's caravan did not travel with Tuaregs whose geographical range covers most of the West and North African countries that extend into the Sahara. In his day the Tuaregs were desert marauders who raided oasis communities along the camel road and, on one memorable occasion, attacked Vischer's own caravan. Vischer was advised by the Commandant of Ghat in northern Libya, 'If you have anything to do with a Tuareg beat him on the nose at once and he will behave. If he thinks that you are impressed by his appearance he will become insolent and a dangerous enemy.' In complete contrast, our Tuaregs were cheerful, knowledgeable, loyal and hardworking. They looked after our camels with great ability, fully demonstrating the *amana*, or trust, in which Tuareg people are obliged by their tribal mores to hold all camels.

Of my twenty-five gelded male camels, nine were riding camels and sixteen were baggage camels. A riding camel – which needs a longer training – commands a price a third more than that of the baggage camel, which can carry loads of two hundred pounds. Among the latter were five skewbald (brown and white) camels that Jasper had read about as existing in the sub-Sahara but had never seen. Four of these remarkable creatures had blue eyes, and the fifth one blue and one brown eye. All five of them were completely deaf, a common trait with camels of their colour. Perhaps this was why they were also the most fractious camels in the caravan. As for their sex, although the female camel can run faster than the bull camels – which is why only females are bred to race in the Middle East – the males, gelded or entire, are the load carriers.

Our guide, Abba, was a Tubbu. The Tubbu are ancient inhabitants of the Sahara and live in northern Niger, Libya and Chad. They have an uneasy relationship with the Tuareg, scratching a living from dates or livestock and treading a very fine line between survival and dis-aster. In the nineteenth century they were constantly battling with the plundering Tuareg and the memories still rankle. I had learnt from Sidi that the Tubbus were agitating for a country independent of Niger and were linked up in this cause with disgruntled Tubbus over the border in Chad. The wily Sidi had chosen Abba precisely because he knew that his ties with the independence movement were strong. His brother had recently been killed in the affray with the Niger army that had forced Sidi to delay our journey by two weeks, and Abba was a well known hero among the militants. He could be difficult, unpredictable and was tiresomely self-important, but he was a good choice. Any recalcitrant Tubbu who had an eye on our caravan as attractive plunder would have been seen off by Abba, whose daily rate of pay of $25 was a compelling encouragement to see us safely through Niger and northwards to Gatrun in Libya. On a number of occasions he reminded me how he had secretly led an American CIA agent into Chad on a mission of such staggering importance and success that his pockets had been weighed down with the subsequent reward from a grateful American ambassador. And then there was the lonely elderly French woman that he had guided into the Tibesti mountains and had received further unspecified rewards.

'I am known as the desert expert,' he would conclude. 'And I am rewarded accordingly.'

Vischer commented that the only real trade known to the Tubbu was robbery and plunder. Understandably, Abba and our team of Tuaregs kept a wary eye on each other.

We spent two days among the Kanembu people of Ngigimi, buying last minute provisions and preparing ourselves for the start of the real journey. Japper, whose legs had been chafed by the saddles on the trek from Kukawa, bought a goatskin and fashioned it into two remarkably efficient gaiters which covered his legs below the knee and lasted the whole journey. Johnny had boxes made for our kerosene lamps and cooker. The professor brought out his acupuncture kit and treated Sidi's shoulder, Argali's back and Japper's seven-year-old bunion. Everyone proclaimed him to be a magician with his needles, although Japper felt that 'my bunion is too callused for a Chinese needle to have any effect.'

Mai Yunusa Mai Manga, was Ngigimi's District Head and Sidi appeared to know him well. His house in the town centre had a fine vaulted audience chamber built entirely of mud. Mai Yunusa Mai Manga himself was a plump, complacent middle-aged man who lolled centre stage on a sofa while he received guests, courtiers and sycophants.

'How do you expect to survive beyond Yat?' he asked. 'The road is stony, your camels will die of exhaustion and so will you. You're too old.' Mai Yunusa was nothing if not blunt. 'Why don't you take a back-up four-wheel-drive vehicle with you so that you can get in when you feel tired?'

I knew that it was going to be tough but I didn't need this rotund, rather self-satisfied man to tell me.

We were all invited to take a shower in his house the next day under a bent pipe capped with a perforated baked bean tin. Surprisingly, the water was heated by solar energy. I should have remained under the tin a little longer. It was the last shower that I would take for three and a half months.

Meanwhile, back at our campsite, the professor had unwittingly begun to entertain the Ngigimi inhabitants who hung about our loads with a display of t'ai chi, 'ultimate supreme boxing.' He did this not for them, but for his own state of health and mental equilibrium. His aim was not to make his body more slim and dynamic, but more flexible and poised. Balancing on one leg, he feinted, shadow-boxed, advanced forwards and then backwards, as if he were play-acting in the slow-motion film of a lost martial art. A leg was elongated to the left and then to the right. When he was satisfied with a performance to one point of the compass, he pirouetted ninety degrees and showed his prowess to another. His mind appeared to be completely closed as his fixed gaze followed the rhythmic flow of his fingertips. The Ngigimi town's people watched him in utter amazement. Was he mad? They had never seen anything like it. Then one or two bolder spirits joined in behind him swaying and ducking, following his flowing gestures with immense care and mimicking his delicate arm and leg movements with the utmost precision. Soon a whole troupe was spread out behind him, weaving and circling, prancing forward and backwards, the professor quite oblivious to this audience participation.

If that was not enough, on waking every morning the professor would submit himself to vigorous slaps and a self-administered body massage in order 'to wake up my body and move the blood'. It was more than his blood that moved. His tent vibrated to this rigorous early morning routine. Initially the unaccustomed noise and movement startled the Tuaregs.

'Is he praying to a Chinese god?' Argali asked me. 'Has he got a problem? Shouldn't we ask him if there is anything the matter?'

But as the days went by, and the professor's self-immolation continued unabated, we all grew accustomed to eccentricities which became as commonplace as Argali's individual interpretation of the morning and evening Muslim prayer.

On 2 November, having spent two days in Ngigimi, we were ready to set off. Japper had numbered our twenty-five camels with gentian violet, so that we could keep track of them individually. Johnny and I were mounted on two riding camels and, at their own request, the professor and Japper were riding baggage camels, tied to the rest of the camels in the caravan. Our caravan looked remarkably shipshape. We had acquired woven white plastic sacking for carrying loads, an ample supply of ropes and all the saddles were new. We said goodbye to Sidi and the charismatic Anna-Marie, who called out that she would meet us in Gatrun. The preliminaries were at an end. Our objective was Bilma, the ancient town in the centre of eastern Niger. At long last, the real journey across the Sahara was about to begin.

4

Away, for we are ready to a man!
Our camels sniff the evening and are glad.
Lead on, O Master of the Caravan
Lead on the Merchant-Princes of Bagdad.
         'The Golden Road to Samarkand', James Elroy Flecker

Ngourti, on the southern edge of the Tintumma, has a tiny market and a huge well, donated by a Canadian aid agency. The well is its life blood. Ngourti clings precariously to its existence and on the day we arrived it was shrouded in grey dust, which made us look as though we had been expertly dusted with wood-ash. Vischer didn't linger there and nor did we. Ngourti is the sort of place where there is little encouragement to linger. The few girls whom we saw appeared to specialize in staining alternate teeth black. When they gave us a rare smile they displayed a kind of facial chess board. We filled up all our goatskins, bought a few tomatoes and limes and pressed on.

The Tintumma plateau begins at Ngourti. It undulates monotonously and seemingly endlessly for a further eighty miles before descending to the oasis of Agadem. Here, the track crosses what is described as the Great Erg of Bilma – 200 miles of shifting sand dunes – which are impossible to portray accurately on maps. The Great Erg is punctuated by tiny oases which cling precariously to outcrops of black rock. To the north of this fragmented rocky spinal cord lies the famous desert town of Bilma, which encompasses a bright green oasis of lush landscape and fresh water, a welcome resting place for many species of migrating birds.

But first we had to negotiate the Tintumma plateau. Vischer, too, had been forewarned:

> The sand in the Tintumma is loose and treacherous and the continual wind which sweeps over the wide space covers up the tracks of a caravan as soon as it has passed. For the first two marches, the guides found their way by the small rocks which rise out of the sand; after that they must go entirely by the stars, or, as the atmosphere is nearly always thick with drifting sand, by their own instinct. A slight error in the direction has proved fatal to many a caravan, for at the southern end there is only one well. A narrow gully leads to it, and this gully is in no way different from a large number which run parallel to it on either side . . . the entrance to the little valley is not more than two hundred yards broad. Both Nachtigal and Rolfe nearly ended their lives in the Tintumma through a mistake, accidental or intentional, of their guides.

If anything, the Tintumma is even more bleak and barren today. Certainly the acacia shrubs and desert trees have diminished dramatically and it seems as though, yard by yard, year by year, the desert is relentlessly advancing south. Fortunately, Abba, our guide, knew the route well, his family home lay tucked away on the frontier of the Tintumma and his brothers, wives and children lived there in splendid isolation.

Trotting behind Abba, and utterly devoted to him, was a little sandy coloured bush dog called Arlit, who survived on the most meagre of rations. As the caravan travelled northwards and the vegetation decreased, Arlit would desperately seek out shade under a withered roadside shrub. Lying there, panting uncontrollably, his long pink tongue dangling from a salivating mouth, he would allow the camels to travel ahead as far as he dared. Then he would rise painfully to his feet and limp along at a trot until he caught up with them. Once reunited with the caravan, he would seek out Abba, who was usually striding along at the head of the camels, and run up to him with a spirited flailing of his long thin tail. When Abba was in uncertain temper, he would shout at Arlit or lob a stone at him as he advanced searching for affection. This was heartbreaking to watch. Having been thus roughly spurned, Arlit would once again seek out shade and a moment of respite from the broiling sun. After a few minutes' rest, the whole sequence would be painfully re-enacted. This loyal, intelligent and immensely lovable dog eventually arrived safely at the Abba family home where he joined his mates, a scrawny pack of pie dogs.

South of the Tintumma, Vischer noted:

> The number of animals we met or saw in the distance was fabulous. Giraffes, ostriches, large herds of sable antelopes, duikers, and dorcas gazelles were seen on all sides, the greater and lesser bustard called among the bushes and flapped heavily over the sand dunes. We did not lack beef for the cooking pots and the good diet, after so many weeks of meagre and badly cooked rations, brought back the old hilarity and the healthy fights to the black followers.

These animals have nearly all disappeared forever, but Vischer goes on to relate a story against himself:

Profiting by the momentary lull in the wind, I rode out to try and bag one of the animals [Addax antelope]. One by one, at an easy trot, away the antelopes moved off into the desert where none could follow. Only one large animal stayed behind, lying down on the sand. It was not sporting, but I left my horse and crawled cautiously nearer, on all fours most of the time, till I thought I could risk a safe shot. I fired and hit, a beautiful head-shot. Then to make sure, I sent him another, and then I mounted my pony and galloped up to the beast. Allah! The antelope was dead and dried to a mummy; it must have been dead for months. And then the wind got up again, and the sand flew about me and hid my shame, and very nearly also the tracks of the caravan; I found it at last, however, and no one seemed to see the humour of the situation.

Today, only a few terrified duiker and an occasional Addax antelope remain and we saw one very dead Fenex fox lying by the side of the track. But the scorpions haven't disappeared. Pale brown or yellow, they come in various sizes and a little one, no more than an inch long, can sting, according to Japper, as efficiently as a colleague twice its size. Although we once discovered six of varying dimensions lying inert under Japper's yellow tarpaulin, no one was ever stung. Japper had brought with him a battery-powered cattle prod which he had used quite frequently on humans and animals to treat the stings from scorpions, hornets and bees. He had also used it with great success on both puff adder and cobra bites. The prod had two electrodes between which passed a charge. Scientific investigation suggests that this charge alters the ions in the poison molecules, rendering them inactive. Several prods around the bite and a few more around a swelling are sufficient and it has proved to be a life-saver in half a minute.

As Japper says, 'If the victim's heart is about to pack up then the cattle prod can kick start it into life. It's far more effective than hitting his or her finger with a hammer and much less painful.'

As we slowly wended our way northwards, the sparse scrub jumped and shimmered in waves of heat. This and the imagined end of a Tintumma horizon which we never reached made the endlessly unfolding plateau seem irreducible – like dry bone. The blue of the sky was veiled in a hot white haze, like the graded wash that fills the painter's sky with vapour. A vindictive sun smote down on the hard-baked earth and frizzling sand, evaporating sweat before it left the pores. Occasionally, a tiny spiral of dusty chaff would start beside the track, dance along a yard or two, and then die down, before springing up again and whirling off into the bush with widening coils. Once more it would collapse, then suddenly rear up and come swirling down on us. From rustling murmur it grew to a rushing, crackling roar, hurling up in its vortex leaves and twigs and small stones amid a thick cloud of dust. Down it would descend, filling our ears and eyes and nose with prickling sand – spitting hot breath into our faces – and then it would dance off into the desert again, swaying and thrashing, just like a living thing, leaving us parched and gasping for breath.

When the wind died away and the atmosphere cleared, I was conscious of shadows gliding across the sand. Day after day, during fair weather or foul, two black carrion crows circled endlessly over the moving caravan. They were waiting in macabre expectation for a camel or a human to die. The crows followed us all the way to Bilma where they were joined by their much less sinister cousin, the Egyptian vulture. I am not someone who shoots, but had we travelled with guns, I would gladly have shot those two crows. Their ominous, unhealthy, ever watchful presence unnerved me. When we stopped for the night, they would flutter to the ground and hop about just outside the limits of our camp, looking searchingly at us with beady eyes, sizing us up, contemplating whether it would be man or beast who would give up first. It would have been immaterial to them. I loathed those crows and felt their influence to be evil.

My camel Pasha and some of the others frequently shook their heads in an attempt to deter the flies hovering around their nostrils. In addition, Pasha would turn towards me and try to rub his nose on the black plastic bag that carried our expedition papers which was tied onto the left side of my saddle. I smeared anti-fly cream over Pasha's nose but this had little effect. Then one day with a vigorous snort and a determined shake of his head, Pasha expelled a one-inch-long fleshy, pink fly bot (larva) that had hatched from an egg laid in his nostril by one of the hover flies. I was amazed to see the size of this unappealing bot which at first had landed on the top of Pasha's head before falling to the ground. Once it hit the sand, it wriggled out of sight. These fly bots set up an intense nasal irritation in a camel. Japper and I sprayed our camels' nostrils and rubbed them with cream, but although this seemed to have a marginal effect for a short period, our poor camels were snorting out these beastly bots all the way into Libya's heartland. The bots only stopped emerging when the weather turned colder and the fly no longer hovered.

Not so the ticks, these were carried along to the end of the road. All our camels acted as hosts to this particular species of *Hyalomma*, which buried into the sweaty sensitive folds of their skin. Pulling the ticks out was resented by our Saharan camels, due no doubt to the sensitive areas in which they buried their wicked little jaws. However ticks can cause more than mere irritation. It has been established that there is a loss of one to three millilitres of blood for every tick that completes its life cycle on a camel. A sufficient inducement for us to continue to pull them out whenever we could.

Frequently, when we pitched camp, we would spot a tamarisk bush which appeared to offer welcome shade and a deterrent to the wind. More often than not we would find that a vast colony of ticks had set up camp first. There was no question of sharing the campsite, and so we would be forced to spend a night braving the desert wind. In the desert, the blood-thirsty tick rules.

By six o'clock in the morning, Johnny would usually be up, scurrying around the kitchen boxes, lighting a fire and making tea. The rest of us were out and about an hour later. It took a further hour and a half to finish off the remains of the previous evening meal, and load up the camels. As we travelled further north, and the night temperature frequently dropped below freezing, our bodies and fingers became sluggish and stiff. It took more time to tie knots and haul on ropes and after cold nights we would not get away until about nine. At about five o'clock in the afternoon we were scanning the horizon for a campsite that would provide shelter from the wind and forage for the camels, and we were invariably settled before the sun disappeared.

A speeding limousine thinks nothing of a twenty-five-mile journey, but on a camel, travelling methodically at two and a half miles an hour, twenty-five miles is a very long day. Over the whole journey, we averaged from fifteen to sixteen miles a day. I was more than happy to slip back into the pace of a world that our ancestors had known for generations. We saw countless things that the speeding motorist never will. A migrating butterfly with battered wings, a dragonfly far from any known source of water, circular tubes of glass that had been fused and formed by a strike of lightning on the sand. Vischer also noticed the glass:

> In many places I noticed thin tubes as of glass, which stood out from the surrounding sand like stems of flowers. The people call this 'desert wax.' The sand had evidently been melted by lightning, and when the wind had brushed away the surrounding loose particles the thin tubes were left standing. There were often between twenty and thirty of these stems of natural glass close together.

Did man first discover how glass was made by observing these remarkable structures?

Travelling continually for seven hours over a featureless landscape with conversation limited by a wind is not always easy. Johnny frequently managed to read a book. I tried this, but after an hour, the camel's swaying gait made me feel sick. If I read, I couldn't concentrate on Pasha. My clever camel immediately sensed this and would strike off on his own line, which was frequently diametrically opposed to the direction in which the caravan was heading. On one occasion I attempted, like Argali, to sing my way across the Tintumma, and struggled to recall all the songs and hymns that were lodged in the crevices of my mind. But I discovered that my repertoire was limited. One can of course ride up to a colleague and talk. But if the wind is howling head on this becomes impossible. So one is left with thoughts that can quickly wing away into realms of fancy unless they are strictly controlled. Vischer doesn't mention such concerns in either his letters or his book, and I have a list of questions that I would dearly like to ask him.

One of those questions concerns alcohol. I know that he drank, because he referred to pink gin in letters home. But when did Vischer's liquor run out? Our whisky ran out before we were a third of the way across the Tintumma. This was a foreseen but nonetheless serious matter. For a while we survived on the professor's *mao tai,* an evil-smelling spirit which tastes far better in China than it does in the Sahara. But eventually, that source too trickled away.

'I brought a little yeast,' said the ever resourceful Japper. 'If we mix it up with our limes and a bit of sugar we should get something after a day or two that will give us a bit of a kick.'

So for mile after weary mile the kitchen camel carried a container which bubbled merrily away and eventually produced a yeasty froth which made you wince and then burp. We managed, however, to convince ourselves that our brewery was well worthwhile. When the limes ran out, we substituted tea and dates which would definitely not have passed the nose of a Master of Wine. But we drank it nevertheless, and pretended that it tasted like sherry.

The mock attack by seven Niger soldiers took us all by surprise. Some were bare-chested, with cloth wrappers tied around their waists. Others were clad in tee-shirts and shorts. They rushed out at us from behind a hill, hollering and shouting and waving their loaded kalashnikovs under the noses of our camels. As they were all Tubbus, Abba soon smoothed down their ruffled feathers and in no time we had dismounted and were shaking hands. They were camped near Ngourti at a well called Karyadiyang. Apparently, they had just been posted to this bleak fold in the hills and their trigger fingers itched to do battle with Lake Chad banditry. So their unproven assault tactics were tried out on us. Sadly, if neither bandits nor travellers materialized the finger itch still had to be assuaged. Abba told me that another band of soldiers had shot, at random, ten harmless domestic camels the previous month. 'Just for the fun of it.' No one received any compensation for this pointless savage act, and it can't have endeared the soldiers to the local Tubbus.

But after we had set up camp that night, Abba whispered to me that they wanted to check our papers, so could I collect up our passports and give them to him. He added that our papers would all be in order if I included a little money — poor Africa.

* * *

'You should teach Abba to drink from big cups,' said the professor, as delicious well sugared, herb-flavoured tea was passed to us in tiny cups by one of Abba's wives. We had reached the well of Bedoaurem and Abba's home. 'The Chinese understand tea and drink it a great deal,' he added, confident of his superior knowledge and culture. 'These cups are too small. You should explain to Abba that big cups are better.' There were times when the professor found it difficult to comprehend other people's customs, or that in these desert dwellers he had met his tea-drinking match. A Libyan poet who celebrates the comprehensive virtues of tea-drinking concludes:

Drink of it at dawn and in the evening, for those two moments are
the most pleasant for gathering together.

It is the drink above all others for men of good company; its taste
is even more delicious when drunk among agreeable guests in
luxurious tents.

It is the greatest gift God has given to those who enjoy drinking; it
is truly their elixir, surpassing coffee or wine.

We make it our rule to drink it unmixed with anything, except
with pure amber.

High praise indeed.

The kindly wife disappeared and shortly returned carrying plates,
mounded with stewed goat and pancakes. As our diet up to this
point had largely consisted of stewed goat and macaroni, the pancakes were welcome, in spite of their being made with sour milk.

We were squatting in Abba's hooped and matted hut, an expertly
grass plaited long-room, which gave welcome shade from the blazing sun outside. It was certainly big enough to accommodate Abba's
two wives and thirteen children. Carpets strung along the walls or
laid on the floor, gave it a cool languid feel. Cut off from anyone for
miles around, Abba's extended family had set up a hamlet of their
own, well away from outside interference. I am sure that his close
blood ties to the leaders of the Tubbu Independence Movement
made this a necessity.

Abba had constructed his own well where we watered our camels
and washed our socks and bodies. Unlike the well in Ngourti, which
was lined throughout its depth with rings of concrete, Abba's well
was unlined. This meant that almost every three years it caved in on
itself and had to be re-dug.

'Two years ago, someone from the Canadian aid agency came
here and promised to come back to help me to line it with concrete,'
said Abba wistfully. 'That was two years ago, but he's never
returned.' It was so apparent that the government had done very

little for the Tubbu, which no doubt explains their current state of turbulence. It was at Abba's well that Japper explained to us the technique of well washing,

'You should wash down from the top of your head as far as possible. Then wash up from your feet as far as possible. And then wash possible.'

The others had gone on ahead, and when I left Abba's well to return to the camp, the light was fading rapidly. Arlit, or one of his companions, was barking interminably. Another dog had started to howl. The walk back to the camp would take about thirty minutes but for some strange reason I felt uneasy. An inner voice was urging me to retrace my steps. I initially resisted, but it wouldn't stop. 'Go back, go back,' it seemed to say. I don't know why I turned and walked slowly back to the well. 'This is crazy,' I said to myself. 'I am wearing all my clothes, my shoes are on my feet. What am I doing?' When I reached the well I walked round to the spot where I had stooped to wash. Lying reflected in the full moon's light, I could just make out two round compact objects – the leather money pouches which contained all our expedition funds. I picked them up and placed them around my neck. Then I peered into Abba's well and saw, deep down in the water, a part reflection of the full moon. It is said that when you see the full moon reflected in water, you have seen it washing its soul and I uttered a little prayer of gratitude to whatever saint had done me such a good turn. Much, much later, I was told that this incident had happened on a day when a candle had been lit for our safety.

Vischer had written:

The same evening we passed a whole forest of acacia-trees. Under one of them lies buried a Tubbu saint, Anna, 'Kaffar Annabe' [the grave of the saint] the place is called. The country now took the familiar look of the Borno bush, with frequent thorn-tress and excellent pasture for camels with stubbly grass in between.

I wanted to find Anna's grave. It wasn't difficult. Shortly after striking camp two days after we had left the our guide's well, Abba led me over a hummock towards a solitary tree. There was no other tree anywhere in sight. Gone was the forest of acacia trees. Vanished was the excellent pasture for camels. This lone tree, planted above the grave of the Tubbu saint, is all that has survived. As Abba and I rode down to the solitary tree, I turned around to see that Johnny was trotting up hectically towards me. When he drew close I sensed that he was greatly agitated.

'What is happening? Where are you going? The Tuaregs won't follow you and they're heading off along the track. The caravan has split in two.'

Our Tuareg herdsmen were not going to go near a Tubbu grave whose occupant could allegedly make tongues of flame leap up from out of the earth.

'A pagan shrine,' said Argali scathingly, when I caught up with him. 'We wouldn't waste our time going anywhere near it. What sort of a Muslim does Abba think he is?'

On 13 November, having slogged for days over the monotonous Tintumma, the black hills of the oasis of Agadem appeared on the horizon, signalling a welcome break from our dreary surroundings.

In January 1823, Denham noted: 'At three in the afternoon, we arrived at the extensive wadey called Aghadem. Here are several wells of excellent water, forage, and numbers of the tree called suag, the red berries of which are nearly as good as cranberries. We broke in on the retreats of about a hundred gazelles, who were enjoying the fertility of the valley. Aghadem is a great rendezvous, and the dread of all kafilas [caravans] and travellers. It is frequented by freebooters of all descriptions.'

In 1906, Vischer found the oasis to be uninhabited, largely due to continued and sustained raiding by the Tuareg. An oasis is an entirely man-made habitation. It ceases to be an oasis as soon as man's control is removed. My journal entry for 13 November 2001 saw

Agadem in a very different light. The cranberries are gone, there are very few date palms and many of the wells were filled up with sand. A hundred people now live in rudimentary mud houses clustered together around a well. Their huts have no roofs, and shade is provided by mats slung over mud walls. How they survive and on what is a complete mystery as it was much too dry to farm.

We crossed over an ancient rock hard lake-bed, where we saw quite clearly the solidified footprints of elephant, lion and ostrich – all long since extinct in this area. We passed the ruins of a French colonial fort – what a posting – where the professor took endless pictures with his prized digital video camera as he scurried in and out of the broken walls that resembled crumbled biscuit. We finally bedded down amidst massive clumps of tamarisk that emerged from mounds of sand piled high against their elongated roots. This fortress of sand harboured thousands of voracious ticks, that pursued us with outstanding tenacity and forced us to alter our camping arrangements. Later our camp was besieged by children bent on trading arrow-heads, beads and ornaments, many quite beautifully made.

The different artefacts strewn across the desert, some of them of great antiquity, never failed to amaze me. We picked up finely serrated arrow-heads of varied shapes and sizes, hand-axes and fleshing tools, all of which littered the road from Agadem to Gatrun. It was a telling reminder, even more so than the prints of extinct wildlife preserved in the lake-bed, of how the environment has changed and of the extent of the population only a few thousand years ago. Vischer, too, picked up these implements, and in an appendix to his book they were identified as from the later stone age. As a very amateur geologist, their discovery was a continual source of wonder to me and I was constantly surprised that they could still be freely picked up, almost one hundred years after Vischer. The professor became the team arbitrator when these discoveries were made and classified all the expedition finds into three categories: 'certainly', 'maybe' and 'rubbish.' How he acquired this sophisticated knowledge I do not know, but he was never in any doubt when he settled on 'rubbish.' It was, in his mind, a certain fake or just a plain lump of rock masquerading as a fleshing tool. There was only one way of dealing with the spurious artefact — throw it away into the desert sands.

After Agadem, we left behind us the last forage that we would find for the camels until we reached Bilma. We had entered the Great Erg. For four days we negotiated dune after dune. Desert sand dunes rise and fall like something incarnate, time-bearing, at once peaceful and yet in their isolated desolation, rather terrifying. At night, surrounded by an unending sea of sand, we lay down to sleep with a majestic display of glittering stars spread over us. Everything was silent and quite still. The stillness before Creation. It was as though our team with the camels was all that existed in the world, and it was infinitely restful. Occasionally a pre-dawn mist lay over a surface so opaque that sand and sky were one. Then, at daybreak, a diffused light would brush the mist and stars away and Johnny would stir to light a fire and make tea.

It was in the dunes that guide Abba came into his own. Without his knowledge of the way ahead, we would have been hopelessly lost. But we were not alone. We had picked up a Tubbu from Agadem who was taking five camels to sell at the market at Dirkou, a commercial town just north of Bilma. Our travelling companion had with him his daughter, a tiny bare-footed tot of about six or seven, who wore nothing to cover her head and was dressed in a nondescript cotton shift. She was a very solemn little thing, who took her difficult and responsible task immensely seriously. Balanced precariously on one of their camels which was roped to the other four, she successfully negotiated the quintet over countless dunes. Day after day she carried out her arduous task, never complaining, hardly uttering. Her competence with camels was staggering. She bedded them down at night and ensured they were fed and watered with the outmost efficiency, while her father chatted away to Abba. Japper commented, 'You wouldn't get a *muzungu* (white) child doing that. After an hour or two it would be complaining that it wanted to go back home to mummy.'

At this point on our journey I gradually realized that we were, at long last, in real camel country. I felt that we had momentarily lost footing in time and had, almost subconsciously, slipped into a part of the world that the internal combustion engine, in spite of its endless versatility, had failed to conquer. The camel reigned supreme and our camels came into their own. In the Great Erg of Bilma, Vischer had had to unload his camels and his men carried their loads over the dunes. Although in places the going was very soft and our camels sank hock-deep into loose powdery sand, they struggled on with loads intact. They snaked, round, up and over the sand dunes, grunting when the uphill going was difficult and surging forward on a downhill slope. The baggage camels were all tethered together. As they descended the steep slope of a dune, little Adam ran up and down the line of camels in a struggle to ensure that they kept an even pace. If they didn't, a tethering rope would snap and the whole caravan would disintegrate.

Denham experienced identical problems: 'The greatest care is taken by the drivers in descending these banks: the Arabs hang with all their weight on the animal's tail, by which means they steady him in his descent. Without this precaution the camel falls forward, and, of course all that he is carrying goes over his head.'

Nothing at all has changed. Slithering down one steep dune, Johnny's camel, Albert, suddenly broke into a trot. Johnny was unprepared for this and fell off, crashing heavily into the sand. The delicate Tuareg saddles are perched high up in front of the camel's hump. Once balance is lost, it's all too easy to fall, and the subsequent drop is much farther than that from a big horse. Johnny was badly lamed and winded, and I was very relieved that he hadn't broken a limb. We struck camp early that evening, and the taciturn Asalik scooped out a pit in the sand in which he lit a huge fire. 'We can help him with Tuareg medicine,' he said to me. The coals were allowed to glow for over an hour and then were removed, leaving a heated hollow. Johnny limped over and was persuaded to stretch out almost naked in this burning bath of sand for three hours. The treatment, to which the professor added some obscure Chinese pills, proved successful. Next morning Johnny's stiffness had begun to wear off.

The Tuareg saddle, though precarious, is a thing of great beauty. At the front it forks from an elongated pommel into three brass-capped prongs, on which the rider can tie his turban, when not in use, or the end of the rope that controls the camel – the *teresum*. The saddle is constructed of wood, and the back support is frequently fashioned in the shape of a mosque and decorated on the back with turquoise, black and blue strips of leather. Rather appropriately, a car seat-belt had been stitched on underneath my saddle and served as a girth.

The rider's legs go either side of the elongated pommel and his stockinged or bare feet are then placed on the arch of the camel's neck. At every stride, pressure is applied with the foot or feet to urge the camel forward. Without this foot contact, the camel will raise its head, arch its neck and become uncontrollable.

The *teresum* is looped through a ring affixed to the camel's right nostril. It is then draped under its chin and held by the rider on the left side of the animal's neck. To make the camel move to the left, the rider's arm is extended to the left. To encourage it to move right, it is neck-reined in that direction. It is a strange feeling at first, and muscles and confidence take a few days to become toned up. But after three and a half months, one becomes aware of what one should be doing.

The camel can usually, quite easily be made to squat down, with a pull downwards on the *teresum* and repeated shouts of encourage-ment. As a camel is usually ready to rest, this is seldom a problem. But when mounting, one needs to take care. If the camel rises when the rider is swinging a leg over the saddle, as some are prone to do, the rider will be tipped unceremoniously backwards into the sand. Some camels make ferocious noises when a rider attempts to mount and they bend their heads round and bare their teeth. Argali used to pinch his camel's upper lip as he mounted, to ensure that his camel didn't stand up too soon. My Pasha protested, but never attempted to bite. All the Tuaregs could mount the camels when they were on the move, by leaping up into the arch of the neck and wiggling onto the saddle. But this was too much for me.

While crossing the dunes, Japper's camel was hitched up behind Argali for security, and Japper was mounted on a tailed baggage saddle. But this caused a problem when he needed to pee. 'Hey, Argali,' he would call out in vain. 'Stop, stop.' But his words would frequently be blown away on the wind and Argali's camel would plod on. The word to urinate in Hausa is *fitsari*, so to relieve the situation, Japper's camel was dubbed FitzHarry and when his rider exclaimed, 'FitzHarry! FitzHarry!' Argali heard and immediately understood.

Japper, Johnny and I took some pride in keeping our faces well scraped and as we were averse to battery-powered shavers, we used water to achieve this. But in the sand dunes south of Bilma, our facial bristles seemed to turn to iron. Even with boiling water and a new blade the effect was minimal. Japper and Johnny hated being covered in iron filings and so did I. But there was nothing that we could do about it. Our faces had dried out, and our bristles told the tale.

* * *

'Hey, John, come up here and bring the British flag.' We were camped in the dunes and the rays of the setting sun were illuminating our little camp in a variety of photogenic shades and shadows. The professor was calling out to me from half way up a dune. He was clutching the Chinese national flag.

'Come, come. The light is good.'

I got up from my sleeping bag and clambered up the dune. When I had caught up with him he asked me why I had not brought a Union flag. I replied that I didn't think it was necessary.

'Not necessary?' The professor stared at me in amazement. 'But this is Sino-British expedition of exploration in the Sahara. How can you come without a flag? Hanns would definitely have carried a flag.' He was genuinely aggrieved and baffled. 'Never mind,' he continued. 'Please photo me holding the Chinese flag. If we cannot have the flags of Britain and China, then we will have just China.'

We had reached the top of the dune and the professor had unfurled his country's bright red flag, topped with the communist stars. He spread out his arms and held it proudly aloft. I took his camera and started to take photographs.

'Good. Very good. This picture will be published all over China.'

I became conscious that a third person was toiling up the dune. Soon Argali's fuzzy head appeared. He was staring hard at the professor and he wasn't at all happy.

'What does he think he's doing?' he asked me in Hausa. 'Who does he think he is? Is he claiming Niger for China?'

A diplomatic incident was looming. I told the professor that Argali thought that he was trying to claim a part of Niger for China. The professor was genuinely shocked.

'No, no. China is a big friend of Niger. We love Niger. Africans are very good. Chinese people like Africans.' The professor couldn't understand what all the fuss was about.

'No,' said Argali angrily. 'No more photos. Tell him this is Niger not China. We have had one colonial power. We don't want another.'

'But tell Argali, we like Niger. China likes Qadhafi. China is a friend to Africa.'

'China might like Qadhafi, but Niger doesn't,' said Argali gruffly.

*   *   *

We passed through a string of oases with melodic and quaint sounding names; Dibella, Zoo Baba, Zoo Karimi, known to Vischer by the Kanuri names of Zo Gana and Zo Kura which correspond to our 'magna' and 'parva.' Each of these uninhabited oases clung to a fragment of the hilly spine which led north, much of it now submerged under sand dunes. That these oases were occupied even in prehistoric times was clear from the stone implements that we found in every one of them.

The type of *rhazzia*, or raid, unleashed on the Zoo oases by the Arabs and Tuaregs, which caused them to be deserted by the Tubbu at the turn of the last century, is dramatically described by Vischer:

> We reached a little depression known as Zo Kura, with good vegetation, grass, and shrubs, where seven water-holes with clear water lay amongst some hillocks. After the painful march we were glad to rest in so delightful a place, which looked like an island amongst the seas of sand.
>
> On the way, Hadji Zaid showed me with pride a place where his people had defeated a rhazzia of Uled Sliman . . . It was four years ago, and the trusty Hadji had himself been in the fray. The Arabs had chosen the hottest part of the year and swooped down from Tibesti when the Tubbus, themselves probably on a raid of their own, expected nothing. Without much trouble they took all the camels, women, and children they found, burnt villages cut down palm trees in the most approved fashion, and hurried off before their husbands had any news of the disaster. Among the sand dunes they thought themselves safe enough to rest a little, but they had calculated wrongly, for the Tubbus had heard of the disaster and by another route reached Zo Kura ahead of the Arabs. When the cumbersome caravan of the robbers slowly climbed one of the heavy dunes, the Tubbus swept down on them; forty of the Arabs were killed with sword and throwing-irons, and the others fled into the desert where the Tubbus pursued them till they died of thirst. We found a whitened skeleton lying head downwards on the slope of a dune, and in its dried-up backbone struck the short iron head of a Tubbu spear . . . Had I met the

Arabs it might have been our most exciting, and probably our last experience.

I related this story to Abba who verified it in even gorier detail. 'My grandfather took part in that battle. It was told to me, over and over again, when I was a boy. I've seen skeletons of those who were killed. My grandfather said that the dune where the slaughter took place ran red with blood. The Tubbus will never trust the Arabs, or the Tuaregs – ever.'

On 20 November, we were camped eleven miles from Bilma, a major landmark on our journey. For days I had pictured Bilma, an ancient city built of mud, with a fort, a lush oasis and salt mines whose output was sold all over the Sahara and beyond. I had been told the tales of the ancient inhabitants of the Bilma oasis, the So, who were gifted with enormous size. They could pluck the fruit off the highest palm tree and when they lay down to sleep their bellies were said to stand out like hillocks. They could reach lake Chad in a day and a half, and the following day return to their homes with an elephant or a hippopotamus under each arm for their evening meal. But Allah had not given them knowledge and they didn't know how to fight. So when the people from the north and the east came (the forebears of the Tuareg and the Tubbu), they were killed or driven away into the desert. The stories of the So are strikingly similar to those of another race of tall people who lived in northern Kenya near Lake Turkana where their graves are still to be seen.

By now, my affection for Pasha was only matched by my admiration for the way he had safely reconnoitered the dunes. He was christened Pasha after Vischer's horse which against all the climatic odds he had ridden, cajoled and led, all the way from Tripoli to Kukawa. How Vischer managed to do this I do not know. It is said that one camel is needed to carry water for one horse in the Sahara and that doesn't include the other loads that need to be carried for a horse's food.

Pasha, the camel, at first had been truculent and unruly. But fully conscious that the best way to an animal's heart is through its stomach, I shared my pocket of dates with him while on the march. 'Hey, Pasha,' I would call out, and he would swivel his head round on his elongated neck and catch a date that I flicked towards him. Just as neatly, he spat out the stone. Soon he would come to me like a dog. But a camel's dual nature also applies to its relationship with the other camels in the caravan. Pasha was determined to get his share – and more – of the food. If he felt his share was not large enough, he would give a rival a smart bite on the withers. This of course could equally well be returned with credit. For ten days, while crossing the dunes, I had been unable to ride Pasha, as my saddle would have aggravated two large flesh wounds that a wither bite had exposed.

Vischer makes an interesting comparison between the domestic habits of horses and camels:

> It was the season for dates, and we bought plenty of them for our ponies and camels. According to the Arabs, fresh dates are excellent food for horses, but under no circumstances should the animals be watered until a considerable time after they have been fed. Later on the march, the non-observance of this rule nearly cost me my two horses. It is amusing to watch how, when they are eating dates, the horses will carefully drop the stone out of each fruit. I have often pitied the horse for his absolute dependence on man, which of course may be due to his domestication. It is worth while to watch a horse after a long march, for tired and hungry though he may be he will neither eat not rest if he can fight or play with another horse; his food is put before him, but more often than not he will carelessly trample on it and spoil it, and when he has been covered with a rug against rain or cold, he will prefer to shift it and wear it round his belly. Camels, on the other hand, are driven off to find their food for themselves, and they will return to camp without giving any trouble in the evening. Eight camels will lie down in a circle and quietly munch

a bit of matting, a few handfuls of dates or some grass, without wasting any of it and without noise.

This last sentence is not strictly true in my experience. When they are hungry, camels will fight over food, as Pasha's wither bites testify, and they do indeed make a great deal of noise while doing so, but ours enjoyed chewing their matting too.

At noon we reached Jetko, a dark and forbidding rock shaped like a miniature Table Mountain which frowned over the southern end of the ancient oasis. Jetko is believed to 'sing' to warn Bilma's inhabitants of an approaching caravan. I had been to the Lake of the Crescent Moon near Dun Huang in China, where the sands are also alleged to sing. This alludes to the deep rumbling noise that erupts from inside vibrant sections of the sand dunes when the wind moves across their surface. Sadly, nothing has yet sung for me.

According to Vischer, the noise is produced 'by the blowing of the wind from a certain direction through the crevices of the torn rock'. The mountain indeed sang for Vischer and, to his astonishment, 'we noticed far out to the west on the round brilliant backs of the sand-dunes, long dark blots; quite imperceptible they increased in size and drew nearer, like the great shadow of a cloud. It was an Absin [Tuareg] caravan of over eight thousand camels and a thousand men.'

How the Bilma oasis accommodated such vast numbers of camels is a mystery to me, and another question that I would dearly love to put to Hanns Vischer.

Jetko did not sing to announce our impending arrival, but as we painstakingly drew closer to Bilma, our hearts began to sing and we forgot about pulled muscles, sore bottoms and treacherous desert sands.

5

A journey of discovery with all its attendant disagreeables.
Major Dixon Denham

Naked light bulbs winked and flared as Agi Marder Taher's television flickered in synchronization with the retching fluctuations of one of the few generators in Bilma that worked. The set displayed a CNN newscaster frenetically chattering about Taleban battles in Afghanistan and anthrax scares in America. He appeared to be conveying this information in the middle of an electrical snow storm. My eyes didn't enjoy it at all, and the inconsistent current which caused the newsreader's strident voice to ebb and flow was excruciating to ears accustomed to the stillness of a desert night. Japper who never watches television unless, as in this instance, he is forced to, turned to our host and opined, 'I think the French girlie on the other channel is somewhat easier on the eye.' Johnny was ambivalent. I was firmly in Japper's camp but the professor, a known television addict, was getting his first fix for over a month and sat staring at the set as if in a trance. The professor was at peace with the world. As well as getting his TV fix, he had also managed to get his video camera batteries charged. This was a constant source of concern for him during the whole expedition and his dying batteries had only just made it to Taher's generator in time.

Earlier that morning we had left our camp about a mile outside Bilma and had walked into the town on foot. Abba led us to the old French colonial fort, a well maintained mud building with a large central tower, where cheerful Niger policemen stamped our passports and dealt with us in a relaxed manner. It was here that Vischer was entertained by Commandant Gadel and a medical officer, De la Jarrige. 'Few "*ententes*" can ever have been more "*cordiales*",' relates Vischer. Not knowing the meaning of *entente*, Vischer's rumbustious black ladies immediately started to fight among themselves and, to quieten their passions, they were made to carry bricks to build the same fort where the Niger army now held sway.

However Denham's arrival in Bilma in January 1823 created an altogether different atmosphere and, for Denham's caravan, the Bilma ladies were clearly a source of attraction and possible temptation:

> On the 12th we reached Bilma, the capital of the Tibboos, and the residence of their sultan, who, having always managed to get before and receive us, advanced a mile from the town attended by some fifty of his men at arms, and double the number of the sex we call fair. The men had most of them bows and arrows, and all carried spears: they approached, Boo-Khaloom [Denham's guide] shaking them in the air over their heads; and after this salutation we all moved on towards the town, the females dancing, and throwing themselves about with screams and songs in a manner to us quite original. They were of a superior class to those of the minor towns; some having extremely pleasing features, while the pearly white of their regular teeth was beautifully contrasted with the glossy black of their skin, and the triangular flaps of plaited

Percy, one of our stalwart team of twenty-five camels

Crossing the river Yobe – the border between Nigeria and Niger

Argali and Ehom skinning a goat, Ngigimi (Niger)

Professor doctoring Argali using Chinese 'needles', Ngigimi (Niger)

Jasper and Johnny plotting the route, Tintumma plateau (Niger)

Sunset in the Sahara

Crossing the Great Erg of Bilma (Niger)

Bilma oasis (Niger)

Cones of salt at Bilma (Niger)

Johnny 'operates' on Jasper's eye

Ancient man's rock art at Yat (Niger)
Above left: cow; *Above right:* desert jinn; *Below:* elephant

hair, which hung down on each side of their faces, streaming with oil, with the addition of the coral in the nose, and large amber necklaces, gave them a very seducing appearance. Some of them carried a sheish, a fan made of soft grass, or hair, for the purpose of keeping off the flies; others a branch of a tree, and some fans of ostrich feathers, or a branch of the date palm: all had something in their hands, which they waved over their heads as they advanced. One wrapper of Soudan [Hausa cloth] tied on top of the left shoulder, leaving the right breast bare, formed their ·covering . . . notwithstanding the apparent scantiness of their habiliments, nothing could be farther from indelicate than was their appearance or deportment . . . the music becomes louder and quicker when they start into the most violent gestures, rolling their heads round, gnashing their teeth, and shaking their hands at each other, leaping up, and on each side until one or other are so exhausted they fall to the ground.

Sadly, our arrival was treated much more mundanely. The line of Bilma's sultans has come to an end and there were no cavorting and seductive dancing girls for us to admire. After the visit to the police, we were told to report to the civil authorities to have our passports inspected, so we were led on from the fort to the offices of *sous prefet*, Taher. During the subsequent conversation, I discovered that he was the grandson of Mai Sidi, a Tubbu chief whom Vischer had met north of Bilma. Vischer described him as 'half blind, deaf, quite lame and over 100 years . . . he passes his life in solitary retirement in a dark hut . . . and except for some occult power has no authority over his tribesmen.' Vischer went on to relate that, 'there are no prisons in the oasis and no judges, but all the men have guns, and the women settle their disputes with the knives or daggers which they all carry and no self-respecting female ever goes unarmed.'

Taher, a bespectacled and cultivated man, was so taken aback at my detailed knowledge of his grandfather that he invited us all to supper. So here he was, entertaining us in his house – the only one in the town built with cement – to a meal of goat, mutton, rice and potatoes, which to our shrunken stomachs took on the appearance of a banquet. But as an *apéritif*, we were being force fed TV.

Japper certainly needed something that was easy on the eye. That morning he had complained about sand that had balled up in the white of his right eye. This had been bothering him for some days but now his eye had become very bloodshot and a thick layer of skin appeared to have formed over the source of irritation, turning it into a tiny, hard and most uncomfortable lump.

In the total absence of a medical De la Jarrige, Johnny had volunteered to take on the role of eye surgeon. It takes a tough nerve and an exceptionally steady hand to perform such an operation with a razor blade. I turned away as Johnny bent over Japper to cut through the tough layer of skin. Japper didn't flinch as our bush surgeon, with painstaking care, slit the membrane, allowing the minute ball of sand to slide free. He hadn't drawn blood and the 'operation' was a complete success, for two days later Japper's eye had healed. *National Geographic* had supplied us with medicines to cope with every foreseen medical disaster. It was ironic that a Wilkinson Sword razor blade from my shaving kit provided our most telling item of surgical equipment.

During the dinner, Taher advised me to buy as much grass as my camels could carry, which reinforced what Adam had been whispering to me. 'We must buy enough forage for our camels. Not one of us, not even Abba, knows what the journey ahead will be like.'

Abba, however, was engaging me with a personal problem. For some days he had been complaining that he was tired. Now that we had reached the comparative luxury of Bilma he had come up to me to say that he wanted to leave us.

'But we are going to go to Dirkou after we leave Bilma. That's the town where your brother was shot dead a few weeks ago. The reason you're with us on such a good rate of pay is to give us security through the turbulent Tubbu country which lies ahead.'

Abba had no better nature to appeal to and I couldn't quite understand why he wanted to leave. It certainly wasn't his tiredness, there was definitely more to it than that and, in the end, I concluded that he just wanted to go home.

But he was breaking an agreement and his contract with Sidi to guide us to Gatrun and, unless I was forced to, I was determined not to lose our Tubbu insurance policy. He suggested that he knew a good Tubbu guide called Ibrahim, who would take us on from Dirkou, where we planned to stock up with supplies for the long and arduous journey into Libya.

I decided to make one of my rare incursions into satellite technology and to attempt to consult with Sidi in Agadez. I had not been in touch with him since leaving Ngigimi and I very nearly abandoned the idea when it appeared to be impossible to make contact. However on the twelfth attempt I got through. It appeared that Sidi was gallivanting in the Air mountains and, in his absence, a kinsman called Mohammed was looking after his affairs. 'Just order him to go,' Mohammed said to me. 'Tell him he must go with you.'

He clearly didn't know Abba. I passed the telephone to Abba and his short fuse burnt up in seconds.

'Forced! Forced!' he yelled, stamping the ground in fury. 'Not even the President of Niger can force me to do what I don't want to do. No man on earth can force me to do anything. Especially a man who is as low-born as a Tuareg.'

Our Tuaregs overheard this rant and shook their heads. 'All Tubbus are unreliable and untrustworthy,' said Argali. 'We all know it and even your own Vischer wrote it down in his book. Nothing has changed, least of all the character of the Tubbus.'

There was no point in attempting to talk to Abba, for he had soared away beyond reason. So I decided not to pursue the matter until he came down to earth. Meanwhile, a visit to the famed Bilma salt mines beckoned.

The mines lie to the west of the town, past Bilma's natural springs which bring such welcome relief to desert travellers and migrating birds. Vischer commented on the large flocks of duck that he saw at the springs. His caravan boys caught great numbers of them when they flew in from the south, presumably from Lake Chad, and flopped down exhausted on reaching the edge of the enticing pools of water. We saw the Egyptian vultures and black and white ravens that Vischer had also noted and, to our surprise, a solitary heron, standing on one leg in the water with a beady eye on a fish.

Beyond the springs lie the ruins of an ancient Kanuri fort whose jagged walls are slowly crumbling into mounds of mud among houses which belong to Bilma's poorest of the poor. To the west of this fort are the mines, which have been dug by hand out of a crusty salt outcrop. Where the deposits are richest, holes are dug in the ground four to five feet deep and of varying diameter. Water then fills the hole and in so doing dissolves the salt. After a few days a crust of salt crystals covers the surface like a thin sheet of ice. This is broken up and the pieces are allowed to sink to the bottom. A new crust then forms and is treated likewise until the hole gradually fills up with salt crystals. These are then extracted and shaped into two commercial sizes, which can be easily transported by camel: a conical cylinder called *kantu* about the size of a traffic cone or a small hump like a tortoise shell, called *kunkuru*.

This mining area is surrounded by a vast open space where for centuries the great camel caravans have camped before they under- take their journey home, laden with the famed Bilma salt. Although the size of these caravans has greatly reduced since Vischer's day, when they could number over 8,000 camels, it was heartening for me to see more than 1,500 camels waiting to be loaded up. We did not see a single vehicle near the salt wells, suggesting that all the salt is transported far and wide by camel caravans, as it has been for centuries. Denham's account of Bilma salt production eighty years before Vischer could have been written today.

Art was employed to obtain Nature; shallow pits were dug, which soon filled with water, and its evaporation left thick layers of salt: high embankments were raised round these, evidently to prevent currents of air. The water is now strongly impregnated; in summer a thick crust is formed, which is the salt in use . . . I however found that their time for gathering the salt was at the end of the dry season, when it was taken in large masses . . . This transparent kind they put into bags, and send to Bournou and Soudan; a coarser sort is also formed into hard pillars, and for which a ready market is found, a single pillar weighs eleven pounds . . . Twenty thousand bags of salt were said to be carried off during the last year by the Tuaricks alone.

The Tuareg salt caravans, called *tarhalamt*, are the only salt caravans of the Sahara which are still functional. The caravan season begins in September at the end of the rainy season, when the Tuareg camels are fresh and fit, having fed on new grass. The camels are assembled in the Tuareg nomad camps in the Air mountains in central Niger, where the strongest camels in the Sahara are bred. It was here during September 2001 that our own camels were bought. As there is very little vegetation between Air and Bilma, fodder for the camels is laid down at regular intervals by the advancing caravan for its return journey. The inhabitants of Bilma and the other salt-bearing oases wait impatiently for the arrival of these caravans, since they rely for survival on the new season's millet which is brought by the Tuaregs who exchange it for their two most important oases products, salt and dates. A barter system operates in the little market near the mine and it was fascinating for me to see for myself that, as in Vischer's day, money does not change hands. After the conclusion of business, the caravans face the strenuous journey back to Air. Already weakened by their outward travel, the camels have to carry home up to 400 pounds of salt each, along a barren unmarked and constantly shifting track. We were very soon to learn for ourselves the dangers and hazards of travelling with weary camels for mile after windswept mile in country where there is absolutely no vegetation.

Bilma salt has a high reputation for both cattle and culinary use and can be sold or exchanged for up to ten times its purchase price. As with the slaves of yore, there is a good profit to be made. So shortly after their return home in the early part of the year, the Tuaregs set out again to sell their salt in the Hausa towns and cities to the south. They then linger in the pastures of northern Hausaland while their camels calf down and set off back to Air shortly before the beginning of the rainy season in June. Once back in their mountain homes, it is nearly time to begin the autumn *tarhalamt* once again.

Since the end of colonial domination, the Sahel countries of West Africa have been ruled by non-nomadic Africans who for centuries have regarded the Tuareg with suspicion and hostility. As a result, the Tuaregs have become politically marginalized and, in addition, since the 1970s, the region has been savagely depressed by a series of devastating droughts which destroyed the nomads' cattle and forced the Tuaregs to take refuge as nightwatchmen or labourers in the cities to the south. Man's interference and the frequent overgrazing of fragile pastures has led to an unprecedented advance of the desert into what had previously been fertile stock-holding land. That the caravans still continue, verified by the majestic sight of those 1,500 camels, was a source of amazement and gratification to me. For the time being, this bleak yet immensely beautiful area of the world has been spared the ravages of the infernal combustion engine.

*   *   *

'We must buy more grass. It will take us three weeks to reach Gatrun and there is no likelihood of our getting grass on the way. We must stay in Bilma another day.'

'Another day, Adam?'

'Yes, to leave without enough grass is very risky.'

The problem was that with nearly 2,000 camels camped in and around Bilma grass was very difficult to buy. No camel grass grew in Bilma, so it all had to be brought in by camel caravan across countless miles of desert sands. Grass was an absolutely essential commodity and could be sold at a huge premium. Little wonder that it was costing me $8 a truss.

'But we can't stay here forever, Adam.'

'We can't leave without grass.'

The days went by. Adam engaged in painstaking negotiation with traders who told him that more grass was expected tomorrow, or the next day, or . . .

Gradually we accumulated twelve large trusses. Adam displayed his versatility with ropes and knots and wove an immaculate fish net around each truss so that it would not collapse when slung on either side of a camel. He had told me that he was looking for a second wife and his skill with a rope would certainly have caught the attention of the prettiest Tuareg girl in Air.

But was twelve enough? Adam thought not. Ehom and Argali thought it was, while the enigmatic Asalik kept his thoughts to himself. On the fourth day the consensus was that it was, and having paid our respects to Agi Marder Taher we set off for Dirkou. This expanding market town, a village of no consequence in Vischer's day, could be reached by Libyan trucks and was a place, we were told, where all the basic provisions could be bought – at a price.

The rocky spine which snaked northwards out of Bilma was Tubbu heartland, and a protecting shield to a string of small oases dotted from south to north amidst a vast sea of seemingly unending sand stretching to the east and west. At one point on this track, we passed a dog that was in sole control of a flock of sheep, without a human being anywhere in sight.

In Vischer's day, harassed by Arab and Tuareg raiders, the Tubbu had lived in the hills and we passed remains of their old settlements. With the cessation of wars and slave raiding, they had come down and settled in the foothills, but with the current independence revolt in full spate, the ringleaders had retreated into rocky crevices where they believed that the soldiers of Niger would never find them.

Abba had told me all this. After sitting in sullen isolation for three days he had come down to earth and back to me. He said that he had changed his mind and that he would, after all, take us on to Gatrun. Once this decision was taken, he immediately reverted to his former self-assured and cocky self. Asalik stared at him in total silence, engrossed with his own private thoughts which no doubt consigned the whole treacherous Tubbu tribe to the dustbin.

Dirkou is a bleak windswept town with houses, constructed of encrusted salt blocks, that huddle on the fringe of yellow desert that stretches away to the great waves of dunes on the western horizon. I went with Abba to a soldiers' tent at the south-western edge of Dirkou for a routine passport inspection. Here, edgy sullen soldiers, quite unlike the police at Bilma, studiously ignored us and kept us waiting for over two hours in a broiling sun, no doubt in the hope of obtaining a bribe.

Meanwhile, Johnny had discovered a passable bar in downtown Dirkou and, after a short flirtation with a coy detribalized lady of the night, he had managed to extract from her the town's commercial low-down. Not that there was much to extract, but it enabled him to buy our provisions at the more accommodating places. He bought supplies for three weeks, plus the welcome addition of three bottles of firewater which was marketed under the brand name of Niger whisky. To our jaded palates it tasted finer that the most precious malt.

At the oasis of Aney, twenty-four miles further north, the army was camped on the hills and there were rumours that they had fanned out through the barren valleys to seek out Tubbu dissidents who had caused the fracas in Dirkou market some weeks before. Aney is dominated, as in Vischer's day, by a remarkably well preserved precolonial Kanuri fort which, before the French established some stability, regularly filled up with Tubbu villagers when Tuareg or Arab raiding parties threatened. There was a feeling that it might be used for this purpose once again, for the Aney atmosphere crackled with suppressed tension and hostility. The tension got to Johnny. When I asked him to dismount he grumbled that he didn't like being given orders unless he fully understood why they were given. The Tubbu were sullen. The soldiers handled their weapons nervously and we were encouraged, politely but very firmly, to move on.

Little had changed in one hundred years. When Vischer arrived in Aney in 1906, he was met by the headman, Abdullah Indini, who told him that it was quite common for the people to be forced to flee to the hills and watch the destruction of their property. He told of the houses being fired and the palm trees, on which the people's very existence depended, being felled. Apparently the wholesale destruction of palm trees, which take a generation to grow, was the way that frustrated invaders expressed disgust at the scarcity of loot. The palm trees are not touched today but, just before our arrival, some of the citizens of Aney had again, fled to the hills.

Once outside the oasis we stopped to load up as best we could with firewood that had to be hacked with a blunt axe and a panga – made in China to the delight of the professor – from iron-hard acacia trees and tamarisk scrub. 'There is no more firewood ahead of us for at least three weeks,' said Abba.

Four days later we reached Sequedine which boasts another well preserved Kanuri fort and is an important village, dominating the unmetalled roads that criss-cross from Libya, Algeria, Bilma and Agadez. It also has salt mines, though not on the same scale as Bilma, and we noticed a few Tuareg salt caravans that had decamped to load up with salt.

The following day, 1 December, we pushed on north-east towards the uninhabited oasis of Yat. As we trailed over a desolate treeless plateau, the wind intensified and blew stinging sand directly into our faces. The desert wind is inescapable. Its relentlessness, more than its strength, is what depresses the spirits. Every voice becomes blurred, every moment is besieged. The wind bellows unceasingly in one's ears. Only a turban can provide a defence and an insulation from its mind-numbing effect. No longer were we shielded by the hills and for the first time since we left Kukawa the sky was overcast. The brilliant blue under which we had laboured for so long, was now dusted with a continuous stain of formless cloud. As the line of hills that we had followed all the way from Bilma gradually retreated, I sensed that we were entering *terra nova*.

It was on this stretch of road that Japper's inventiveness overcame the difficulties of trying to smoke a cigarette while riding a camel in a biting head wind. The glowing end would flare and disappear before Japper had time to take more than a couple of a satisfying puffs. We had bought milk in over a hundred small round tins, a popular West African size and very useful for travel through the desert. Japper bored a hole the diameter of a cigarette into the side of one, and another small hole in the top so that air could enter and keep the fag fired. The lit cigarette end was then stuck into the tin which Japper held and smoked like a pipe. This proved to be an essential item of smoker's riding kit and Japper puffed merrily away on his Kenyan Sportsman cigarettes, sure in the knowledge that they would not burn out in under sixty seconds.

Yat surprised me: dominated to the west by a large black hill, which Vischer had captured in a delightful water colour, it contained water, date palms, camel grass and the ostentatious dum palm with its magnificent nutty fruit. But why were there no people here? Surely this relatively fertile little spot could support human life? There seemed much more for man in Yat than at, for instance, the Agadem oasis where a hundred souls appeared to cling precariously to life as their date palms withered around them and grass for their flocks was reduced annually.

'They've all emigrated to Sequedine,' said Abba mysteriously. Yet even in Vischer's day the oasis had been uninhabited and it was deserted when Denham and Clapperton arrived there eighty years before. Barth had arrived in the deserted oasis exhausted by fatigue and almost totally blinded by the glare of the sand in the heat of the day. Argali, ever sensitive to matters of the spirit, muttered something about jinns and restless souls. 'Maybe,' he pointed out, 'there are too many jinns in Yat for comfort.'

However, if it wasn't the jinns, then there must be other malevolent spirits in the air at Yat. When Vischer's caravan arrived from the barren and desolate deserts to the north, the women, sensing that the flesh pots of Bilma were nearing, decided to sort out their finery by the well at Yat so that they could enter Bilma dressed in full fig. Vischer records:

> Boxes and cases disclosed the most wonderful clothes. Zouave jackets from Tunis and long silk robes from Egypt, old umbrellas from Tripoli and many bits of brilliant silken rags and handkerchiefs. All were washed and scrubbed, and before nightfall the grass around the camp was covered like a great mosaic, with a hundred bits of different colours.
>
> All were in their best humour now, and to end this happy day in a fitting manner, a tremendous battle took place between the women.

But the prize for the greatest spat in Yat must be awarded to Denham and Clapperton who became involved in a monumental row with each other. It appears that matters between them had been deteriorating for some time and Denham's continued arrogant and dictatorial manner particularly provoked the resentment of the sensitive and small-minded Clapperton. This had driven Clapperton to what Denham described as 'open mutiny' but it was not until they reached Yat that their mutual resentment burst into flame. The 'little quarrel' as Dr Walter Oudney, who was travelling with the two

explorers, discreetly described it, was recorded in letters exchanged at Yat between the two men. The mind boggles when one
realizes that two adult males had sat down in their respective tents,
pitched in this remote oasis, to formally exchange an acrimonious
handwritten correspondence. Denham wrote:

> I had hoped that a mutual disposition to amicable Cooperation
> would have made our journey of discovery with all its attendant
> disagreeables at least one of Harmony but . . . that unfortunately
> appears impossible.

Clapperton retorted from his tent:

> With respect to amicable cooperation and harmony every one
> who belongs to the mission or ever has belonged to it will give me
> the credit of contributing all that was possible to the happy object
> and as Major D. craved my opinion on that subject let me tell him
> I suppose that it must have arisen from his having quarrelled with
> and brow beat every person belonging to the mission or who has
> ever been attached to it.

At which point things took an altogether much nastier turn.
Denham wrote:

> I should neglect my duty were I any longer to delay setting before
> you in the strongest light I am able the continued extreme impro-
> priety of your conduct both public and private which I regret to
> say is no less discreditable to the mission and the country than to
> yourself as an officer and at the same injurious in the highest
> degree to our Interests at the present moment.

Clapperton took the letter straight to Oudney and asked him to
put into writing what he thought about it. Oudney wrote: 'How
your conduct public or private has or will tend to injure the interests
of the Mission I am at a loss to conceive.'

Denham hastened to enlighten him, alleging that it was common knowledge among the Arabs of the caravan that Clapperton was involved in homosexual relations with one of his Arab servants.

On learning this, Oudney dispatched by messenger a letter to Colonel Hanmer Warrington, the British consul general in Tripoli saying that Abdullady, the man on whom the allegation was centred, 'is a man apparently above forty and very ugly.' Oudney believed that the charge was the invention of Abdullady to further his own ends. But it did not stop there. The consul general forwarded Oudney's remarks to the Colonial Office in London and his accompanying letter reflects the feelings that such an accusation would arouse in 1823.

It is indeed painful to be under the necessity of referring to a Subject which must be as disgusting to you to read, as it is for me to write. I have received the accompanying correspondence. Great God!!! May it prove Impossible that the Spirit of Ill Will, or rancorous feeling, can lead Men to forget the first and Last attribute of Christianity 'of doing, as we would be done by'.

A more Infamous, Vile, diabolical Insinuation to blast the reputation of Man was never before resorted to, and I have not the smallest hesitation in the Presence of my God to say that it is false, malicious, and conspiring against the future happiness of an Individual.

Lieutenant Clapperton I know little of, but in that little, I would with my life answer for Him that he never would disgrace Human nature by such foul and damnable Conduct.

Even two years later, when they were safely back in Tripoli, with all their perils behind them and assured of the fame they had so richly earned, Clapperton still had not heard a retraction from Denham's lips.

Our problems at Yat were of a less histrionic nature. I knew from Vischer's writing that he had found rock art here and near the well, which still provided sweet drinkable water, we saw the rock carvings that he had sketched, little spindly stick men, camels and Tuareg symbols. But we were saddened to see that they had been desecrated with recent graffiti of the 'Ali loves Amina' variety, not something the Bradshaw Foundation, who had donated funds for the recce, would be too pleased to receive photographs of. So after we had set up camp, I encouraged our team to spread out to see if we could seek out undiscovered examples. After searching for upwards of an hour, we struck gold. To the south-east of the well, which stands in the centre of the oasis, there are further rocky outcrops, and it was here that we found a wealth of desert rock art, some of great antiquity. We discovered minutely detailed portraits of animals that have long since vanished, such as elephants and giraffes. There were others of copulating cattle, people with spears, phallic symbols, ancient Tuareg script and jinns – some defaced by later carvings – but others, pristine and unspoiled. Many of these pictures were carved on rocks which must also have tested the climbing agility of the sculptor.

'I expect that they carved them in these inaccessible places to get away from their wives,' said Argali perceptively.

These rock carvings had not, to my knowledge, been recorded by previous travellers. As our cameras clicked away, we all shared the excitement of what we believed was a notable 'first'.

The elephants and giraffe portraits puzzled us most. How long ago was it since men at Yat had seen an elephant? It has been said that the Romans were possibly directly responsible for the extinction of the elephant to the north of the Sahara. The principal cause was the demand for beasts to provide sport for the Games. Augustus tells us that 3,500 African animals were slain in twenty-six Games. Pompey showed 600 lions at a time, of which 315 were males. Furthermore, the elephant was persecuted, then as now, for its ivory, immense quantities of which used to be transported to Rome. There was also a culinary use. According to Pliny, the cartilage of an elephant's trunk was a particular delicacy of the Roman kitchen. Of course, the Yat climate of today could not support any of the animals carved on the rocks, but it is interesting to comprehend the sheer scale of the numbers that the Romans slaughtered.

At Yat, Vischer had written about jerboas and locusts. I was angry that Abba had chased, caught and killed, quite pointlessly, one of the stunningly beautiful and quite harmless long-tailed jerboas with hind legs shaped like a tiny kangaroo. We had been searching for rock art and on our return found the poor creature propped up against a grassy mound so, as Abba proudly related, 'you can take its photograph.' As for the locusts, Vischer's caravan discovered a swarm of them and all the Africans immediately broke ranks to scoop them up. They returned in triumph to their cooking pots, pulled off the locusts' wings and stuck them head down into the hot ashes of their fires. When their legs ceased to waggle they pulled them out of the ash, pulled off their heads and munched on the crisply roasted body. Vischer affirmed that they tasted very good, something between a shrimp and a whitebait. His only regret was that he had no wild honey to spice them up. The Africans maintained that they were good for the blood and they clearly provided a welcome change from Vischer's normal caravan fare.

When the professor and I spotted a small swarm, we scrambled hectically about in a vain attempt to catch a handful. However, they were no longer at the 'hopper' stage and eventually flew off, leaving us gasping and perspiring on the top of a rocky outcrop. So we were unable to spice up our daily fare of macaroni and cabbage with roast locust.

Those who know me would be the first to affirm that I am to mechanical devices what oil is to water; something that just does not mix. Mechanical objects, be they as large as a car or as small as a cigarette lighter, hold no fascination. The devices invariably take umbrage at this lack of interest and affection and retaliate by rendering themselves malfunctional. For me, a camel (or a horse) is much preferable to a car and a wooden match to a cigarette lighter. These are animals and objects that I feel comfortable with and, in most cases, can control. I entertain no finer feelings for machinery and, to my continual cost, have little inclination to maintain it. I am not proud of this weakness, nor am I proud of my attitude. It's just an undeniable fact.

So it seemed to me inevitable that at some stage of our journey the satellite telephone, that was guarded and controlled by my uncertain hand, would cease to function. And at Yat, with its hint of malign and mischievous spirits in the air, this is exactly what happened.

Jasper's son Simon was to marry on 30 November and, not unnaturally, Jasper wanted to confirm that he had indeed acquired a new daughter-in-law. But the telephonic connection between Yat and Jasper's ranch in Kenya was not proving an easy one to make. We tried countless times and I zapped out the numbers in quick succession to try to get through. But I zapped once too often on a mis-dialled security number and was given the mysterious command to 'enter your emergency PUK number.' As already related, our instruction booklet for this piece of remarkable modern technology was in Arabic, but although the acronym PUK featured quite frequently, the Arabic lettering scrolled on either side of it told me nothing. Neither did the lettering disgorge its secrets to anyone else in our caravan when I desperately sought help. Argali and Ehom spoke Arabic, but they could not read it. The telephone's menu included an item called 'help.' This was something that by now I needed urgently. But it appeared that all the help-line attendants were on an extended lunch break. I couldn't even manage to extract a 'bear with me.'

Johnny, who is quite definitely a friend of machinery, came to the rescue through the resources of our GPS which up until that point we had hardly used. The GPS boasted an email device, but the required current drained its batteries at an alarming rate and the batteries couldn't be charged directly by the solar charging device, so it had to be handled with great sensitivity. Which is why it was entrusted to Johnny's safe pair of hands. Eventually, via Burundi, England and the USA we acquired our PUK number and our wayward phone immediately reverted to normal behaviour.

Incidentally, when Japper finally did get through to the family ranch, he was told by his wife Jill that Simon's wedding had been postponed until the end of December.

Yat was nothing if not an oasis of surprises. No sooner was the satellite phone back on air than I received this message from a co-trustee of our Wild Camel Protection Foundation.

'There's a German photographer called Carsten Peter who would like to join you at his own expense. Would you like him to come?'

Long pause while this startling information sunk in.

'How long he is able to come for?'

'Twelve days.'

'Twelve days? That's very short.'

'Well, he thinks the risk is worth taking. He's a very good photographer and the *National Geographic* like his work. They've used three of his pictures for their magazine covers.'

I pondered on this novel development. One of the practical reasons for undertaking this trans-Saharan journey had been, paradoxically, to attract attention for the cause of the critically endangered wild, two-humped or Bactrian camel that lives in China and Mongolia. Pasha and our other stalwart single-humpers, unknown to them, were making great strides to save their double-humped progenitor. We needed an illustrated story that would give publicity to the plight of the wild camel. If we managed to get a *National Geographic* article, it could mean more than just an account of our trans-Saharan journey.

'Do you know what's he like?'

'I haven't met him. He sounds dedicated and very serious. But he's prepared to put up funds for the flight and for the time that he spends with you. He won't cost you anything.'

It was a risk, but I had already decided that it was a risk worth taking.

'Fine, we'll look forward to meeting him. Where will he join us?'

'At Gatrun.'

The line went dead and my mind raced. What would Carsten Peter be like? Would he fit in with the team? These were the imponderables. However, the meeting with our new team member seemed a distant prospect. The road that lay immediately ahead of us was the one that had been littered with the bones of slaves and was, I was told, still strewn with the carcasses of dead camels.

Gatrun was two and a half weeks away. In my mind, the whole journey divided into totally distinct phases. Ngigimi, Agadem, Bilma, Aney, Yat. When I looked beyond Yat, it was to the next target. The target beyond that one was something that I could hardly envisage. After Yat, my immediate target was Tummo on the Niger/Libyan border. Beyond Tummo lay Vischer's 'howling wilderness' and at the end of that bleak desert was the oasis of Tejerri. After Tejerri we would set out for Gatrun. I found it almost impossible to project my thoughts beyond Tummo. This was the way my mind worked, step by painful step, oasis by oasis. When we had safely reached one oasis or landmark, I then thought about how we would reach the next. Carsten Peter's arrival in Gatrun, and the possible problems that his arrival would pose, seemed much too far away for serious consideration at the moment. The chance of an article in *National Geographic* was of interest, but it paled beside the overriding objective of completing the journey successfully. The immediate problem was the road to Tummo. The map gave me the stark, unremitting picture; it was bleak, rocky and devoid of any vegetation.

'You wait until you see it,' I had been advised by a French traveller in Bosso who had recently crossed the track in a jeep. 'You won't believe that so many camels could die on one stretch of road.'

Denham had seen more than dead camels:

> During the last two days, we had passed on an average from sixty to eighty or ninety skeletons each day; but the numbers that lay about the wells at El-Hammar were countless: those of two women, whose perfect and regular teeth bespoke them young, were particularly shocking; their arms still remained clasped round each other as they had expired; although the flesh had long since perished by being exposed to the burning rays of the sun, and the blackened bones only left; the nails of the fingers, and some of the sinews of the hand, also remained; and part of the tongue of one of them still appeared through the teeth. We had now passed six days of desert without the slightest appearance of vegetation.
>
> While I was dozing on my horse about noon, overcome by the heat of the sun which at that time of the day always shone with great power, I was suddenly awakened by a crashing under his feet, which startled me excessively. I found that my steed had, without any sensation of shame or alarm, stepped upon the perfect skeletons of two human beings, cracking their brittle bones under his feet, and, by one trip of his foot, separating a skull from the trunk, which rolled on like a ball before him.

And things hadn't changed when Vischer made the journey eighty-three years later. In an unpublished letter sent to his family, he reminds us whose skeletons these probably were:

> A caravan might include anything between fifty and a hundred slaves. They would be driven with whips, always headed for the next hill on the horizon, where they would be told, there would be water. Those who fell by the wayside were left to die. The skeletons are most numerous on the steepest and rockiest parts of

the route and also around the waterholes, because these would often be found to be sanded up and the exhausted slaves would be forced to re-dig them immediately upon arrival. We marched for long stretches, day after day in the searing desert winds. During these last fourteen days we have marched for one hundred and fifty-two hours and covered seven hundred and fifty kilometres, the longest march being sixteen hours. So I had to be a very hard taskmaster which I found distasteful. The women were worse than the men. Even after ten hours marching in the burning sun, they would fight among themselves like wild cats.

It was this next stage of the journey that had provoked the sardonic District Head of Ngigimi to tell me that I was too old and that I would never make it. 'You'll die, just like the slaves did years ago,' he had observed with a chuckle. 'We'll hear all about it on the radio.'

6

Kick on, John. Kick on.

Bertie Hill, former MFH, Dulverton West

The eight uniformed soldiers who had fanned out into a horseshoe on the open plain, stood rigid, with cocked kalashnikovs pointing straight at me. I had reined in Pasha, dismounted, collected the team's passports and walked in a straight line towards the centre of their semi-circle, a distance of about fifty yards. The rest of our party was standing beside their squatting camels. A person on a camel, or a horse, always looks intimidating to someone with their feet on the ground. We didn't want these particular soldiers to feel intimidated.

We had arrived at Madama, the last Niger checkpoint before entering the barren no-man's-land which stretches for over twenty-five miles before reaching the Libyan border post. The border, according to the map, was not precisely defined. How right the cartographers were.

Moments earlier, the soldiers had come roaring out of their old French colonial fort (and the pages of Beau Geste). With the exception of their officer, they had all been seated in the back of an open jeep with a large machine-gun mounted behind the cab which, much to our relief, was pointing at the sky. The jeep had screeched to a halt, the soldiers had jumped out and proceeded to form their supremely hostile half circle. They were smartly dressed in khaki battle fatigues, they looked extremely well drilled and exuded an air of suspicion and barely suppressed tension. The superficial efficiency of Madama seemed quite unlike any other border post that we had visited. Was this because the Libyan army was not that far away? Clutching tightly to our papers and passports, I felt that the scene must have looked like something out of an old Western movie, but I certainly didn't feel like John Wayne.

The officer-in-charge stood in the centre of the horseshoe with his eyes firmly fixed on my face. I moved slowly towards him with a pounding heart. His face was set in rigid lines, his eyes were cold and hard. I forced a smile and held out my hand.

'Hello,' I said in Hausa. 'How are you? We've come to report to you.'

The kalashnikovs pointed straight at me. For a few moments he stared at me in absolute silence. 'Is he drugged?' I asked myself. Then when he realized the nature of the language that I'd used, his features relaxed and he smiled. Hausa had done the trick, he made a gesture to his soldiers to lower their guns.

'Do you speak French?'

'I'm afraid not, can we keep the conversation in Hausa?'

I handed over the passports and travel documents and he passed them to the soldier on his right.

'We'll study these,' he said. 'Where are you going?'

'Tripoli.'

He stared at me in utter disbelief. We were to get many such stares in the future when responding to similar questioning.

'You'll get your papers back when we have checked them. Meanwhile make your camp over there.'

He pointed to an open space that was strewn with the detritus of other caravans; plastic bags, bottles and rusting cans. Other travellers who had camped there before us had clearly been detained for a long time.

'How long will your checks take?'

The officer grinned and shrugged his shoulders.

'As long it takes. It depends on whether we like the look of you.'

I walked round the semi-circle and shook each soldier by the hand. The officer called out to his jeep driver who started the engine. Then he climbed into the cab, his men jumped in the back, and the jeep accelerated rapidly from a standing start sending up a shower of gritty sand in my face. They raced back towards the old French fort and disappeared, leaving me to turn and walk slowly back to the caravan.

'I wish I'd taken a photo of that scene,' said Japper.

We pitched camp. Our camels were soon munching away at desiccated acacia bushes and the remains of chewed up tamarisk. They were hungry, the journey to Madama had not been easy and there was, no doubt, worse to come. Our passports were eventually returned, stamped and approved at four o'clock. We were grateful that it hadn't taken any longer but it was by now too late to set off. So we prepared to bed down for the night amidst derelict vehicles, coils of wire from hay bales and the sun-bleached bones of dead camels. Even in Barth's day, he had found the ground at Madama to be 'strewed with bones'.

That evening, an unusual trail of clouds, a seemingly unending sequence of corrugations, puckered and blazed in the setting sun. As the sun dropped to the horizon, a rutted blood-red canopy spread over us like a vast umbrella. Our camels standing on a nearby hillock were silhouetted against a breathtaking backdrop of vivid colour.

Camels, soldiers and blood. The three images merged into one and seemed to me to be fittingly appropriate to Madama.

Since leaving Yat five days before, we were heading into a cold north-east wind and I discovered that I now craved sugar in tea, which normally, I would be quite unable to drink. Two or even three heaped teaspoons had to be shovelled into my rusting tin mug and well stirred before I was able to drink it. It was bleak barren country, strewn with the carcasses of camels and as a twenty-first century touch, two burnt out jeeps. My dead camel count had already topped one hundred which made me worry about how long our forage would last. Fortunately, we came across a few wind-ravaged acacia trees. The lower limbs had all been eaten away by other hungry camels. Our Tuaregs, at risk of being torn by the vicious thorns, climbed up the trees and chopped down branches so that our camels had something to eat, apart from our precious grass. How the camels cope with the long white and extremely sharp thorns I will never know. But the higher you climb up an acacia tree, the smaller the thorns get until they eventually disappear. Unlike the Bactrian camels in the Gobi, our dromedaries don't seem partial to the tamarisk bush, even when they are hungry. They just nibble at it rather dejectedly.

While travelling in this barren stretch we passed quantities of most unusually constructed volcanic rocks. Some were long, thin, tubular and hollow, some kidney shaped and others shaped like a small bowl with the lid permanently affixed. We smashed one of these brittle bowls and it split neatly in half. To our amazement it contained red ochre coloured powder which we thought must be iron ore. In the same area Vischer and Denham had discovered these relics of volcanic violence and, like us, they had marvelled at the weird and wonderful shapes that nature had sculpted amidst scenes of indescribable turbulence. My prize find was an absolutely perfect spherical rock. Others had picked up similar objects, but nothing that was so exquisitely and perfectly formed as my simulated billiard ball.

'Victor,' said the professor, struggling to find the English word for a volcano. 'In Africa there were big victors and little victors.'

He was trying to explain his theory on the size and frequency of volcanic eruptions on the African continent.

'In middle Africa, there were big victors like this – whssssssssss.' His eyes glittered behind his spectacles as he flung his arms out wide. 'In North Africa, there were little victors like this – whsss.' This time his equally graphic demonstration was suitably muted. 'That is why we find all these interesting pieces near the hills, because the victors here were only little ones. They did not get thrown very far away.'

The professor was adamant and no one attempted to argue or to contradict his intriguing explanation. When later we found more volcanic rocks, we would turn to each other and remark sagely that they were there because a little victor had occurred nearby.

On the third night after leaving Yat, when camped in a rocky hollow where we had piled up our loads to give us a little protection from a cold, gusting wind, we had two unexpected visitors. A Fenex fox and his vixen arrived at three o' clock in the morning to see if they could carry out a pre-tasting of next morning's cold macaroni breakfast that had been left standing on the lid of the kitchen box. The Fenex fox is similar to the bat-eared fox which is common to East Africa and sports large round ears and eyes with the allure and appeal of a bush baby. Silently levering ourselves up from our sleeping bags, Jasper and I watched as, with their snouts, the thieving conspirators expertly flipped off the lid of the breakfast pot. Unfortunately, the professor spotted them, too, and began to bellow and holler and throw things before I could capture the Fenex fox photo of the year. But they were an intrepid and no doubt hungry pair and later returned to run off with Argali's much prized wooden cooking spoon. He was not in the slightest amused and grumbled away during gaps between his morning prayers. How these foxes survive in a wilderness where there appears to be no life at all one cannot imagine. Their territory must be vast.

As we trudged slowly northwards after leaving Madama, our heads bent by a fierce north-east wind, a bus appeared coming from the north and no doubt heading for Sequedine. I have seen many overladen buses but never one that was topped up to the extent of this one. The chassis was practically buried in a mound of turbaned men, veiled women, beds, bicycles, bric-a brac, goats and sheep.

'Very bad,' grumbled the professor. 'In China only thirty passengers on a bus. No more. The police should not allow this. Very danger, very bad.'

Shortly afterwards, the solitary flat-topped mountain called Emi Madama appeared on the horizon. It has been nicknamed, Ko Karama 'the bewitched mountain', because for two or three days it seems to be getting closer, yet then appears to recede as a caravan approaches. Vischer, travelling from the north, commented on this strange sensation and exactly the same experience held true for us. It was the slaves who gave it the name Ko Karama, as they were driven forward by the Arab traders.

Two of our camels were now peeing blood. The Tuaregs said that it was due to something that they had eaten and Japper concurred. Abba was complaining of kidney pains and Japper twisted his knee when mounting, to add to his saddle sores. We passed many more dead camels and when we halted, the professor dosed Abba with Chinese medicine.

At long last, Ko Karama stopped receding. We passed just to the west of this great table mountain which, with its gnarled sides that dramatically cut away to black smooth and no doubt slippery rock on top, rises up from the red desert. On the horizon to the east we spotted another landmark, an isolated conical mountain called Fezzan. Vischer had stopped for water near Ko Karama at a well called Bir Ahmer, but we were still carrying sufficient water to take us to the Niger/Libyan border crossing at the Tummo mountains, so had no need to seek out Bir Ahmer.

When planning the expedition my main concern had been water. I hadn't appreciated that the problem, at this stage of the journey, would be the shortage of forage for the camels. As the weather was cold, the camels didn't need much water to drink. In addition, if a camel is travelling on short rations, it is not wise to provide water too frequently. Too much water in a camel's system without the compensating bulk of food can engender colic. At no point on the whole journey did the camels appear to crave liquid. It was grass, date palm leaves or acacia scrub that they wanted.

10 December 2001 was a beautiful day and the desert sparkled under a sky of brilliant blue. Although it was cold, mercifully the wind had completely dropped. Ko Karama gradually slipped away behind us, until it was left shimmering in a magical haze on the horizon. After a further two hours of travelling across a vast stone-strewn sandy plain, we passed five isolated and grotesquely shaped pinnacles of rust-red rock that rose to a height of over fifty feet. They reminded me of *yardangs*, the ancient eroded land forms that are found north of Lop Nur in the Gashun Gobi desert in China. They rose up quite unexpectedly out of the fine sand and were covered in flaky red shale, which would have made them extremely difficult to climb. We had seen nothing like them previously and, as the sky was a brilliant blue and the atmosphere clear as crystal, the overall effect on the senses was stunning. At three o'clock, we spied the Tummo mountain range which straddled the border, quivering above a mirage of water on the horizon ahead of us. As we drew closer and the mountains acquired stability and substance, they seemed to have been strangely cut, as if some unseen hand had skimmed their summits with a sharp knife leaving them uniformly flat-topped. This supernatural hand then appeared to have iced them with dark black chocolate which had trickled down their sides.

The next day was my birthday, and Johnny miraculously produced three miniature bottles of British Airways red wine, that he
had secretly stashed away since our flight out from England. I discovered a battered tin of anchovies in my bag and we wrapped the
savoury fishes around sweet Marie biscuits that had survived the
journey from Maiduguri. This luxurious delicacy formed an *hors
d'oeuvre* to accompany our last dram of Niger whisky. We then
topped up with in-flight wine. This bacchanalian flourish was made
in the full knowledge that our liquor was now finished. From now
on, we were on the wagon. As a climax to this birthday orgy, we all
burst into individual song over a smouldering campfire. The professor was easily the most vocal and rendered his homeland's communist songs in a strident fruity baritone.

Next day, a truck laden with baled lucerne drew up as we trekked
north through the foothills of the awesome jet black Tummo mountains. Noting our dire shortage of fodder, the driver spontaneously
unloaded four bales and presented them to us. An astonishing act of
generosity. He told us, somewhat ominously that we would not be
able to buy any grass until we reached Tejerri, five days away.

Denham had graphically described this country we were passing
through:

> These [the Tummo mountains or El War] were the highest hills we
> had seen since leaving Fezzan: the highest peak might be five or
> six hundred feet. They had a bold appearance, and were a relief to
> the eye, after the long level we had quitted. This was the eighth
> day since our camels had tasted water; they were weak and sore-
> footed, from the stony nature of the passes in these hills of El War.
> At night it blew a hurricane . . .

When Denham did find water, Dr. Oudney recorded:

> Several of our camels are drunk to-day; their eyes are heavy, and
> want animation; gait staggering, and every now and then, falling

as a man in a state of intoxication. It arose from eating dates after drinking water; these probably pass into the spirituous fermentation in the stomach.

An hour after loading up the hay bales, we reached a military camp where, to my astonishment, cheerful and efficient soldiers casually checked our papers and waved us on. The only words of English that any of them understood were Manchester United. There was much laughter, hand-shaking and back-slapping at the mention of the magical mantra. Is all Libyan officialdom like this? I thought to myself. Are all Libyans so obliging, friendly and generous? I had erroneously assumed that this was the official border post and that we had been waved cheerfully into Libya, along a track that was normally barred to foreigners, by Manchester United football supporters. The British ambassador's standing soared in my estimation and I felt that he must have tremendous pull with Libyan security. I didn't know at the time that the real border post lay twelve miles ahead and that things there were going to be very different.

We saw it from over a mile away. A white concrete carbuncle abutting a hummock of sand-coloured rock, the only feature in a windswept plain. There appeared to be two, possibly three, dilapidated buildings, one with a flapping corrugated iron roof and a radio mast hoist at one corner. The buildings seemed abandoned. So much so that, as we drew closer, I began to wonder whether we had reached the Libyan border post at all. Old truck tyres, rusting cooking oil canisters, coils of wire from hay bales, all the waste of caravans and itinerant trucks littered the ground. There were also over thirty skeletons of dead camels, some skewed into a posture of agonising death. I could hear the wooden shutter of a window banging rhythmically in the gusting wind with the consistency of a ticking clock. I scanned the wasteland, searching in vain for a solitary bush, tufts of grass or remnants of unused hay, anything that might give our hungry and travel-weary camels something to munch. There was nothing.

The buildings appeared to be surrounded by heaps of stony desert gravel, that had been mechanically piled up to form a series of haphazard mounds.

'A relic from the war with Chad,' Argali explained. 'They're bunkers for soldiers to shelter behind in a shooting match with an enemy.'

I then noticed that hundreds, maybe thousands of them, fanned out beyond the buildings in all directions. Mound after mound had been scooped up at random as far as the eye could see. The plain was spotted with these incongruous kennels for the dogs of war.

When we were a hundred yards from the buldings, Ehom motioned us to stop. He had seen someone. There was life here after all and it was clearly not politic to advance closer. The camels were ordered to squat and we dismounted. Just as we did so, the wind gusted black plastic sheeting in our direction and it flapped at our feet like a malignant dervish. With a frightened bellow, three of our camels lurched to their feet and broke their tethering ropes. For a moment our tightly disciplined caravan split up in confusion as our Tuaregs scattered after the camels with yells and shouts.

Ten minutes later, when order was restored, three men, dressed in khaki sweaters, faded jeans and sandals, advanced slowly towards us. They were not hostile, they were carrying no weapons and they were certainly not in a hurry. As we were shortly to discover, the occupants of Tummo police post had no conception of the meaning of the word 'urgency'.

*   *   *

'Hello, Bridget. Is that you?'

I had managed to contact Bridget Brind at the British embassy in Tripoli at the first attempt. Allah was on side.

'Welcome to Libya. How are you?'

'We're fine but we're holed up at the border post at Tummo. All our papers are in order. They've checked our passports and visas, there's no administrative problem, but they won't let us through. They've told us that the Tummo border crossing is barred to foreigners. They say that an order to allow us to enter Libya must come from Tripoli, via Sahba, Murzuk and Gatrun. They won't budge unless approval comes down from on high.'

Silence. Bridget was, as they say, thinking it through.

'I have a contact in the Libyan security office and he speaks good English. I'll try to get hold of him but I might not be able to do so until tomorrow.'

Tomorrow was a Thursday. No one in Libya worked on Friday. The end of Ramadan, the Muslim fast, would possibly fall on Saturday which could mean an additional holiday on Sunday and Monday. I was conscious that we could be here for days unless a positive decision was taken very quickly. It was 12 December. Carsten Peter was due to arrive at Gatrun on the 18th and Gatrun was at least six days away, separated from Tummo by one of the worst stretches of desert on the journey – Vischer's 'howling wilderness.'

'Thanks, Bridget. There's a policemen here called Ahmed who speaks Arabic and operates the radio. Could you tell him that we're not spies or international terrorists masquerading as camel drivers?'

Ahmed, a squat black-skinned Arab with a sharp wit and a ready smile, also spoke Hausa. He had confirmed to me that his boss hadn't the authority to let us through. I had bandied the name of the head of Libyan security and how our trip was sanctioned by his office. I'd also played the China card.

'We're travelling with a gentleman who is a highly respected and important Chinese government official. He's undertaking a major study of the deteriorating environment in the Sahara and is making comparisons with similar conditions in the Gobi desert. China is a good friend of Libya. I am sure that you wouldn't want to upset him.'

The officer-in-charge of the border post had eyed Professor Yuan in utter amazement. By this stage of the journey the professor's skin was blackened by wind and sun and the post-operative folds of his turban made him look, quite frankly, ridiculous. A more unlikely senior Chinese government official it would be hard to imagine. But I had been taught a Libyan lesson which was to be repeated many times in the future. The authorities were friendly and accommodating but they were working within a security system where a sanction for our onward journey could not be taken at local level or even at regional level. The decision could only be made in Tripoli. In essence, Libya is a tightly controlled police state and decisions, even minor ones, can only be made at the top.

Bridget spoke to Ahmed who was impressed to be holding a conversation with an official at the British embassy. But there was nothing that could be done until his boss was instructed to release us.

'I'll try to ring my friend's office. Telephone me tomorrow morning at nine o'clock and I'll tell you what he says.'

Pressed for time and with no forage for the camels, there was nothing that we could do but wait. Conscious of our plight, Abba asked me if he could use the telephone to ring a friend in Gatrun. If he could track him down he said that he would ask him to hire a pick-up to bring us bales of hay. Gatrun was 180 miles away. The cost would work out at $12.50 a bale. Needs must, I thought to myself as I handed him the telephone. Whether we stayed at the border post or were allowed to press on we must have hay.

That evening the policemen made a friendly gesture and sent us a leg of freshly killed mutton. Apart from corned dog, it was our first meat for a fortnight. We gnawed with delight on mutton bones smothered with beans that we had bought in Maiduguri market. It was a culinary decision that all of us, except Johnny, were shortly going to regret.

That night an unrelenting and cold wind swept over our caravan and the dreary landscape. I felt chilled in my heart for a different reason; our camels had eaten the very last of our forage. At nine o'clock as instructed, I rang Bridget. Her message was short and to the point.

'I spoke to my contact in security twice yesterday and he confirmed that there is no problem. He said that he will ring Gatrun personally and give the authority for you to enter Libya.' She gave me his telephone number. 'If you don't hear anything in a couple of hours I suggest you ring him yourself. He speaks good English and we've always found that he does what he says he'll do. The embassy can't really help any more. It's up to the Libyans now. Good luck. I hope that we'll meet in Tripoli in February.'

'Could you do one last thing? Please try to get a message to my trustee in England to tell Carsten Peter, the German photographer, not to wait for us in Gatrun. He should try to come down the road to meet us.'

'I'll do my best.'

I was acutely conscious that I was now on my own and that unless I got hold of Bridget's contact to-day, tomorrow was Friday and the end of Ramadan was imminent. At the fourth attempt I got through to the smooth-talking security official who told me that the telephone to Gatrun was not working but that he would try to send them a fax. This puzzled me because I thought that a fax line and a telephone line were one and the same thing.

'Don't worry, in one, two, or maybe three days' time you'll be allowed to enter Libya.'

The only relief that lightened my deepening gloom was Argali's discovery of a small quantity of grass that had been buried in the sand some distance from our camp. A caravan on its return journey was going to suffer but the fortuitous find would be enough to keep our camels going for another day. It was difficult, in the circumstances to keep the team's spirits up. Border posts are not salubrious places. This particular border post, where a howling wind swept over dead and hungry camels, was not a place that anyone would opt to dally. I couldn't wait to get away. But when?

As it happened, the word came through that evening. Ahmed ran over to us grinning and proclaiming his only word of English, 'Okay, Okay, Okay.'

'Welcome to Libya,' he continued in Hausa. 'You're free to go. Here are your papers and passports. All stamped and signed.' He grinned at me. 'Of course if you don't want to go, you can always stay as our guests and celebrate the end of Ramadan.'

'Thanks, Ahmed, but we'll leave tomorrow morning as soon as we can.'

My journal dated 14 December relates that: 'We set off into the howling wilderness, a lifeless ancient desert where man hurries through.'

What my journal does not relate was that something had begun to hurry through Japper, the professor and myself, and the prime suspect was the Maiduguri beans. Caught on the hop on the march, it was a constant and very public embarrassment for the next few days, as we would dismount rapidly and scuttle off as far as we could before nature forced us to squat, especially for Japper, who is not the swiftest of movers.

Something quite bizarre occurred on our first day in Libya and fortunately between dismounts. We were trekking through an extraordinary area of multi-coloured rock, some of which was a delicate shade of lilac, when at midday we saw a vehicle approaching from the north and for a moment my spirits rose, sensing that Abba's hay merchant had made good time. But it turned out to be a Tunisian who was flabbergasted to see Europeans and an Asian travelling with camels. He insisted on taking photographs of us which amused Japper no end.

'It's the first time that I've ever seen the natives taking photos of the tourists,' he said.

It was in this area that Vischer recorded:

All around a great mass of hills showed, black peaked, strewn with yellow and red rocks with patches of bright sand in between, and beautiful purple shadows . . . As we waded and tumbled through the red sand which covers the slopes, we passed a large heap of camel bones. They were the remains of a caravan from Bilma which had been killed by the intense cold during the winter months. Hadji Zaid, [Vischer's guide] had been held in the neighbourhood by the cold. The wind from the north-east froze the water in the skins and paralysed the camels, who refused to get up, being unable to stand on their stiff legs.

Passing through this area Clapperton noted yet another camel virtue. When their caravan descended onto a level plain composed of clay, sand and gravel, one of their heavily loaded camels put his near fore into a deep hole. This caused the off fore to stick out in front of the camel's body:

It was quickly unloaded and the people dug away to bend the other leg under the body and then hauled the other out of the hole. Fortunately the poor animal had received no injury and it was loaded and proceeded on as if nothing had happened. Had the same incident happened to a horse or mule, he would either have had his near leg broke or the off shoulder out of joint – but the camel though to appearance is a very stiff looking animal, it has the most flexible joints of any large animal I have seen.

When we pitched camp that evening there was no food for the camels. The entire country was one great desert and the landscape was utterly barren. Extremes of heat and cold had broken rocks and stones. The wind had scattered them about in wild confusion and carried away loose soil where grass might have grown. Consequently, there was not a blade of grass in sight.

'These camels can go on to Cairo,' said Adam, 'but, like a car, they must have petrol to keep them going. They can't travel on an empty tank.'

That first grass-less night was terrible. We bedded down by a cluster of rocky stones that marked ancient graves and used their cover as protection from the wind. The hungry camels hovered around us, staring at us pathetically. 'What are you doing?' they seemed to be asking. 'We worked hard for you all day. Where is our food?' I felt shamed. Next morning the fetid smell of their breath confirmed, if confirmation were needed, that their stomachs had ground all night on nothing. We were doubly cursed, both by their breath and by our own liquid stomachs.

We continued for a further two hours. My head was full of the horrors of starving camels and my tally of dead camel skeletons by the side of the road was now well past 1,200. There were so many that I had given up counting. At about two o'clock Argali abruptly turned his camel's head and set off on his own to the north-west. I watched as he reined in his camel and jumped to the ground. He squatted down for a moment and then he turned and shouted to the other Tuaregs to bring over all the camels.

I always think that on this stretch of the road three miracles occurred. This was the first, although it was later to be tinged with sadness. Argali had spotted a campsite that had been used by another caravan that quite clearly had plenty of forage, of a kind. They had been carrying millet stalks. Their camels had fed and the remnants were strewn over the ground. What was left was manna from heaven for us. We unloaded the camels and allowed our hungry animals to eat. They scrambled to wolf down what they could. One camel, a little white gelding that had always laboured uncomplainingly day after day, became too eager. It started to cough and rasp. It was quite clearly choking.

'It's got a stalk stuck in its throat,' said Adam.

A tin of cooking oil was flushed down in an attempt to loosen the obstruction which appeared to be caught in its windpipe. No success. The camel began to retch in a violent struggle to breathe. Argali pushed a stick down its throat in a vain attempt to dislodge the corn stalk. The Tuaregs tried everything they could but with a sudden and dramatic gasp the poor beast died. I was very upset, having been determined, if I could, to complete the journey without losing a camel. Jasper wanted to take some meat from the dead animal but the Tuaregs would have none of it.

'If you want to cut off meat then you can do it,' said Argali, 'but we won't help you.'

This was in contrast to Vischer's experience when, in almost the same area one of his camels became *batal* or useless and to shorten its suffering they shot it. 'Within twenty minutes nothing was left on the ground except the feet and some odd bits. All had been cut up and divided, and on the back of his brothers the poor camel continued its road to the south. Even by his death the good beast had helped the caravan, who went forward, singing and content, their faces turned towards the black mountains [Tummo], a good well, and a good meal of camel meat.'

Eighty years earlier, Denham recounted a similar experience in rather more gruesome detail:

> Four camels knocked up on this day's march: on such occasions the Arabs wait, in savage impatience, in the rear, with their knives in their hands, ready, on the signal of the owner, to plunge them into the poor animal, and tear off a portion of the flesh for their evening meal. We were obliged to kill two of them on the spot; the other two, it was hoped, would come up in the night. I attended the slaughter of one; and despatch being the order of the day, a knife is struck in the camel's heart while his head is turned to the east, and he dies in almost an instant; but before that instant expires, a dozen knives are thrust into different parts of the carcass, in order to carry off the choicest part of the flesh. The heart, considered as the greatest delicacy, is torn out, the skin stripped from the breast and haunches, part of the meat cut, or rather torn, from the bones, and thrust into bags, which they

carry for the purpose; and the remainder of the carcass is left for
the crows, vultures and hyaenas.

The firewood that we had carried from Aney was exhausted. That
night, we cooked over glowing dried goat droppings that had been
used to stuff the dead camel's goat-skin panniers. These were carried
on all the baggage camels to stop our loads rubbing their backs. The
heat they generated was much less than the heat of firewood, but it
was greater than that given off from dried camel dung which we
were forced to use when the goat droppings ran out.

At eleven o'clock the next morning, when we spotted the pick-
up coming towards us, my spirits soared. Abba's friends had responded to his plea for hay but as the vehicle drew nearer I could see to
my confused alarm that it was empty. It was not carrying a single
bale.

'They've come for money,' said Abba casually. 'Give them $300
and they'll bring you thirty bales.'

'Abba is taking $50 for himself,' whispered Asalik. 'Two fifty is a
fair price.'

'I'll give you $250, $300 is too . . .'

I hadn't time to finish the sentence before Abba exploded into one
of his short-fuse tantrums.

'If you don't like the price, then you won't get the hay,' he said
with an incoherent splutter before stomping off into the desert, only
to sidle back an hour later.

I knew that $250, which included the hire of the pick-up, was
exorbitant, and I was also fully conscious that my expedition finan-
ces were very tight. I talked to the driver who was quite happy to
settle for $250. This was what he had been expecting before Abba
inserted his own commission. The driver turned the vehicle towards
Gatrun to collect the hay.

'It will take us two days.'

'We have nothing for the camels. Please be as quick as you can.'

I wished him God-speed and prayed that he would hasten, half wondering whether we would ever see him or the pick-up again.

Both the professor and Japper were still in a bad way. There was some discussion as to whether our condition was caused by the Maiduguri beans or by maggoty dates. Little matter, the end result was exactly the same and for all of us except Johnny the daily agony continued. So much so that the professor unwittingly ruffled Tuareg feathers when he was forced to squat behind the only available shelter in the landscape – a pile of stones. These turned out to mark the resting place of another dead traveller and his act was considered, not unnaturally, to be sacrilege.

'Tell him to go anywhere he likes in the desert, but not behind piles of stones,' said Adam who was particularly upset. 'We are all men, we know his problem, we understand.'

That night, for the first time in days, the wind dropped. I poked my nose out of my sleeping bag and stared up into a depthless blaze of stars which curved in a brilliant mass from horizon to horizon. In this desolate desert, where nothing living made its home, I felt as though our planet was as cold and lifeless as any distant star. The camel caravan could have been crossing the moon. Only a wheeling satellite which winked and flashed across the sky, brought the comforting, though fragile reassurance, that I belonged to a world of life.

Next day the second miracle occurred when we found another former campsite of a passing caravan. On this occasion, the camels had been fed on grass and by the time we arrived, the remnants had been half-buried under drifting sand. We all scrambled about, scraping up fragmented green stalks with our fingers. Separating grass from sand to form life-saving mounds of nourishment, just enough to enable our caravan to keep moving slowly forward.

We rejoiced when the next evening the pick-up arrived with enough hay to ensure that we would reach Tejerri. Abba's friends hadn't let us down and run off with our cash. We allowed the camels to gorge themselves, until they too had left wastage in the sand to ensure the survival of another hungry camel caravan should it pass this way. The professor, whose stomach had defied the most up-to-date anti-diarrhoea tablets that National Geographic could provide, had starved himself for four days. At long last he felt able to break his self-imposed fast and both Japper and I, who had suffered extremes of discomfort, were also on the mend. It was not only the stomachs of the camels that had obtained relief.

On the evening of the following day, against the backdrop of a cloud-furrowed scarlet sunset, the third miracle occurred. We came to a soldiers' post situated on a rocky outcrop in the middle of nowhere. It had been established as a mobile customs post and was set up to catch the unwary smuggler. Libya is totally 'dry' and no doubt one of the main group of renegades that they were out to catch were alcohol smugglers. We submitted to their lengthy search with good grace. Like the police at Tummo, they were neither hostile nor officious. Just resolutely efficient. I think that they must have had word of our imminent arrival because they expressed no surprise that there were four foreigners on the road with a caravan of camels.

Now that our camels had fed, I was anxious to press on to Tejerri as soon as possible and the arrival of Carsten Peter was uppermost in my mind. We were two days behind our agreed rendezvous time and I wanted to link up with him before he was persuaded to return to Tripoli, having lost heart that he would ever see us. Unfortunately, the soldiers took their time. All our loads had to be unloaded from the camels, searched, and tied back onto the camels again. The search wasted three hours' travelling time and after we were cleared by the soldiers the setting sun forced us to settle down to camp about half a mile from the soldiers' customs post.

That evening, having pitched camp, Argali walked off on his own into the desert. He had spotted something lying in the sand and had set off to investigate. He returned, cradling something under his long flowing gown. As he called out to me a huge grin spread slowly across his face.

'Hey, John, I've found something that will interest you.'

I strolled over to him.

'Turn your back on the soldiers, I want to give you infidels a present and I don't want the soldiers to see us. They could be looking at us through binoculars.'

I turned my back as instructed and Argali handed me a litre bottle of Johnny Walker Red Label whisky. I couldn't believe my eyes, and stared at Argali, stupefied. One cannot readily imagine finding whisky in the middle of the Sahara.

Argali busts into roars of laughter. 'I thought you'd like to have some of your own medicine,' he said. 'There's a sack over there and it's got more bottles in it. I think some whisky smuggler must have taken fright when he saw the soldiers and thrown his precious cargo overboard.'

Japper and the others were not unnaturally staggered at Argali's discovery and Johnny set off to retrieve a second bottle. I felt that it would be unwise to upset our guardian angel by taking more and to do such a thing would display an unwholesome greed. Furthermore, the owner might return in the night in an attempt to retrieve his sack of spirit. That evening, in sight of the flickering hurricane lamps of the soldiers, we christened our amazing find. We were careful to control our human spirits that had soared after days and nights of deprivation. Like the camels, our stomachs ground on nourishment and warmth. The camels' breath didn't smell in the morning but I suspect that ours did.

I later learnt that it was a truck parked near the soldiers' camp that had jettisoned the whisky and they had formulated a plan to retrieve it. Incredibly, they had no objection to us taking two of their bottles and even offered Argali a lift to Tejerri. I jumped at this. Argali could go and try to find Carsten Peter, tell him we were on our way and, if necessary, bring him out to find us.

Much later we learnt that at this exact moment, candles had been lit for us in London and Chishinau, the capital of Moldova.

About one o'clock on 19 December a pick-up arrived carrying Argali and Carsten Peter who brought post and much welcomed vegetables which we had not tasted for days. The cucumbers were especially delicious and we wolfed them down like bananas. The pick-up left, minus Carsten and his staggering amount of photographic kit but we fortunately had two unladen camels which could carry it. We passed the old fort of Tejerri (mentioned by Vischer) and camped near tamarisk bushes, swarming with ticks, just outside the town. Our relief at having finally crossed the 'howling wilderness' was palpable.

Carsten Peter was tall, fair and forty-two. He appeared to be extremely well organized, a man of experience in adapting to rough conditions and highly motivated. Above all, he appeared to have a sense of humour, an asset of great value. Fortunately no volcanic eruption, no big or little victor, had taken place in the world in the last few days, because he had made it his particular specialty to be present at such scenes of spectacular geological activity. His reward had been a number of cover photographs for *National Geographic* magazine, the peak of photographic professionalism.

But first of all, we had to get one or two things straight.

'Do you have a back-up vehicle or any form of motor transport?' he asked.

'I'm sorry, Carsten, we're undertaking this expedition entirely by camel.'

He considered for a moment.

'But how can I get away from the caravan to take shots of you from a distance?'

'I'm afraid that you'll have to go either on a camel or on your own two feet, there's no other way.'

'And do you have radios so that I can keep in touch with you when I leave the caravan to take photographs?'

'Sorry, we're not carrying anything like that.'

'It will be tough for me, very tough indeed.'

'I feel the toughest thing for you is that you can only join us for eleven days. That's a very short time on an expedition that may last for three and a half months. Can't you stay for a few days longer?'

'Maybe that is possible. Let's see how we go.'

He had wound a turban round his head with the expertise of a man well practised in the art.

'Have you been in the Sahara before?'

'Yes, but I've never tried to cross it on a camel.'

'Good, now's your chance.'

That evening, a number of curious Tubbus, decked out in flowing gowns and turbans of blue and white, visited our campsite. They spoke Hausa and Kanuri as well as Tubbu and were eager to learn about our travels and what we were trying to achieve. They also wanted to learn what their town was like when Vischer paid them a visit. They squatted down in a semi-circle as I translated Vischer's account of what had happened to him when he visited Tejerri almost one hundred years ago. Rather disconcertingly, Carsten began to snap away in the background. Although the weather conditions that Vischer faced were strikingly similar to our own, the behaviour of the Tejerri Tubbu, the grandfathers of the little group seated in front of me, were very different. They had sided with some renegade Tuaregs in an attempt to wipe out Vischer's caravan.

7

But who are ye in rags and rotten shoes,
You dirty-bearded, blocking up the way

James Elroy Flecker
'The Golden Road to Samarkand'

Vischer described Tejerri as follows:

In the evening we marched into Tejerri and put up our tents on the great caravan camping ground south of the village under the walls of the Tejerri castle.

Tejerri itself is rather larger than Gatrun [not today], though the low huts, partly in ruins and all crammed together in a slight rise in the ground around the scraggy old fort, look equally miserable. The high walls of the ancient fort, rising out of the black mass of houses, gave the whole scene a most imposing if somewhat forbidding aspect.

The inhabitants were Tubbus. There were also a great number of Borno slaves and everyone seemed to speak Kanuri [as they still do].

Today, there are a great number of date palms which are a welcome sight for the traveller from Niger. The fort has, for the most part, crumbled and the oasis seemed to us neither forbidding nor imposing, just a place of utter relief.

It was at this oasis of Tejerri that Hanns Vischer survived a serious Tuareg attack. Vischer had continually been warned about the untrustworthy nature of the Tubbu and three days previously Tubbu camel drivers had stolen some of his camels. He had lingered in Tejerri to try to retrieve them. He related that the Tubbus at Tejerri have their faces veiled like Tuaregs [not so today] and that their manner of greeting is well in keeping with their robber nature. Both parties stop at a short distance and holding on to a sword, gun or preferably to both, squat down and begin their greeting with endless repetitious enquiries and questions after health, relations, camels, and country. However, they always kept carefully to strictly neutral ground. I didn't see this practice in Tejerri but had noticed in Niger that Tubbu males placed a hand on the hilt of their dagger or sword when exchanging greetings.

An unpublished letter to his family recounts what happened:

> The enemy was reported to be close at hand. Memories of my Cadet Corps training came flooding back and I tried to recall the lessons dinned into us by Old Wirewhiskers! There seemed to be no doubt that battle was about to commence. I mustered my troops, ten men equipped with Winchester rifles and four with long Arab breechloaders. The latter's only effectiveness was really in the noise they made! Every rifleman was issued with an extra twenty-five cartridges, so that each had fifty rounds. The women were ordered by me to brew up and hand out strong, black coffee to make sure no one dropped off to sleep.

I mounted my horse and set off to patrol the surrounding area, paying special attention to any clumps of palm trees. Every now and then I would gallop back to the camp to make sure that everyone was awake, but I soon found this to be unnecessary, because to a man they all had the vertical breeze-up, both in their hearts and in their trousers! Furthermore, it was a bitterly cold night, so they shivered and clung desperately to their weapons!

Decisive action was called for, because not only would the enemy be at our throats at the slightest provocation, but the Tubbus were ready to join in on the winning side, as soon as they could see who had the advantage.

As I reconnoitered the surrounding area, I twice heard and glimpsed the shadowy figures of camels and riders in the uncertain light of the stars. I immediately opened fire, whereupon they vanished into the night as if spirited away.

At 2 a.m. three Turkish gendarmes appeared, having come from Gatrun with a letter from the local garrison commander with scarifying reports of a band numbering more than one hundred Tuaregs and Arabs, who were intent on attacking my caravan!

As soon as it was dawn, Hadji Zaid (the Tubbu pilgrim wise to the ways and wiles of his own people) and I mounted our horses and set out to reconnoitre the situation. We eventually located and made contact with the enemy, who was well ensconced in the lee of a small hill. Ssssseuuuuu! Came back the first bullet as it sped over our heads! An old soldier back in Malta told me that when fighting with Africans, it was best to stand foursquare in the open and face them – whereupon they would take aim, fire and miss! I posted Hadji Said behind me to hold our horses in the shelter of a hillock and guard our rear. Having taken up position and located the enemy, I decided that it was time for battle to commence and opened fire. One opposing gun was silenced. Then, one after another four camel heads were crumpled to the ground. Simultaneously, various well-armed spectators, who had been lining the surrounding hillocks, vanished like rats down a hole. We then decided to call a halt to the encounter, re-mounted and withdrew to our camp, one and a half hours' riding distance away.

In best military fashion Vischer regrouped and went on the offensive:

Salvos of shots were directed at us from the hillocks, throwing up little spurts of sand all around us. The trusty Wespi carbine came into action again. With careful aim and a steady rate of fire, five of the enemy's guns were silenced and eleven camel heads crumpled to the ground. The Wespi was a credit to its makers, and a thorn in the side of the Tuaregs, which they won't easily forget. When fighting takes place, the camels are trussed so that they cannot rise to their feet and bolt. Therefore, all that is visible on the skyline are their long necks and heads which weave slowly to and fro. One camel actually broke loose and bolted, careering about in the cross-fire. One of my fusiliers hit it in the backside and it sped on its way towards us, so I was able to grab it and secure it. By this time the day was drawing to a close and with sundown the fighting was broken off, allowing me to withdraw my forces. We marched back to our camp, where we were anxiously awaited.

The rabble element in the village, supported by a considerable number of the Tubbu, had seized the occasion to prepare for a pillaging raid on my camp with a view to making off with various pieces of baggage. My friends among the Tubbus, together with the camp women had managed to keep them at bay but things were getting tense. The minute we appeared, the would-be raiders made off, like the varmints they were.

What were the Turkish Gendarmes doing all this time? Let it be said, here and now, loud and clear that Hanns and all like-minded, freedom loving citizens cannot abide cops, gamekeepers and heavy-handed flatfoots. These sorry relics of a bygone age are maybe necessary to deal with drunkards and escort them home, but certainly not to intrude their big feet and coarse features into any decent, law-abiding company. Having got that off my chest, let it be said those Turkish 'heroes', were a half-hearted, timid and ineffective lot and were highly relieved when I told them to go off and have a good rest.

That evening we had confirmation that the Tuaregs had struck camp and withdrawn to where they had come from – with clipped wings and tails between their legs! We had succeeded in driving them off, so the way was now clear for us to resume our journey.

Though Vischer did not have much to say for the local gendarmes, the Turkish authorities approved his taking the law so efficiently into his own hands, writing later to his family: 'En route Mr Vischer was attacked by Tuaregs. He repulsed their attacks by making a point of killing only their camels, thereby depriving them of their means of pursuit. This was considered a noble act by the people there who venerated him and said devout prayers for him . . . The Tubbus took fright after examining the camels of the Tuaregs and finding that they had all been shot through the head. Finally we would add that a legend has grown up around him here which regards his presence to have been the visitation of a Saint.'

As for Major Denham, almost a hundred years earlier he had experienced a much more agreeable time. As usual, he found the young girls very pretty. But he noted that over the main entrance door of the now crumbling castle, there was a large hole which opened to the gateway underneath. Denham was told how a woman had recently dropped a stone on the head of an attacker as he advanced through this gate. This action, which killed the assailant instantly, saved both the castle and the oasis from a full-scale attack.

Abba had left us at Tejerri and gone ahead to Gatrun by lorry, leaving us with a replacement Tubbu guide, a friend of his who lived in Tejerri called Sidi. As Abba's contract finished at Gatrun, we were letting Sidi have a dummy run. If we liked him and he liked us, we would hire him to guide us north to Tekertiba, a dwindling oasis north of Murzuk.

Sidi guided us through a straggling line of villages that run northwards along the line of a depression from Tejerri to Gatrun, the most important town in the oasis and a link to the southern city of Sahba and the road network to Tripoli. This strip of land is well watered and is fringed by a low ridge of hills, which protects the ground from shifting sand dunes to the east. The highest point on this ridge is Ras el Tejerri, a mounded hill situated at the northern end of Tejerri.

We passed an impressive number of solid square mud castles and the remains of walls and trenches, evidence of how this area had been fought over for centuries. Some of these castles appeared to be of Berber, or possibly Roman origin. These fortifications, with their large courtyards and deep wells, had been used for centuries as strongholds against outside attack. However, the unexpected attack from outside that we sustained took a more unusual form. We had no mud walls for protection – only synthetic sleeping bags.

At one of the campsites, halfway between Tejerri and Gatrun, Japper and I had set out our sleeping bags in a sandy hollow. A group of our camels, both forelegs hobbled for security, had come up to us and squatted down nearby. They started to masticate on rich lucerne and clover and their obvious satisfaction was music to my ears. I sensed their deep contentment as I lay back under the stars, listening to the methodical cud-chewing going on all around me as I drifted off.

'Aieou,' I cried out as a heavy weight landed on my left thigh and roused me abruptly from a deep sleep. I thought that I had been assaulted. Convinced that we were under attack by robbers, I struggled to free myself from my tightly fitting sleeping bag, half expecting the blade of a knife to come slicing through the flimsy material. As I wrestled with cords and zips, Japper, who was sleeping nearby, let out a more modest squawk as the assailant thumped his shin and left ankle. But this was not a Tuareg or a Tubbu. Our attacker was a camel.

When the first glimmer of light had started to streak across the early morning sky, the camel nearest to us had decided that it was time to fill his stomach. Rising unsteadily to his feet, he unaccountably blundered on his hobbles all over us. Camels will not normally tread on prostrate people and his hobbled front legs must have accounted for this unpremeditated error of judgement. It was a shock for me, but for Japper it was painful and more serious.

Nearly ten years earlier his ankle had been damaged by a bull camel that he had imported from Pakistan to Kenya. It had taken a long time to heal and now an ankle had once again been damaged, this time by a camel toenail that had dug into the ankle joint. Japper did not need this on top of an upset stomach which was only slowly adjusting to a normal diet. He had already decided to leave us at Gatrun and return from there to Tripoli and Kenya in time for his son Simon's wedding at the end of December. It was a rare slice of misfortune that one of our camels should send him home with a limp, especially as he had done more than anyone on the expedition to look after the camels' welfare. By checking them over every day and treating saddle sores and minor wounds, he had ensured that they remained fit for travel. They had now unwittingly determined that his travelling ability was limited.

*　　*　　*

'Is that really me?'

I stared at the long-haired, wind blackened, sunken-eyed reflection in the cracked mirror of Abdul Aziz's hairdressing saloon in down town Gatrun. The mirror was slewed at an angle that painfully distorted even further the wild man image. I was mildly shocked.

Since leaving Kukawa on 24 October, precisely two months earlier, I had not seen my face in a mirror. Although I had shaved fairly frequently as best I could, the razor had been guided through the gulleys and over the weathered contours of my jaw by the fingers of my left hand. Now I was face to face with reality – and it wasn't a pretty sight.

The next day was Christmas day and Japper's last and I felt an overwhelming need to look and to feel spruce. A shave and a haircut had been a top priority ever since we had pitched camp about a mile to the west of Gatrun. I wanted to shed the mad professor image that tousled locks conveyed and wallow in the luxury of a personal shave. Poor Abdul, he was slightly unnerved at the sight of his extraordinary customer.

Of an indeterminate age that hovered around forty, he was plump, dressed in a dirty white shirt, and soiled fawn trousers. He had pointed to a map to indicate that he hailed from Egypt and had a disconcerting tic that caused his head to jerk involuntarily to the left every ten seconds. Our communication was limited to sign language and I wondered idly whether his hand would keep his gleaming cut-throat razor on an even tack around my three-day-old whiskers. He held up a pair of scissors and a pair of clippers in each hand and waved them in front of me. I suddenly understood what he was asking. Did I want my hair cut with the scissors or shaved with the clippers? I pointed emphatically at the scissors and moments later he had dived into my greying locks with unrestrained enthusiasm. As soon as the first furrow had been ploughed, I realized that the damage was done. I was about to be scalped and when he concluded the tonsorial operation I felt that he might just as well have used the clippers. I was shorn like an old tup in midsummer.

When he finished lathering my face I closed my eyes. Either the old tup was going to end up as dead mutton or he would get a decent shave. Fortunately, I received the latter and hairless and tingling from scalp to chin I left the grinning Abdul feeling light-headed and light-hearted. It is quite wonderful what a barber, even one with a tic and a blunt razor, can do to cheer up the day.

It had needed cheering up because earlier I had visited the local and national police offices, the security office and the customs, all of whom were eager to get sight of our passports, papers and visas. All the offices were, without exception, sparsely furnished and urgently in need of a coat of paint. The occupants were curious, polite but authoritatively emasculated. Gatrun administration appeared to be powerless to act without sanction from on high.

In the customs office, the middle-aged, greying and unshaven officer who reclined on a couch on the other side of a wooden table, gave me a weak grin that exposed three gold-capped lower teeth. He then proceeded to drop his bombshell.

'You are required to pay customs duty on your twenty-five camels,' he said, without taking his eyes off mine.

'Customs duty?' I spluttered. 'But we were given special permission to come into Libya with our camels at Tummo. Here is the certificate, signed by the officer-in-charge.'

'That is a military certificate, you weren't given authority to evade customs duty. The tax comes to $50 per camel, and that is $1,200.'

'But camels are coming into Libya from Niger every day. The owners can't possibly be paying $50 per camel.'

'That is the law,' said the customs officer enigmatically.

Our expedition budget had not allowed for camel customs duty and I did not have the money.

'Can I telephone the security office in Tripoli and ask them to speak to you?'

'As you wish.'

I went out of the office into the morning sunshine and dialled the number that Bridget Brind had given to me in Tummo. Amazingly, the helpful official was not only in the office but he answered the telephone. After I had explained our situation, he promised to speak to the head of Libyan customs in Tripoli on our behalf, but I sensed a lack of enthusiasm. Having helped us to enter his country, I suspect that he felt that it was now up to us to make our own way. He said politely but firmly, that it was not necessary for him to speak to the Gatruni customs officer as that officer would not be able to make a decision, one way or the other.

I then decided to telephone Mustafa at Sukra Travel and for the very first time got through to him at the first attempt. But he gave me short shrift. Piqued that Sukra had made no money out of us, he told me in as many words, that we were now on our own.

'You should have sold your camels at the border and hired fresh camels from Sukra. Then you wouldn't have had to pay customs duty.'

'But we would have had to rent camels from you.'

'That's your problem, not ours.'

Sukra was definitely not on side.

So the camel duty scam remained unresolved which is why I had felt an urge to call on Abdul Aziz for a facelift. The scissors and the cut-throat had done the trick and I returned to camp with a spring in my step.

On arrival I was immediately confronted by an irate Abba.

'I want my pay,' he shouted. 'Where is Sidi's brother Hadira? He was supposed to have arrived from Agadez by truck and meet us here on the 19th, it's now the 24th. I've been cheated.'

He railed on. All the money for the guides and the Tuaregs had been made over to Sidi at Ngigimi. I had parted with Abba's cash, and had no responsibility or money to pay him.

'You'll have to be patient, Abba,' I said as gently as I could. 'Hadira must have been delayed. I need to meet up with him too to find out if Sidi's contract can be extended to Tripoli from Gatrun. I need to know whether Ehom, Argali, Adam and Asalik will stay with us. My contract with Sidi runs as far as Gatrun.'

'That's not my affair,' said Abba angrily. 'I want my money. If I don't get it I will take the nine camels that Sidi hired to you in lieu of my pay.'

'Then I will have to go to the police.'

'The police! You won't get anywhere with them. The chief of police is a Tubbu. If I speak to him he won't lift a finger to help you.'

There was little point in prolonging this illogical rant. I turned away. But the spring in my step had subsided, Gatrun was turning up a number of unsuspected problems. My only slight consolation was that Vischer had experienced similar difficulties here with his Tubbu guide, Marabut Senussi, observing: 'Although there could not be the slightest doubt that the guide purposely kept us here, I could do nothing but wait. I felt scarcely justified in shooting him, as he deserved.'

Though not nearly so wily and deceitful as Marabut Senussi, Abba's uncontrollable temper and his inability to listen to reason was a trial, not always lightly borne.

*   *   *

Near the Gatrun market stands an old Italian fort that was being rebuilt and refurbished by one Mohammed Tahir, a Hausa-speaking Tubbu, and a Gatruni entrepreneur. The fort was built entirely of mud and a visitor enters into a large courtyard through two ancient wooden gates which are surrounded by massive rectangular mud walls. The courtyard is lined on two sides with individual mud-built rooms for travellers, some of which were under construction when we arrived. Down one side of the courtyard is a long cool room fitted with chairs and a dining table and in a corner on the opposite side there is a rudimentary shower system of the holed tin variety. Mohammed, who was about forty-five, had travelled widely throughout East and Central Africa. He was gushingly friendly, offering refreshment and tea and refusing to accept payment. The reason for this exceptional friendliness puzzled me, it couldn't be love at first sight. The more, this much travelled man, chattered away in Hausa, the more I had an uneasy feeling that something wasn't ringing true. He was hoping to persuade tourists to use the fort as a travelling base. Johnny, who befriended him immediately, metamorphosed into a tourist and hired a room which appeared to have all the comforts of a monk's cell. However, there was a positive bonus to this for the fort was hard by the market, and this proximity enabled Johnny to stock up with supplies for our onward journey without having to trek back and forth to the camp.

Meanwhile, Carsten Peter, when on his way to meet us, had off-loaded a significant package into Mohammed Tahir's care, a Fortnum & Mason Christmas hamper that my ever efficient Wild Camel Protection Foundation co-trustee had personally packed to ensure that Libyan customs could not place sticky fingers on any alcohol and thereby prevent its safe arrival in Gatrun. In the event, brandy butter and cherries preserved in port had slipped through. On Christmas Eve, we dispatched a camel to the fort and as the sun started to slip behind the palm trees, a Fortnum's Christmas hamper was laid to rest in the soft sand in the centre of our camp.

How we revelled in the contents. Our Christmas lunch consisted of goose liver pâté, mince pies, a magnificent Christmas pudding and all the traditional accompaniments – except alcohol, which no doubt explains why in the party photos we appear to be somewhat subdued. Abba, sulking and skulking moodily in the background added a piquancy to the paper-hatted celebration. De-fused crackers (so as not to alarm customs) disgorged silver-plated gifts and exotic candles.

After the feast, visitors began to appear: representatives of the Gatrun Historical Society who alleged that in 1798 the explorer Hornemann had written in his book that all Tubbus were cowards – I certainly did not concur and refuted the suggestion; a guide who wanted to take us to Murzuk – I had already hired Abba's protégé, Sidi; a Gatruni merchant wanting to purchase our camels – how, pray, were we to travel to Tripoli? Lastly the local police came to the camp for the fourth time because they were puzzled by certain stamps in our passports. Then, in the late afternoon, Japper left us to travel by 'share-taxi' to Tripoli, thence onwards to Nairobi. I was saddened to see him go. He had been a wonderful member of our team, full of practical common-sense, versatility and humour. Argali had tears in his eyes as he shook his hand for the last time. 'A good man,' I overheard him mutter, 'a very good man.' Japper had covered 1,000 miles out of a total distance of 1,500. A remarkable feat.

Next day, Hadira had still not arrived. Although the Tuaregs had indicated their willingness to accompany us all the way to Tripoli, Hadira had to sanction this and agree a fee. I had managed to contact Agadez by telephone and had been told that the truck in which he was travelling had broken down north of Sequedine. So to avoid the muttering of Abba, who by now was nearly incoherent, I left with Carsten, Asalik and two camels on an early morning photo call in the old township.

All the ancient mud towns that we encountered in these southern Libyan oases had been abandoned, allegedly by a Qadhafi inspired edict in the 1970s that decreed that the citizenry move into new concrete soviet-style apartment blocks and houses. A far cry from the narrow, picturesque streets that Vischer must have wandered. Whether this proclamation was done in the name of modernization or security, I have no idea, but not a single person lived in any of these ancient dwellings. The houses had had their roofs removed to ensure that the evacuees would not return.

Asalik and I pottered through the romantic ruins mounted on our camels. Though the taciturn Asalik certainly wouldn't have seen it that way. For the romance stopped at ground level where rusting tins and plastic detritus littered the streets. Gatrun old town had descended into a rubbish dump. But if one raised one's eyes there was much to see including Carsten leaping from rotting rooftop to weathered wall like a mountain goat, snapping hectically all the while. I had been disconcerted to learn from Carsten that professional photographers only use their expensive gadgetry when the sun is either setting or rising (or shortly before or after).

'What if I fell off my camel at midday and broke my neck? Wouldn't you take a photograph for posterity?'

'I shouldn't think so,' he replied with a soft laugh. 'I wouldn't be able to find a publisher.'

The morning sun rose, shining through the serrated leaves of the date palms. As it did so, it transformed dirty brown walls of cracked mud into ever changing displays of burnished gold. The overall effect was stunning and I decided that Carsten had a point. But it was a point that provoked mild conflict at a later date when he wanted to elongate his evening programme to take silhouettes of camels on dunes after sunset. The weary camels (and their human attendants) were not prepared to act out bit parts after camp had been pitched at dusk. Everyone, man and beast, was too tired.

'Carsten's a perfectionist,' I had been told by a friend at *National Geographic*. 'He's never satisfied with his pictures. He's always aiming for something better and is his own most stringent critic.'

I discovered that every word of that observation was true and I grew greatly to respect Carsten's commitment and professionalism. That evening he persuaded Johnny to squat almost naked under a leaking water tank from which water cascaded into the street. The result didn't say anything about our expedition, but it said a great deal about Carsten Peter's opportunism and imagination.

The phlegmatic Asalik could not, of course, see the point in any of this, but nevertheless went quietly along with the strange behaviour of his temporary paymasters.

Back at base, the professor was busy making Chinese dumplings.

'Good defence for stomach,' he remarked on our arrival.

Defence was one of the professor's prime considerations and he was constantly defending himself from sundry bugs with an impressive array of Chinese potions. Chairman Mao had designated flies, mosquitoes, rats and sparrows as the four great natural evils. The professor had no doubt had this maxim drummed into him in his youth and with respect to the first three evils he was on constant alert. In common with most other Chinese his other obsession was for food and the rigours of our spartan expeditionary diet must have been very tough on him. Normally, Chinese dumpling making is an assembly line process with one colleague pounding the dough, another rolling it and cutting to a desired shape, and yet another inserting a meat or vegetable filling. The professor combined all these skills into a creative display of dumpling construction, using mutton from Bilma that he had carefully marinated with red-hot peppers and cooking oil and concealed in a tin for the past three weeks. The end result, cooked in a frying pan over glowing goat droppings, was delicious and complemented his latest discovery – brandy butter spread lavishly on Gatruni bread rolls.

The professor's meat preservation techniques were not too far removed from Denham's observation made at Murzuk, although fortunately, the end result was different:

> The Inhabitants of the richer class have however a method of preserving their meat which enables them all the year to enjoy a little Soup. In the Winter Season when the passage of the desert between Mourzuk and the Vallies to the South of Tripoli is not attended with such difficulties for Animals, many flocks are passed over by the Arabs – these are brought up and dressed for the purpose of being preserved in large Jars, fat is poured boiling into the Top of the Jar, so as to entirely exclude the air & the Contents will remain good for many months. As soon however as the Jar is uncovered the preserve becomes sour but this they consider as nothing, therefore the repast with which you are furnished as a supreme luxury, after all is but a nauseous mess of stale, greasy stew which not infrequently disorders the stomach more than a twelve hours fast.

Meanwhile Argali was not neglecting our camels. They had fattened noticeably on limitless supplies of lucerne and clover and for the first time for many days were looking content. I had read in a book written by Major Glyn Leonard in the late nineteenth century, which embraced the totality of camel management, that tobacco was good for them. 'It livens the blood and acts as a wholesome tonic.'

I had idly imagined a caravan of pipe-smoking dromedaries or Bactrians sporting lighted cigars. Argali showed me exactly what Leonard had in mind. He was, like many nomads, an inveterate chewer of tobacco and Japper had bought him and the other Tuaregs a number of packs from Kenya to keep their blood up. When Argali had extracted all the juice that he required from a plug of tobacco lodged tightly in his cheek, he would walk up to one of our squatting camels, open its mouth with both hands and deftly spit mashed tobacco down the camel's throat. Whether it livened their blood I do not know, but they certainly did not object to this force feeding in the slightest.

About four o'clock in the afternoon, Hadira unexpectedly materialized. He arrived, undramatically, on foot and I was mightily relieved to see him. I soon discovered that he was the very antithesis of his younger brother, Sidi. Calm, with a shrewd and measured approach, he soon settled Abba and reached an equitable agreement with me over the onward journey to Tripoli. Adam was to leave us and the seven camels that we had hired from Sidi would return to Agadez in his care. The other three Tuaregs would continue the journey with us to Tripoli. We would all miss Adam, a hard-working man of wit, resource and good humour who had succeeded in keeping Abba's volatile temperament on an even keel for most of the journey.

Hadira reminded me of a wise Emir of Gombe whom I had known many years earlier in Nigeria. Surrounded by young and impetuous councillors, who frequently disagreed with one another, this wise, impeccably dressed Muslim, would listen to their arguments in complete silence. When they were finally exhausted, the Emir would pause to reflect and then turn to them with consummate friendliness and say, '*Za mu yi haka.*' – We shall do it like this. And they did, respecting his wise council, even though he was illiterate and some of them had received higher education abroad. Hadira was certainly not illiterate, but he brimmed with the same common-sense, tempered by a strong Islamic code of conduct.

When Denham left Gatrun, he was given a divine insurance policy.

> Much necessary arrangement had been made here by laying in a stock of dates, etc. for our long journey: and at eleven A.M. we left Gatrone. The maraboot [holy man] accompanied Boo-Khaloom [Denham's guide] outside the town, and having drawn, not a magic circle, but a parallelogram, on the sand, with his wand he wrote in it certain words of great import from the Koran; the crowd looking on in silent astonishment, while he assumed a manner both graceful and imposing, so as to make it impossible for anyone to feel at all inclined to ridicule his motions. When he had finished repeating the fatah [first chapter of the Kur'an] aloud, he invited us singly to ride through the spot he had consecrated, and, having obeyed him, we silently proceeded on our journey, without even repeating an adieu.

Maybe I should have asked for a repeat performance because on leaving Gatrun we immediately ran into trouble. We had not travelled more than two and a half miles when a jeep, emblazoned with the Libyan customs emblem, caught up with us at speed. The officials were irate. We had not received clearance for our camels to move. I replied that, 'Mohammed Tahir had told us that everything was in order and we were free to leave.' Not unsurprisingly they said that Mohammed Tahir had no authourity to say any such thing. After a lengthy discussion, they agreed to take Argali back to Gatrun carrying all our passports, visas and papers. They knew, of course, that we could not move without them.

When Argali returned Hadira was with him.

'The situation is serious,' he said. 'They have heard nothing from the Head of Customs in Tripoli. You could be delayed here for days.'

I decided, yet again, to ring the Libyan Mister Fix-it. But this time he sounded world-weary, as though he really didn't want to involve himself with something so mundane as camel customs duty. Perhaps he had become Hare-weary.

'I can't get hold of the Head of Libyan Customs,' he said. 'I suggest you pay the duty if you don't want any further delay.'

'Thanks for all your help. I'll take your advice.'

This of course was easier said than done. My funds were not sufficient to pay $1,400. Fortunately, Hadira came to my rescue. He told me that he had a good friend who was the head of the Gatrun secondary school.

'He will lend you the money at no extra cost, provided that you refund it in Tripoli before you leave.'

And so, this kind schoolmaster, whom I had never met before, lent me, in the event, $1,000, having persuaded the authorities to reduce their charge to this amount. I have no idea what motive compelled Mohamed Tahir to send us the spurious message that we had been cleared to leave. I suspect, however, that personal financial gain was at the bottom of it.

On 29 December we were free at last. Hadira agreed to meet up with us in Murzuk and, without benefit of a parallelogram, we set off into the desert heading for that ancient township.

I had a read a good deal about Murzuk and its importance in the days of the great camel caravans. Notwithstanding its unsavoury reputation with former explorers for pestilence and disease, Murzuk held out for me a certain romantic allure.

8

God be thy guide from camp to camp: God be thy shade from well to well.

'Gates of Damascus', James Elroy Flecker

'This place is full of jinns,' whispered Asalik, sidling up to me.

We both stood and stared, as our hobbled camels charged from one cluster of stunted date palms to another. Having reached a clump of greenery, they would stop and crane their necks forward to eat. Then, in unison, they would abruptly jerk their heads upwards and gaze about them, wild eyed and tense, before frenetically rushing off in another direction. Normally, when we camped and had unloaded the camels, they would rest for a moment before rising slowly to their feet. We would then hobble their forelegs with coiled rope to prevent them from wandering off too far and they would set off individually, at a restricted walk to the nearest forage, whether acacia, date palm, tamarisk or grass. However, here in Mestuta, a lush little oasis midway between Gatrun and Murzuk, things were very different. The camels had first grouped nervously together in a herd and stood gazing uneasily round about them. Then hunger propelled them towards the date palms. Hardly had they reached their target and stooped to feed, than their heads were up and they were off again, not at a restricted shuffle but with great thrusts of their hobbled forelegs so that they sprang forward in uncoordinated leaps towards the next green foliage.

'The jinns are trying to ride them. They are playing with them.'

To us it had seemed perfect, a picturesque but unoccupied ancient fort which, given the odd crumble or two, was unchanged since Vischer's day. Mounds of sand gave our campsite shelter from the wind. There was ample food for the camels, immature date palms, tamarisk and grass after a punishing twenty-two-mile trek. A glorious sunset lit up the little oasis like a film set and fingered the derelict fort with blood-red shards of light. It was a New Year's Eve to remember, but not for the camels. For two hours until the fiery sky faded to a quilt of sparkling stars, they continued to charge about in this manifestly unsettled state. We had never seen them behave in this way before and we were never to see it again.

At last, when the sun had given way to a bright moon, they half settled for the night, huddled together in a group. They had been too distracted to eat and there wasn't much cud for them to chew on.

Hearing a noise beside me, I poked my nose out of my sleeping bag.

'Happy New Year. I've brought you the last of the *mao tai*. Share it with me and let's drink to the New Year.'

'Thanks so much, Professor, happy New Year.'

Before we pitched camp, the oasis of Mestuta had doubled for Ko Karama, seeming to retreat as we edged closer. The ancient fort had been hidden from us by a central hummock of sand and on that hummock a tent was pitched. Soldiers had been making a lightning raid on the oasis to catch the unwary smuggler. The mobile customs unit was back in operation again.

Dead camel on the treacherous road north of Tummo (Libya)

A Fortnum & Mason hamper arrived at Gatrun (Libya)
to brighten Christmas 2001

The old fort Murzuk (Libya)

Mestuta, an uninhabited oasis full of desert jinns (Libya)

Ibrahim Kwaidi at Wunserik
(Libya), grandson of Vischer's
friend Sheikh Ahmed

Shikou, our Tuareg guide in Libya

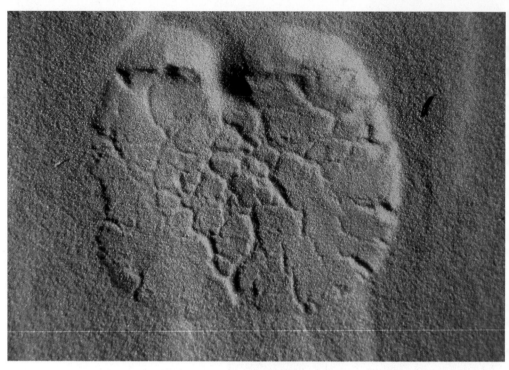

A camel's footprint after travelling nearly 2,000 miles

A sheepskin boot for a sore camel's foot

Lake Um el Mar, north of Tekertiba (Libya)

Shadows across the Sahara

The last stretch of the road to Misda (Libya)

Journey's end – Misda (Libya)
Johnny, Argali, Asalik, JH, Ehom and the Professor

'How is Manchester United?'

The commanding officer had come up to me and, discovering that I was English, had asked the obvious question.

'Fine, just fine,' I replied airily.

'Any whisky?'

'I beg your pardon.'

'Any whisky? It's New Year's Eve. We should celebrate.'

'Sorry, we're not carrying any. This is Libya. No alcohol.'

He was wearing a tee-shirt on which was ironically emblazoned 'Pour yourself a Pepsi'. But the request for whisky was not made in idle jest.

After I had dismounted from Pasha, a young wild-looking soldier jumped up into his saddle when my back was turned. Pasha rose unsteadily and the soldier, who was unused both to camels and Tuareg saddles, grabbed hold of the three-pronged pommel to steady himself and the left-hand section snapped. After we left Ngigimi, I had assiduously protected that saddle pommel by binding it with white cloth. I wasn't best pleased.

The soldiers, having persuaded Ehom to allow two of the camels to be used as temporary water carriers, pointed out a place to camp. The casually dressed officer had retreated to his tent, but no sooner had we settled to unload the camels than he and five other soldiers started running down the hummock towards us.

'I have been ordered to search your loads.'

The joking, smiling demeanour that we had first encountered had disappeared. In its place was the brusque, officious manner of a man who, I guessed, had been reprimanded by his superior at the other end of a radio for not subjecting us to a thorough search. An army battle-dress jacket covered the Pepsi tee-shirt. A peaked hat was rammed firmly on a woolly head and, with Manchester United quite forgotten, the search through our equipment and loads began.

They were particularly interested in the wooden kitchen boxes which they no doubt judged were ideal for carrying guns. I could see our quartermaster's gorge rise as his meticulously ordered supplies and cooking equipment were flung haphazardly onto the sand.

Then careless and clumsy hands started to rifle through our possessions and when they reached Johnny's leather bag that contained his personal belongings, I saw him tense and the veins on his temples puff up. His colour rose alarmingly and just for a moment I feared that one particularly rough-handed soldier was going to be hit.

'Take it easy, Johnny,' I muttered as I noticed his fists clench and unclench.

At length, the search was complete. Having discovered neither weaponry nor alcohol, the soldiers relaxed. The officer-in-charge apologized for his action, adding that there was nothing else that he could have done.

'I was acting on orders,' he said, with a shrug of his shoulders. The tee-shirt was back on display and the peaked cap had disappeared. 'Camp where you like. You're not our concern any more.'

We decided to move as far away from the soldiers as possible. The selected route had led us into this grove of restless, camel-riding jinns.

New Year's Day was cold. Frost covered my sleeping bag and we estimated that the temperature at six o'clock in the morning was three degrees below freezing. Water had frozen in our kettles and in spite of our resolve to leave soldiers and jinns firmly behind us, our limbs and joints were stiffened with cold. So were the frost-encrusted coils of rope. It consequently took a long time for the loads to be hitched to our camels.

When our new guide, Sidi, led us across the desert of Murzuk we found that it too was strewn with artefacts. This delighted the enthusiastic Carsten whose interests seemed to be turning away from photography and more and more towards archaeology. We all picked up more immaculately serrated arrow-heads, axes and other ancient implements and once again I marvelled at the quantity.

'The jinns are chasing us from Mestuta,' said Argali with a laugh when I asked him to explain a strangely patterned track that seemingly led from somewhere to nowhere. In the Murzuk desert we discovered a number of these odd trails and I just might have started to believe Argali had I not seen a large tuft of grass and then a twig being bowled over and over in the sand by the ever present wind. The fractured lines in the sand were caused by rollicking vegetation, not roistering jinns, though I later learnt that some desert dwellers still believed jinns were the real culprits.

However, the pace that guide Sidi set was neither rollicking nor roistering and it certainly wasn't in tune with ours. He treated us like tourists on a three-day safari and seemed not to appreciate that we had already covered over one thousand miles and were anxious to kick on. Shaped like an amiable duck, swaddled in blue cloth and a black turban, he waddled flat-footed in front of our caravan, more often than not to the accompaniment of a Muslim chant intoned at the pitch of a castrati. Coupled with this lack of urgency, was a finely tuned religious fervour, which induced sung prayers at half past five in the morning and a full prayer session to Mecca five times a day. As I understand it, a Muslim travelling through arduous terrain does not have to be quite so assiduous with his daily prayers. He was a zealot and our Tuaregs, including the religious non-conformist Argali, considered him to be a nutcase.

He had brought with him a large nylon tent, also coloured blue and he hastened to erect his superior sleeping quarters as soon as we set up camp. Later, he attempted to sell it to me, muttering that I would be much more comfortable, ensconced under canvas. His general lethargy and religious fervour prolonged our daily trek by at least an hour and caused our Tuaregs to mutter, once again, that no Tubbu could be trusted to do anything properly. But at least he knew the general direction to Murzuk. However, as soon as we left Mestuta we were in sand dunes which dwarfed those of Bilma's

Great Erg and our new guide Sidi did not impress, often leading us into soft sand which tired both man and beast.

Denham recorded that on this particular stretch between Mestuta and Murzuk he did not see one living thing that did not belong to their caravan, not a bird or even an insect. Things have changed. I stared in astonishment at two dragonflies flitting over the dunes. Where were they going? Did they know where there was water? What were they doing in this lifeless wasteland? Later I spotted a butterfly hitching a ride on a somnolent professor's sock on his shoeless foot. It was carried along for at least twenty minutes, impervious of, or possibly attracted to, the smell. Had it been blown off course? Where was it heading?

On this pre-Murzuk stretch of the journey I travelled on a replacement camel. A food fight in Gatrun between Pasha and FitzHarry had inflicted two deep bites on Pasha's withers and as my Tuareg saddle's tree rested on top of the wound, friction prevented it from healing. Sidi had acquired Pasha on a temporary basis, using the tailed saddle which enables a rider to carry loads slung underneath him. The weight is taken up by four horizontal sticks which rest on the sides of the camel and not on the withers. When this type of saddle is in use, the camel has to be tied fore and aft to other camels in the caravan. Pasha who was nothing if not a free spirit, disliked being shackled to his mates in this embarrassing fashion and plodded along in disgust with both wounded withers and wounded pride.

On 3 January we woke to an abrupt weather change that made us feel that we had reached Europe, as we arrived at the oasis of Murzuk, the former capital of a fertile region known as the Fezzan. Sidi led us straight to the town refuse dump, surrounded by ramshackle hovels, barking dogs and urchins, and suggested we camp there. For the first time on the whole journey I became angry. It was a disgusting place, surrounded by the rotting carcasses of domestic animals, camel bones, rusting tins and disused plastic containers. As there was water nearby Sidi seriously considered we would want to camp there. Argali took charge and led us to a good campsite to the south of the town. This resembled a large bomb crater, which afforded both shelter and privacy. In the centre of the crater, which was really a scooped out sand dune, there was a grove of date palms. The palms were lush and fruitful and Sidi fretted that angry farmers would drive us away. We ignored him and the camels settled to chew on date palm leaf. The trees were mature and the damage the camels inflicted scarcely noticeable. Sometimes I despaired of our new guide. Dried date palm fronds blazed lustily and burnt rapidly, but they warmed our sheltered hollow, our spirits and the father of the Murzuk chief-of-police who arrived in the evening to find out what we were up to.

Denham's entry into Murzuk in 1823 was as inauspicious as was our entry via the rubbish dump.

> It was three in the afternoon before we arrived at the wells near Mourzuk. Here we were obliged to wait until our camels came up, in order that we might advance in form. We might, however, have saved ourselves the trouble: – no one came out to meet us, except some naked boys and a mixture of Tibboos, Tuaricks and Fezzanese, who gazed at us with astonishment, and no very pleasant aspect.

Later, Denham was annoyed to discover that his Jewish servant had ridden on ahead of him into the town. Sheik El Blad, the town's governor, had mistaken him for the esteemed Englishman, who he had been told, was arriving to pay his respects.

> The servant of mine, mounted on a white mule with a pair of small canteens under him, had preceded the camels, and entered the town by himself: he was received with great respect by all the inhabitants – conducted through the streets to the house which was destined to receive us; and from the circumstances of the

canteens all covered with small brass shining nails, a very high idea of his consequence was formed.

He was told that the error was caused because, 'We thought the English were better looking than Jews . . . but then God made us all, though not all handsome like Mussulmans, so who could tell?'

Murzuk had an evil reputation among the early explorers on account of the health risk from its stagnant pools. Dr Oudney, Denham and Clapperton's long-suffering travelling companion, also recorded:

> The Fezzanians have a horrid practice of throwing the carcases of all the animals that die in heaps close to the gates and under the walls of the Town, then suffering them to lie & rot until dried & consumed away by the powerful effects of Sun. I have well said in stating this to be the treatment of the remains of all Animals, for very little more attention is paid to human bodies – they are merely laid on the sand & sometimes not wholly covered even with that – a few boughs from the date tree thrown over them completes the ceremony – and as the branches sink and the sand is carried away by the wind, the body becomes exposed some-times a few days after its being deposited. These Cemeteries above ground are to be found quite round the Town.

Prolonged residence was usually the lot of those nineteenth-century travellers and Vischer's twentieth-century experience was no different. Caravans usually broke up and dispersed on arrival as it was an important trade centre. Onward travellers, including impa-tient European explorers, sometimes waited months before all the necessary guides, servants, equipment and supplies, and in partic-ular the camels, were brought together to form a new caravan. One of these explorers, Ritchie, sickened and died while submitting to an enforced stay in Murzuk and was subsequently buried in the township.

In 1869, another traveller, Alexandrine Tinne, known to the Fezzanis as Bint-el-Rey (the daughter of the king) on account of her great charm and spirit, had met in Murzuk an explorer called Gustav Nachtigal. They agreed to attempt to make the journey to Borno and, while waiting for fresh camels and supplies to arrive from Tripoli, Alexandrine Tinne was invited by a Tuareg chief, Jchnuchen, to visit his camp which lay a few days' journey to the west. Dr Nachtigal, in the meantime, had gone on a reconnaissance trip to the Tibesti mountains. When he returned to Murzuk he found that Miss Tinne, and two Dutch sailors who were with her, had been murdered by Tuaregs belonging to the very tribe whose chief had invited her to visit him. Little was done to punish the murderers and the crime is recalled to this day as an example of a betrayal of trust by an unscrupulous Tuareg chieftain.

Whereas these early explorers, on entering the township, had to pay their respects to the Governors of Murzuk, be they Arab sheikh or Turkish pasha, we, in these more prosaic times, had to call at the police, customs and security offices. The professor, Argali and I did the rounds, carrying the team's passports. We trudged from one office to another and were subjected to a series of indifferent interviews. But, without fail, the reply that we were travelling with camels from Nigeria to Tripoli never failed to surprise.

'Aren't you tired?'

'What are you doing it for?'

'Why don't you continue by bus?'

The incredulity of our interrogators was heightened when we stated quite simply that, 'We are travelling with camels.' In Niger and to a lesser extent in Nigeria that reply was accepted and understood. In Libya it provoked utter disbelief.

Eventually, our papers and documents would be scrutinized, stamped and approved; our eccentric answer to 'Method of transport?' accepted. The last call was at the Office of Internal Security. As one might expect, security was so tight in Internal Security that we did not even see the person who checked our papers, let alone enter his office. A gloved hand accepted our documents through a hole in the wall. After they disappeared, a tiny grille banged shut. The subsequent wait in the main street of Murzuk was a lengthy one.

The professor who, by this time, was tired and hungry, slumped slowly to the ground with his back resting on the outer wall of the building. Then, much to the amusement of Argali and myself, he fell asleep. Moments later, he began to snore. Not a rippling, pedestrian purr but a full-blown, nasal, Chinese rumble. Passers-by stared in amazement at a foreigner sleeping on the streets of Murzuk. The professor's khaki sun hat dropped from his head and fell to the ground. I carefully turned it over and placed some Libyan currency notes in the crown. The professor snored merrily on and passers-by now looked askance at the only Chinese beggar who had ever graced the Dendal, or main street, of Murzuk. Forty-five minutes later our passports were handed back to us through the hole in the wall. The professor, sensing that the vigil was over, rose sleepily to his feet, stooped to pick up his hat and stared in astonishment as a stash of Libyan banknotes floated to the ground.

'Where are all the Libyan women?'

The professor stared about him as we walked away from the security office.

'How do these people make babies? They have no women at all.'

The purdah rule appeared to be strictly enforced in Murzuk. There was not a woman in sight.

Things were different in Vischer's day. He found that the women of Murzuk gave the town all its vitality and colour. Free from the restraining laws of the northern Arab, the Fezzani girls in Murzuk had no use for the veil and believed little in the sanctity of the harem. Vischer heard their laughter ring through the streets and the market, as if their jests were verging on the improper. He discovered that they had the most cheerful manners in which the eternal feminine spirit, the gaiety of the African and the wit of the Tripolitanian, blended together to produce the most delightful female. He noted that their complexions were all shades from ebony-black to *café-au-lait*; so refreshing after the veiled figures that he had encountered in Tripoli. With their large silver earrings, heavy bangles and anklets, shrill but not unpleasant voices, henna-dyed hands, coal black eyes and shining white teeth, their whole appearance expressed for Vischer, a vibrant defiance of the melancholy desert that surrounded them.

A century earlier Denham recorded that the Arabs believed nothing male could flourish in Murzuk and that the air in the town was only good for women and mares. Like Vischer, he confirmed from his own observations that vivacity, strength and good looks are all on the side of the female. In a village just outside the township, he was brought a bowl of fresh milk by the beautiful Ohmal-Henna, the sister of a friendly merchant called Abdi Zeleel.

Denham described her:

> Dressed, with only a blue linen barracan, which passed under one arm, and was fastened on the top of the opposite shoulder with a silver pin, the remaining part thrown round the body behind, and brought over her head as a sort of hood, which, as I remarked, had fallen off, and my having taken her hand when she set down the milk had prevented its being replaced. This accident displayed her jet black hair in numberless plaits all round her expressive face and neck, and her large sparkling eyes and little mouth, filled with the whitest teeth imaginable. She had various figures burnt on her chin with gunpowder: her complexion was deep brown; and round her neck were eight or ten necklaces of coral and different coloured beads.

After suitable Arabic salutations she confessed:

> You were the first man whose hand I ever touched – but they all said it did not signify with you an Insara (a Christian). God turn

your heart! – but my brother says you will never become Moslem – won't you, to please Abdi Zeleel's sister? My mother says God would never have allowed you to come, but for your conversion.' By this time the hood had fallen back, and I again had taken her hand, when the unexpected appearance of Abdi Zeleel, accompanied by the governor of the town, who came to visit me, was a most unwelcome interruption. Ohmal-Henna quickly escaped; she had however, overstepped the line, and I saw her no more.

Ah, the delights of old Murzuk. After nearly 200 days of desert travel they were definitely not experienced by any member of our caravan. If these good-looking, vivacious females still flourish, it is strictly behind closed doors.

However, there was another aspect of old Murzuk that was quite horrific. Denham explains how slaves waiting to be sold, the twenty per cent that survived the blistering journey from Borno, were generally kept in the slave dealers' houses. He feigned an interest in purchasing some and was taken to inspect the slave dealer's choicest specimens.

Three young female slaves were led out and displayed before him. They were dressed in a blue linen cloth which passed under one arm and was fastened on top of the shoulder of the other by a wooden skewer. This skewer was roughly pulled away by the dealer and the poor girls were left quite naked to the waist. Their favourable points were then shown to Denham as though they were cattle or horses displayed for sale in a country market. Their tongues were pulled out, their throats and ears were looked into and they were subjected to rough and indelicate questioning. They were then forced to retire and another group of three was led into the chamber. At length, all the prospective candidates were herded into the room and those that were finally selected were put on one side like sheep separated from the flock. Bargaining then commenced. Once again they were stripped and their defects pointed out, scrutinized, denied and asserted. Denham, who by this time was quite upset, said that the price was too high and left the house. The unfortunate females retired, waiting to be displayed again when another prospective purchaser arrived.

Denham was shaken by his experience with the slave dealers in Murzuk and was later to write: 'It is here that the advocate for the barter of human flesh (and shall it be said that in the 19th century such Advocates are to be found) should come in order to turn his heart.' Eighty years later, the slave trade was mercifully coming to an end when Vischer arrived in Murzuk. The Turks ruled, but their rule was disintegrating and Murzuk was partly used as a penal settlement for dissidents – another Devil's Island. It could be reached only under conditions which spelt death to all but the most robust, and it was remarkable that the colony of international prisoners that Vischer met there survived to tell the tale. Locked up in the vast fort of Murzuk were rebellious Young Turks and forty-five Bulgarians. Among the traders seated in the market-place Vischer discovered one of these Young Turks selling tea and sugar. When no customer appeared, he took comfort in no less an author than Baudelaire.

Vischer was enchanted to find a market trader reading such a great work of European literature as *Les Fleurs du Mal* and discovered that Samy Bey was a former officer in the Turkish navy who had been condemned to 101 years exile and sent to Murzuk to undergo his penal servitude. Vischer and Samy became good friends and he later became Vischer's interpreter. These Young Turks never complained and Vischer discovered that they were a great force for good in the town. They had founded a school where the children of the township's poorest received a free education. When not actually thrown into chains, as they were from time to time, these cheerful exiles advised the Governor as clerks or secretaries and taught in the school. After years of solitary confinement which would have killed

most people, Samy had managed to acquire a little house and gar-
den, married a local Fezzani and soon found means to make himself
indispensable. He borrowed and lent money and traded in the
market. Rogues and rascals, thieves and robbers, traders and farmers, everyone seemed to know and like Samy Bey.

As for the Bulgarian captives, they had been driven across the
desert, heavily chained like slaves of old in the charge of some brutal
policemen. Cut off from their homes, with no means of commun-
icating with the outside world, at the mercy of the local authorities,
who gave them just sufficient bread to keep them alive, few had any
definite knowledge of the offence for which they were suffering.
Vischer found that they strove to make the best of their lot, although
none knew if they would ever return to their homeland.

Vischer stayed in Murzuk for over a month which coincided with
the celebration of the Sultan of Turkey's accession to the throne.
Poles and flags appeared along the Dendal, and everything was
covered with branches of date palm. Drums were beaten, bugles
blown and children recited poems and songs in honour of their far-
off ruler. When darkness fell, the whole of the town was given over
to dancing and singing, a favourite pastime of old Murzuk. No
sooner was music heard in the streets than women ran out to dance
and sing. Vischer describes how, Aisa, a brown beauty with a well-
oiled head, would lead the chanting and the other girls would throw
themselves into the chorus. Most of their songs were love songs and
one gives a different slant on the slavery question:

> He who is your friend in words is not always your friend;
> He who in his heart is your friend he alone is a friend.
> When you meet him receive him well;
> Forgive him all his faults and be patient with him.
> My heart desires, but fruitless desire is misery,
> My desire is painful, it leaves me no quiet.
> I die for the little Arab girl,

Her brown eyes have been made by Allah himself,
Whosoever sees them can neither read nor pray,
I wish I were a Negro, I would sell myself,
I would go to the slave market that she might buy me.
I have cast my eyes on a star,
I remember for ever her beautiful form.

In Murzuk today there is no longer street dancing to the rhythms of carefully crafted songs of love. State-controlled television force feeds the Fezzanians with a depressing diet of soap opera, football and pop music, interspersed with carefully controlled news. Argali and I discovered this for ourselves when we decided to try our luck with roast chicken and tea in a little roadside cafe. The chicken, served on a metal plate, was tough but welcome after weeks of macaroni and the odd goat. The tea, weak and sweet, was equally welcome. But the television, operating at full blast, was excruciating. Argali is a big man and he was hungry. His head was down and I am sure that he did not notice the howls of pubescent pop stars, for not once did he look up at the screen. It was in this little cafe that I realized to the full just how lucky I was to be travelling in the desert with camels.

Earlier that evening, when we had at last finished with the authorities, the professor and I set off to visit the old city and the fort. The latter, has been carefully preserved and the massive mud walls are punctured by a beautifully constructed curved wooden gate. The great doors stood ajar and slanting sunlight filtered through the gate's arches and bathed the minaret of the fort's ancient mosque, which tilts to the north like a miniature Pisa. A large market covers much of the internal area, but the dungeons and buildings of the Turkish administration have long since disappeared. In 1850, Barth made a striking sketch of Murzuk, from the roof of the British consul's house, and this depicts the fort towering over the Dendal. When Vischer stayed in Murzuk the house of the consul, a Mr

Gagliuffi, who had been stationed in Murzuk for the purpose of stopping the slave trade, was in ruins. In the sketch, camels are being driven along the Dendal and the substantial merchants' shops flank it on either side. However, some of the houses in the background appear to be dilapidated for, even in 1850, Murzuk was in decline. Barth commented that the township was too large for its scanty population of 2,800 people and that a large part of the town's habitations was in ruins.

One interesting remark that Barth makes, which had particular relevance to us, was that 'the place, is usually in great want of money.' Our attempts to change US dollars into Libyan dinars, were extremely frustrating. There were no banks and no one wanted to change our money. Johnny and Carsten chased from one potential money-changer to another before finally settling on a non-native of the town who was at last prepared to change our notes. The exchange rate that they were given was, not surprisingly, abysmal. This problem in every oasis township that we visited remained with us all the way to Tripoli.

Today, the old city to the south of the fort is much more dilapidated than the fort that we had seen in Gatrun and those we would find in the oasis towns we were to visit further north. Only the fort, which housed the political prisoners of Vischer's day, remains as a pointer to Murzuk's strategic importance during previous centuries.

The Young Turks, the Bulgarians and the other political exiles have long since gone, but there are others who have travelled to Murzuk from afar, as Johnny and Carsten, who set off into the town to replenish our supplies, soon discovered. Ghanaians have settled in as bakers. Nigerians and citizens of Sierra Leone are chancing their arm to make a living in modern Murzuk, selling carpets, running roadside food stalls and labouring to build shops and houses. Conscious that our route would lead us on to the bleak and barren Hamada el Homra, one of the toughest and coldest deserts in the

Sahara, I bought a thick, multi-coloured blanket from a Hausa man who sold them by the kilo.

Exiled Ghanaians are particularly friendly and helpful. I discovered them teaching in South Africa in Bophutatswana University, during the bad old days of apartheid. I came across them trading far from home in Botswana and publishing in Zimbabwe. The migrant Ghanaian is the gypsy of Africa, taking on whatever trade that he surmises might make him a fortune. The Ghanaians in Murzuk were no different and happily guided Johnny and Carsten to money-changers and suppliers of basic foodstuffs.

Denham, Clapperton, Dr Oudney, Vischer and Barth had all spent over a month in Murzuk, in spite of its evil reputation for pestilence and disease. We spent twenty-four hours there. Our enforced delay at Gatrun had pushed us behind schedule and, having satisfied the four different police offices that we were bona-fide travellers and secured sufficient foodstuffs for ourselves and our worthy camels, there was no compelling reason to linger.

Hadira, true to his word, had found us and our campsite by following the cracked footprints of our much travelled camels. Early travellers would have been allowed to bring their camels into Libyan townships but today no camels are allowed to enter a Libyan town's precincts. Hadira had brought with him, as promised, all the papers from the Gatrun customs which confirmed that our camel importa-tion duty had been paid by his friend, the schoolmaster. He now proposed to head by road for Tekertiba, our next oasis stop, to try to find us a replacement guide for Sidi whose contract ended there. Sidi had never travelled the camel road further north than Tekertiba and I needed a guide with both a sense of urgency and a sure knowledge of the way ahead. To the north of Tekertiba lay massive sand dunes and to the north of the dunes spread the formidable Hamada el Homra. A reliable guide was essential, but for once, Hadira's judgement let us down. The man he chose made the defi-ciencies of both Abba and Sidi pale into utter insignificance.

9

Pull out, pull out, on the Long Trail — the trail that is always new!
Rudyard Kipling

'What are you going to do with your camels when you reach Tripoli?'

Hassan M. Hassan had succinctly articulated the nagging question that had been surfacing on and off in my mind for weeks and was now niggling on a daily basis.

What was I going to do?

I had talked glibly of selling them when we completed the journey, but the only potential buyers were Arabs. Whereas Tuaregs have an innate sympathy for the camel and its welfare, the Libyan Arabs we encountered had made it quite clear that, for them, camels are valued as a source of food and a very tasty food at that. The young dromedaries that we had met being driven along the road from Niger, had all been heading for Libyan Arab cooking pots. I had

formed a mental picture of an avaricious, wild-eyed merchant testing the sharpness of a well-honed blade on his thumb and was
determined that our camels should not fall into the hands of this
kind of butcher. Well over two months into the expedition I was
greatly attached to our camels and especially to Pasha. I was thankful
that so far all but one had survived and was committed to taking the
caravan safely through to journey's end. I wanted to sell them to a
person who had a vested interest in keeping them alive. But to
whom?

We were sitting in Hassan's tent in Tekertiba. It was chilly, and
outside burnt a fire over which mutton kebabs were roasting. Hassan
was the senior partner of Mukhtar Ansari of Fezzan Tours whom I
had met on my reconnaissance mission to Tripoli, and who had
efficiently spirited Carsten Peter from Tripoli to Gatrun and safely
engineered Jasper's flight to Nairobi. Dressed in a long brown burnous, Hassan, exuded hospitality and warmth. He was rotund and
jolly with a lively face that periodically creased into a tangled web of
laughter lines.

We had entered Tekertiba on the afternoon of 7 January, and were
now settled in a Fezzan Tours campsite, from where Hassan and
Mukhtar organized short trips for tourists into the nearby sand
dunes. The campsite was dominated by these dunes. They took off in
dramatic style, rising abruptly at the northern edge of the lush oasis
of Tekertiba, which was dotted with date palms and an exquisite
shrub, whose mauve flowers, composed of innumerable florets,
continually changed colour in the fluctuating sunlight.

An idea formed.

'Have you thought of taking your tourists into the dunes by
camel? Wouldn't this be more of an adventure for them than taking
them up there in a four-wheel-drive vehicle?'

Hassan M. Hassan was quick to spot the link.

'Your camels are tired, they have come a very long way. They are
very thin.'

'A month's rest with good food and you wouldn't recognize them. They would be so fit and full of life that tourists would be up in the dunes in no time, if they hadn't fallen off in their excitement at being mounted on such splendid animals.'

'Will you have a little water?'

Hassan smiled benignly as he held out a large plastic water bottle which advertised the name of a local spring.

I took a long draught and nearly choked. This wasn't ordinary water, this was firewater; clear as crystal and sharp as a Tuareg's knife. I stared at Hassan.

Hassan's laughter lines spread slowly all over his face. 'That's how we beat the ban,' he said with a chuckle. 'Eighty per cent of Libyans distil raw alcohol. We bottle it in water bottles, so that it doesn't attract undue attention. Then we drink it. I'll give you some to take with you.'

'Will it make us go blind?'

'Not my brew. It's a very high quality.'

It wasn't as good as vodka but it was much better than the professor's *mao tai*. I wiped my mouth on a paper napkin.

'Are you interested in buying the camels?'

'Maybe. We think that they could be a tourist attraction. Especially after their illustrious journey.'

'I would sell them to you on one condition.'

Hassan raised his eyebrows.

'That they are not to be killed for food.'

'I can promise you that.'

There the matter rested. Fezzan Tours was definitely interested at a price of about £150 per camel. If I had not sold them to another buyer for a higher price, I was to contact Mukhtar before we reached Misda, just south of Tripoli. What a relief it would be if I could find a safe home for them.

A few days earlier, we had left Murzuk and set out on the four-day journey to Tekertiba. Sidi the guide, who had slept in Murzuk and not with us in the camp, arrived late and delayed our start by over an hour. Having initially led us to the town's premier rubbish dump, it was not the best way to pick up brownie points with the caravan team. He was consequently subjected to a number of expressive Tuareg curses. We followed a line of date palms that led us north of the Murzuk oasis and then stopped at a well to take on water. The camels were laden down with fresh bales of hay which was a great relief to me after their pre-Gatrun hardship. One camel had choked on grass in the night but fortunately was none the worse next morning after being force fed with cooking oil, the great camel lubricator. Pasha's fighting wither wound was better but as a precaution he was still being ridden by Sidi. Other camels had saddle sores and rubs but, given the distance they had covered, almost 1,700 miles, they were in amazingly good shape. Meanwhile, Sidi's pious fervour seemed to be increasing by the hour and his castrati-pitched renditions climbed heights that other singers dared not reach. This endeared him even less to the team.

As we advanced through the day, the desert gradually changed from a featureless gravel plain to a stony plateau covered with clumps of camel grass. At 5.15 in the evening we pitched camp near some palm trees which appeared to flourish among rolling sand dunes. That night, as I played endless games of backgammon with Carsten Peter, huddled around a palm frond fire, the professor's comments on the state of our mental health amused us all.

'Madams, that's what we all are, madams.'

'I beg your pardon, professor?'

'I tell you, John, we are all madams and you are the number one madam.'

'What do you mean?'

'Madams, people with no head, crazy people.'

'Oh, madmen. Now I understand. But why are we madmen?'

'We are madams because we could get a bus that would get us to

Tripoli tomorrow. Yet you want us to take another month to get there!'

'Well, put like that, I take your point.'

'I tell you, John, you are the number one madam around here for bringing us all this way by camel. And I am a Chinese madam for agreeing to come with you. Every Libyan who sees us knows that we are all madams.'

I had known and worked with Professor Yuan Guoying since 1995 and in all that time, never once had I questioned him about his past. I felt it would be politically inept for me to do so. For instance, I never mentioned the Cultural Revolution, although he must have experienced that traumatic and hysterical time at an impressionable age. The professor's past was, for me, a no-go area. Therefore it came as something of a shock, and certainly a surprise, that after the 'madam' conversation, he suddenly settled to talk to me about his experience as a university student in Lanzhou, during the Great Leap Forward, that period at the end of the 1950s and the beginning of the 1960s when Chairman Mao forced a totally new agricultural system onto a country that for centuries had relied on the age-old practices of its peasant farmers. The result was a disaster of gigantic proportions and millions of people died. I listened enthralled as the professor explained how his sister's husband had died of starvation and of how, as university students, they would go out into the fields to scavenge for leaves, grass, anything that they could find that was remotely edible. He told me how over 100,000 people had died in Lanzhou city alone, and the effect this searing experience had had on him.

Then the door closed. The chink of light that he had allowed to shine in on his past disappeared. I did not question him in an attempt to find out more. Maybe our meagre and unvaried diet had prompted these thoughts or maybe it was a necessity, after weeks of talking trivia, to communicate at a deeper level. Whatever the reason, I took this intensely revealing conversation as a great compliment.

When in China, engaged on work to protect the wild Bactrian camel, it has always struck me most forcibly that a Chinese person in their late fifties or above must have experienced change that is quite impossible for us to comprehend. We in England survived a terrible war, but the ideology of our country was not stood on its head and then decades later turned upside down again. We have never had to conceal our thoughts from members of our own family. We have never had to guard our speech so that we only expressed opinions that conformed with the government's viewpoint. One can only speculate on what terrible secrets lie buried behind the mask of Chinese inscrutability and one can only hypothesize at how the professor was reacting to the liberating, yet disciplined, crossing of a vast African desert, where there were no political restrictions, and where the individual was totally free.

All the 'madams' awoke the next morning to an eerie sight. There had been a heavy dew in the night and my sleeping bag was soaked. But the dew had settled prior to a great fog which, as day broke, gusted towards us in rolling clouds. We watched in astonishment as it advanced at a quickening pace. Soon it engulfed us, reducing visibility to a few yards and covering us and our camels with tiny droplets of moisture. As we packed up our camp and loaded the camels, I wondered whether some mighty hand had mysteriously transported us to Europe. But for the sand and the palm trees, we could have been in England in November. The unpredictable dramas of the desert are endless and on that very same morning there was another one.

Before the fog engulfed us all, I had risen earlier than usual. The previous evening, I had persuaded, Johnny, an assiduously early riser, fire-maker and kettle-boiler, that he take a lie-in and allow me to light the fire and make the morning tea.

'Thanks, I'll do that.'

So at first light, having shaken off the dew like a dog, I managed to light the kerosene cooker and the kettle was soon singing merrily away. Johnny, as I have already mentioned, was a stickler for routine. This was a laudable trait that ensured that the fire and lamps were meticulously serviced and lit at precisely the required time on a daily basis. As he had been the early morning pot-boiler for two and a half months, his routine was inviolate.

One of Johnny's most prized possessions was his mother's thermos flask, a heavy metal convenience of pre-second world war vintage, that she had generously allowed to be taken to the desert. Now, when Johnny had boiled the first early morning kettle, he filled the thermos full of hot water. He then refilled the kettle, so that when the rest of the team approached for a morning cup, he had a reserve of hot water waiting in the thermos, in addition to a singing kettle. A sound and eminently sensible strategy.

Unaware of the strategic role that the thermos played in the great scheme of things, I failed to fill it with hot water. I did however pour the first kettle of boiling water into a saucepan, where it inevitably cooled rather quickly, and placed the refilled kettle on the kerosene hob.

Johnny, refreshed by his early morning lie-in, advanced towards the fire to claim his cup of tea. He went straight to his mother's thermos and picked it up. It was empty. He stared at me incredulously.

'The thermos is empty.'

'Sorry, Johnny, but there's a boiling kettle and a saucepan of hot water.'

'But the thermos? Why didn't you fill the thermos?'

Fortunately, Carsten provided an immediate distraction which focused attention elsewhere. All of us had to pee in the morning and some of us had to pee in the night. However, when Carsten felt the urge, he didn't extricate himself from his sleeping bag and walk away from the camp. He hopped in the bag to the desired spot, unzipped his bag, peed, and then having zipped up all round hopped

back to his berth. Carsten chose exactly the right moment to provide this singular entertainment. The thermos was forgotten.

On any expedition of this length, be it in the Sahara or Antarctica,
the trivial can become magnified into a thing of huge import and
significance. Only in retrospect, does one realize the triviality of the
initial irritation. On this occasion, a drama was narrowly averted.

Two days later, we found ourselves on a prairie covered in ump-
teen acres of six-inch-high, young wheat. For centuries the central
Fezzan had been renowned for its fertility. It is the bread-basket of
modern Libya and underground reservoirs of water have allowed
generations of Fezzanis to cultivate crops here. Herodotus described
it as a corn-bearing land, rich in palms. Leo Africanus in 1600
describes it as, 'an ample region, containing great store of castles
and villages, and being inhabited with rich people.' Because the
Fezzan was so fertile, its potential wealth attracted every victorious
army that swept across North Africa. The Romans penetrated to the
Fezzan in 20 BC. Pliny relates that Consul Cornelius Balbus threw
the ruling Garamantes out of the area and turned it into a Roman
province called Phasania. However, centuries later, after successive
invasions by Vandals, Moors and Byzantines, the Fezzan became
depopulated, its villages were burned and its gardens and palm
groves destroyed. This left the inhabitants reduced to depending on
the passing caravan trade and, when this failed, and the oases were
no longer able to support them, they were forced to emigrate.

It was clear to us that today, fuelled by oil money, the productiv-
ity of the Fezzan is being restored, through cultivation undertaken
on a vast and highly mechanized scale. Judging from the prodigious
amounts of water that are being used, one could question whether
the region's underground water reserves are being unduly taxed.
This was certainly the query in my mind when we passed enormous
mobile overhead irrigation conduits spraying vast areas with untold
gallons of water. Green and yellow John Deere tractors with prodigious pneumatic wheels scurried about like restless ants. We trav-

elled along a track through the wheat in the face of a very cold wind. Wrapped up against its penetrating grip, it seemed incongruous that in this frigid climate, we should be advancing through an endless expanse of lush wheat which stretched to the horizon. Under these conditions, the wheat should have been yellowed and shrivelled by the cold. It wasn't, it was green and healthy and, for the first time on the whole of the journey, I was conscious that we had moved firmly into the twenty-first century. Our camels alongside the lumbering John Deere mammoths could not have provided a greater contrast.

My mind soon returned to more immediate matters. Sidi had lost his way and was trying to head us towards a motor road which I knew from the map, lay too far to the east of our intended route. The Tuaregs were reluctant to impose their will on a guide. After all, the guide was supposed to be the expert and was being paid for the job that he was doing. However, the very last thing that I wanted was to follow a motor road and so, after a brief confrontation with Sidi, Argali, who knew this area, took over. After two hours, the fields of wheat were left behind us and we were back once more in familiar territory, a broad stone-strewn and totally infertile desert plain.

It was four o'clock, campsite selection time, and Argali had gone on ahead to seek out a suitable place, preferably one that held something for the camels to eat.

'Look, John, look over there.' Carsten, who always rode atop a baggage camel and was hitched up behind me in the absence of Argali, was pointing excitedly at the horizon.

'What is it, Carsten?'

'Look, the hills in the distance have detached themselves from the desert surface. They appear to be floating in the air. It would make a wonderful photograph. If you could lead me far enough away from our camels, then I could take a picture which would look as though the caravan was floating in space.'

I hesitated. Far enough away would have to be a long way indeed for the mirage conditions to take effect. We would then have the difficulty of catching up with the rest of the camels at a time when campsite selection was paramount. I didn't want to be negative. Carsten had a tremendous enthusiasm and it would be counter-productive to dampen it. He had also had one or two frustrated attempts at taking pictures on an earlier occasion, when I had wanted to pitch camp.

'Where do you want to go?'

'Over there.'

He pointed to a slight rise on the eastern horizon. The caravan was heading to the north-west.

'All right, but I am going to have to trot over there, otherwise we will never catch up with them when your photographic session is finished. Hold tight.'

Trotting on a camel is a question of balance and a precarious balance at that. Unlike a horse, where the rider's feet are encased in stirrups, a camel jockey cannot rise to the trot. He cannot sit to the trot either, because a camel's trot is more violent and the rider gets thrown further into the air than when perched on a trotting horse. It's uncomfortable on one's bottom and on much else besides.

Pasha, who I was thankfully riding once again, enjoyed trotting and would willingly do so, but not if he was trotting away from the other camels. Like horses, camels are herd animals and do not like to be separated from their fellows.

My camel trotting experience was limited and I was totally self-taught. Pasha started to twist his neck round to the left in an effort to force me to change direction. 'I don't mind trotting,' he seemed to be saying, 'but not in the direction that you are taking me.' What happened next, was a series of short, sharp bursts at the trot, followed by an abrupt halt and a subsequent camel neck wrestle. Carsten, who was entirely at the mercy of Pasha was jolted violently up and down at the trot. Then he would watch helplessly while I wrestled with Pasha to keep him on track. When I eventually won the battle, Pasha would break out into another short burst of trotting. In a very short time, in spite of the cold, I was pouring with sweat, red in the face and beginning to regret that I had ever agreed to take Carsten on a photographic session at all.

'Is this all right, Carsten? Can we stop here?'

'No, please go a little further.'

Thankfully, Carsten's camel was prepared to follow Pasha and allow him to play the lead role. Had he developed a mind of his own, then goodness knows what might have resulted. On we went until at last we reached the ridge that Carsten had first pointed out. We stopped to try to spot the caravan. By now they were a string of dots on the western horizon. Although camels travel at two and a half miles an hour, it is amazing how rapidly they can pull away from you, especially if you are travelling in a different direction.

The mirage was still sending hills into the sky and, indeed, as Carsten had predicted, our camel caravan was starting to drift slowly upwards into the ether. This was the shot that Carsten was after. If he could take it now, all the effort and energy that we had expended would have been worth while. However, the next problem was to make Pasha stand still. He knew exactly where his gelded brothers were and he also knew that they were slowly disappearing into thin air. Pasha had been stopped in the middle of nowhere, and was determined to rejoin his brother camels as quickly as possible.

He attempted to surge forward. I pulled on the *teresum*. Pasha spun to the left and Carsten's camel was obliged to follow. We started to circle round and round as Carsten struggled to extract his camera from his brightly coloured camera bag. Not an easy task when his camel was being forced to pirouette in an ever decreasing circle. The bag almost fell to the ground. In Carsten's eyes, far more important than his own welfare, was the safety of his precious and expensive cameras.

'Stop, John. Stand still. Please stand still.'

'That's what I am trying to do, Carsten.'

Pasha would not stand still for a second. He was determined not to give Carsten a chance to focus, let alone press his camera's button.

'The camels are disappearing. They'll soon be out of the area where the mirage is having an effect.'

I knew what Carsten wanted, I certainly knew what I wanted, but with Pasha's mind firmly set on forward movement, immobility was impossible. Our caravan, quite literally, shimmered away over the horizon. One moment they were there, floating over the desert, the next moment they had totally disappeared. The photo opportunity had gone. All we could do was to try to catch up with the caravan before we lost them forever.

'I'm so sorry, Carsten. There was nothing that I could do.'

'It's not your fault.'

I was wringing wet. Perspiration was pouring down my face. No doubt, the thermal vest, the three sweaters, a waistcoat, a tweed jacket and a Barbour jacket in which I was encased helped to account for this. The instant I pointed Pasha's head in the right direction and gave him a nudge forward he was off. Not at a gentle trot but at a brisk trot that on two occasions almost broke into a gallop. Mindful that it is a long way to fall from a camel and conscious that a Tuareg saddle is a precarious piece of travelling equipment, I held on as best I could. I fervently hoped that the frayed seat belt, that acted as my saddle's girth, would hold. It was a sound item of kit when we had set out from Ngigimi, but 1,200 miles later it was beginning to show signs of wear and tear. Camel control had gone. Pasha was in charge and he knew it. I was by now oblivious of Carsten, oblivious of anything except survival.

Twenty minutes later we caught sight of the caravan and so did Pasha. This was the moment that I had been waiting for. The moment when I could exercise control. Pasha was slowed to a fast walk. Carsten, whose turban had unwound and was flowing out behind him like some enormous white totem, was gasping. Fifteen minutes later we had caught up with the caravan.

'We enjoyed watching you,' said Asalik. 'You looked just like a Tuareg.'

'I certainly didn't feel like one. I wasn't riding Pasha, I was being taken for a ride.'

'It would have made such a good picture,' said Carsten sorrowfully. 'It would have been something very special for *National Geographic*. If only you could have stood still.'

Asalik had found a date palm frond and a number of succulent dates were still attached to its forked stem. He handed it to me and I held it high above Pasha's head. With great excitement, Pasha stretched his long neck round and upwards and with remarkable agility picked the dates off one by one, neatly spitting out the stone when the date was in his mouth. I have a remarkable mental picture of a human hand and a camel's head reaching upwards to pluck a date off the same branch.

Vischer's experience with camels and dates was similar:

The camel which I rode from Bilma to Borno soon became attached to me, like a dog, and would follow me about everywhere. We Europeans of course have to get used to the beast. The way a camel will turn his head round during the march to give one a long thoughtful look is at first disconcerting. In time, however, I succeeded in interpreting the dumb request, and thenceforward always kept some dates ready for him; the large lips would take the fruit out of my fingers with extraordinary neatness. Many a night to guard against the piercing wind, I slept alongside my good warm animal, which took me to his bosom like a mother. [I did this regularly when travelling with camels in northern Kenya. The only subsequent problem was that the camel's ticks decided to migrate onto a new, and no doubt more succulent, host.] A little hissing sound would bring him to his knees, and a light touch on his neck with my foot would set him off at a trot. The rope attached to his nose-ring was never pulled tight, and a gentle movement to the right or left would guide him anywhere.

The desert has a sobering effect and in these harsh wastes, living creatures draw closer together and come to realize their dependence on each other. The large hulking form of the camel, like some relic from another age, is completely in harmony with the desert and perfectly designed to deal with whatever nature throws at it, be it sandstorm, treacherous dune or lack of water.

In the haunts of man, camels look grotesque and totally out of place, but in the wide, waterless plains they are part of the overall picture, the true friend and companion. And man, in his usual heartless and unfeeling fashion, returns their stoic kindness by burdening them with loads and driving them forward until the time comes when, old, tired and worn out, they join the skeletons of their brothers by the roadside.

Denham lost a much loved, desert travelling companion, in this case, his favourite horse. He too experienced similar emotions to those shared by myself and Vischer:

> I was not at all prepared for the news which reached me on returning to our enclosure. The horse that had carried me from Tripoli to Mourzuk and back again, and on which I had ridden the whole journey from Tripoli to Bornou, had died, a few hours after my departure. There are situations in a man's life in which losses of this nature are felt most keenly; and this was one of them. It was not grief, but it was something very nearly approaching to it; and although I felt ashamed of the degree of derangement which I suffered from, yet it was several days before I could get over the loss. Let it be however remembered, that the poor animal had been my support and comfort – may I not say companion? – through many a dreary day and night; had endured both hunger and thirst in my service with the utmost patience;

was so docile, though an Arab, that he would stand still for hours in the desert, while I slept between his legs, his body affording me the only shelter that could be obtained from the powerful influence of a noon-day sun: he was yet the fleetest of the fleet, and ever foremost in the race. My negro lad opened his head, and found a considerable quantity of matter formed on the brain. Three horses at the Arab tents had died with similar appearances; and there can be little doubt but that it was the effect of climate, the scarcity and badness of the water, and the severe exposure to the sun which we had all undergone. The thermometer was this day in the hut 103 degrees; the hottest day we had yet felt.

Before reaching Tekertiba, the old camel road winds through a spectacular gorge that leads down from the plateau of Murzuk, which we had just crossed, to the Wadi Gherbi and Tekertiba. Just before it narrows to a steep pass, the rocky surface is littered with the blackened remains of petrified trees which Vischer was told the Arabs called 'the bones of some old sons of Adam'.

Vischer, approaching from the north and leaving Tekertiba behind him, describes this scene as follows:

The next day we left the Wadi Gherbi, [river Gherbi near Tekertiba] and, passing the black mountain which lies across the valley, we turned south into a narrow path leading up the cliff to the plateau of Murzuk: the old path is worn deep into the rock, and in many places regular steps have been cut out by the numberless caravans that pass through. The sand-stones on either side bore many crude Arabic inscriptions: names and verses from the Book. About half-way up the slope portions of great black tree-trunks lay across the path and on the side of the hill. They were the remains of fossilised trees which had been piled up here in prehistoric times. . . . The black colour of the fossils contrasts beautifully with the red of the rocky slope, and the forms were so perfect in every detail that at first sight they might readily have been taken for newly cut trees which had been left lying about the path by some woodcutter. Fragments of petrified wood can be found anywhere on the stony plain up to the gates of Murzuk.

He painted a beautiful watercolour of the gorge and the black petrified trees which littered the route. Nearly one hundred years later the scene was instantly recognizable. Water, which is found quite near the surface in this part of the Fezzan, is probably the remains of some ancient river which, over the centuries, grubbed up the trees and left them strewn about for us to discover, thousands of years later.

*   *   *

Hadira, as promised, had arrived in Tekertiba with a new guide who agreed to lead us to Misda. I had been advised by Hadira that it would be impossible to advance beyond Misda to Tripoli with camels. The land was comprehensively farmed and the suburbs of Tripoli had advanced many miles to the south since Vischer's day. There were roads everywhere and the journey north of Misda would be extremely difficult, if not impossible. Misda lies 120 miles to the south of Tripoli, but it does lie within Tripoli city's municipal author-ity. Reluctant as I was to accept this advice, I had seen modern Tripoli and its traffic for myself. We would not have been allowed to enter the city with camels and even if permission had been obtained, they would have spooked and possibly caused an accident. This was one area of Libya that has changed considerably since Vischer's day. So, regrettably, the decision was taken. We would end our journey, within Tripoli's municipal authority, at Misda.

The guide who had been selected to take us over the sand dunes and the daunting Hamada el Homra, was a Libyan Tuareg called Shikou. He was a mountain of a man, swathed in a dark blue, locally dyed turban. The dye is made from powdered indigo plants, and I had seen them used to dye cloth and turbans in the famous dye-pits of Kano. A turban, once it is dyed, dried and pommelled with a special stick, ends up stiff, as though starched, with a shiny dark-blue sheen. Unfortunately, the dye can be transferred to the wearer, and many Tuaregs seem to be permanently stained indigo in this way. This had happened to Shikou. When he wanted to talk, he would pull down the visor that the turban formed, to reveal an expressive light brown face streaked with dark-blue stripes, which reminded me of a strange animal I had once encountered in Kenya, a 'hebra,' a cross between a zebra and a horse. Shikou's body was encased in flowing camel-hair robes which were covered with an ancient coffee-coloured burnous.

The overall effect made Shikou appear to have walked straight out of the pages of the Bible or the *Lord of the Rings*. I had once been involved in a production of *Aladdin*. He would have made a redoubtable genie. His eyes were wild and bloodshot. He had a predisposition to talking loudly and not always coherently, but he was Hadira's choice and I had great faith in Hadira's judgement. Unfortunately, he didn't speak a word of Hausa, the language in which I communicated with the Tuareg team. This was a major disadvantage, as we were later to discover. Our Niger Tuaregs sized up their Libyan tribesman somewhat warily, but if there were doubts over Shikou, he enjoyed the benefit. I did however wonder, even at this very first meeting, whether he could just be a genuine indigo-stained 'madam'.

After another depressing attempt to change money in Tekertiba at a reasonable rate, I returned to the camp through the date palms and flowering shrubs, to find the professor engaged in a lively conversation with a trader whose eagle eye had spotted his compact Chinese short-wave radio. Although this prized possession had never managed to pick up Beijing, it had been able to receive the Chinese language Free Asia programme which was broadcast from Washington. However, the outpourings from America were not to the professor's taste and he had become increasingly frustrated with his radio's inability to connect with mainland China.

'Free Asia is western propaganda, nothing that they tell you is true.'

The trader had never seen anything quite like it and was buzzing around, proffering Tuareg trinkets, swords and knives as an inducement to barter for this Chinese short-wave miracle.

The professor switched to diplomatic mode.

'The Chinese people love Colonel Qadhafi. He is a great leader of your country and was a good friend of Chairman Mao. For Chinese/ Libyan friendship and solidarity, I will let you have my radio, cheap, cheap.'

For $20 it was very cheap, cheap and the trader knew it. He gave the professor two silver Tuareg earrings and a necklace, as a present for his wife.

When we returned from the evening meal with Hassan B. Hassan, we bedded down with his firewater swilling around inside us to the accompanying roar of a disgruntled lorry which seemed to be engaged in an arduous and unending attempt to travel backwards. This struggle to reverse was not a light task. Maybe the vehicle was stuck in sand but, for whatever reason, the noise continued for nearly two hours. I gritted my teeth and prayed for starlit nights in dunes far away from grinding gears.

These dunes that we were to attempt to cross are one of the most extraordinary tracts of country in the whole of Libya. They contain the quite striking, sand dune lakes. Even today, it is not known exactly how many there are. Some guide books list thirteen, others more, others less. These lakes some of incomparable beauty, are set at the foot of massive sand dunes some of which, Denham judged, were too difficult for camels to cross. The dunes, higher and infinitely more complex structurally than those south of Bilma and north of Mestuta, are extremely taxing for camels. If the animals are fresh, the crossing is hard enough. If they have travelled 1,700 miles, as ours had, the crossing becomes a supreme feat of endurance.

Some of the lakes hold fresh water, others salt. At the little lake called Trona, which Denham, Clapperton and Vischer visited, the salt and natron were exploited and Vischer found that these products were carried by camel to the coastal towns where they were in great demand. In 1906, the Turkish government owned and exploited the mine, but the mining was done by a people who were shy and retiring, so much so, that Vischer hardly saw anything of them. He recorded that: 'A solitary Turkish policeman was in charge of the place when we passed. Of the inhabitants we saw little; they are negroes of a retiring disposition, and look very poor, but negro poverty has always a cheerful aspect, very different from the squalid Arab misery.'

Eighty years earlier Denham had recorded that 400–500 camel-loads of salt and natron were taken annually from the lake, each load weighing about four hundredweight (200 kilos). In some of the lakes live a minute and very primitive species of shrimp which Denham called worms and examined under his microscope.

> They are caught in a long hand net, by a man going some way into the lake, and after allowing the net to remain some time at the bottom, it is taken up, or drawn a little along the ground; and in this manner several pints are sometimes caught at one time. It is found to be almost impossible to preserve them alive for a few hours after they are taken from the lake. It was past sunset before we saw any of the people of the town; but by the promise of a dollar, a small basin full of these insects was procured for us before daylight in the morning.

We were to pass one lake which teemed with these tiny prehistoric creatures. The bright blue water held them in such vast quantities that they seemed to form a constituent of the very liquid itself. Nobody fishes for them today. The lakeside inhabitants, rogues, robbers or Vischer's people with a 'retiring disposition', have all been moved during the clearances of the seventies and resettled in Sahba and other towns and cities. Their former settlements are totally deserted. In an attempt to ensure that they will never return, the corrugated iron roofs of their houses have been stripped off and taken away.

10

Freedom is a forbidden fruit and I have tasted it.

Hanns Vischer

When corrugated patterns overlaid on crested dunes are made by the wind, and when those dunes stretch to the horizon, time is suspended. One sees exactly what Denham, Barth or Vischer saw. One hundred, two hundred, one thousand years; dunes may have twisted and shifted, but in a desert's true heartland there is neither change nor decay. It is here, that one is able, without the slightest mental effort, to remember time.

'God is Great,' intones the pious Muslim bowing low to Mecca. 'We Thy unworthy servants do give Thee most humble and hearty thanks,' mumble I, the imperfect Christian, struggling to recall that most biddable of prayers when confronted with unsullied creation. Grains of sand, specks of dust, the true desert hones humility, not only is it unchanging, but utterly unforgiving. In a pristine state it is awesome. The desert shares this characteristic with the vast icy wastes of the Arctic or Antarctica, which is why men of the desert, such as the explorer Sven Hedin, have been drawn to and inspired by an Amundsen or a Shackleton.

It was therefore a rude and unwelcome shock when we discovered, on first climbing the great dunes to the north of Tekertiba, a disorderly zigzag of vehicle tracks. Time's suspension vanished. This was the present, where vehicles careered up and over sand dunes for the thrill and where four-wheel-drive Toyotas whisked day trippers out to the nearest sand dune lake – Mandara – for a night in the sand in exchange for a $300 dollar bill.

The Great Erg of Bilma has defeated the four-by-four and the Erg, where everyone moves with a camel, has remained timeless. In the sand dunes north of Tekertiba, the internal combustion engine has overcome the shifting sands and shattered the illusion of suspended time.

In *Mister Johnson*, a novel by Joyce Cary set in northern Nigeria, there is a moving little scene. The villagers are inspired to construct a dirt road through virgin bush to link them to the outside world. They labour for months, overcoming numerous setbacks, until finally the connection to another road is made. The first truck to drive down the new road roars towards the villagers who are lining the track to cheer. But it doesn't stop. It races down the road, lurches through a large puddle and soaks all the villagers in the process. When our camel caravan was passed by a tripper truck the trippers cheered and spooked the camels which broke their tethering ropes and ran in all directions. I remembered *Mister Johnson*.

'I need time, John,' Carsten had urged the evening before in Tekertiba. 'The sand dune lakes are a very important photo source if my pictures are going to get into *National Geographic*.'

The conflict between Carsten and the onward progress of the caravan had surfaced. Not a conflict of personalities, but of priorities. Our camels were tired, we needed to push on; Carsten wanted to take high quality photographs. It was not easy to resolve, but Carsten had, at his own expense and risk, come a long way to find us and so it was agreed to make an extra day's detour to the north-east, to take in two additional lakes, Mafu and Gabron.

We camped on the first night by the rather disappointing Lake Mandara, having travelled over spectacular multi-coloured dunes whose yellow and orange pastel shades were highlighted by a setting sun. There was rubbish and a criss-cross of vehicle tracks by the lake. Vischer encountered different problems.

> We fell down by this salt lake and had soon stretched our mats alongside the 'vapor el Sahara' – the ship of the desert. We wanted nothing but sleep. Weeee . . . began mosquito no. 1, Wooeee . . . another and so on. At first I was indifferent, then angry and lastly hopelessly resigned, when – like an inspiration from the gods – I thought of the yellow liquid in the little bag beside me. Oh golden fluid, invention of the gods and confusion to the devil. I rubbed and rejoiced. You could hear the brutes approach, smell and die. 'Alhamdelillahi! Allah Akbar! Las illa, illalalaher.' It was VENI, VIDI, ASPHIXI for those pests of Satan and I slept smiling until morning.

His 'pests of Satan' did not trouble us. Maybe when the people were cleared from the lake in the 1970s, the pests of Satan had followed them.

Lake Um el Mar, just to the north of Lake Mandara, which we reached on 9 January, was exquisitely beautiful. Massive dunes, stretching from the lake's eastern shoreline, were silhouetted in clear blue water. I hoped that Carsten, who was behind me, was snapping away. We trekked north-east over the biggest dunes that we had yet encountered until we entered a long valley, lined with date palms and tamarisk bushes, that led us to Lake Mafu and onwards to Lake Gabron. We were followed through the valley, for the first time since we left the great Erg of Bilma, by black carrion crows which cast unnerving shadows in the sand and once again made me wish that I had a gun. Lake Mafu was grey and disappointing, but Gabron, surrounded by a substantial number of ruined buildings, was quite

beautiful. There must have been a large population here that survived principally on the primitive shrimp. Now that the shrimp was
no longer caught by villagers, its numbers had multiplied for the
clear blue water was thick with the ever-wriggling deep red crusta-
cean. Besides the crows, only a pack of hungry feral cats remain to
stare at us out of the date palms leaves as we cook supper. They set
up an unnerving and slightly hostile mewing as we tucked into our
Tekertiba supplies and the dregs of Hassan's firewater. The latter
induced the professor to burst into another round of patriotic communist songs which fortunately drowned the caterwauling from the
date palms.

It was seventy-seven days since we left Kukawa. The Tuaregs had
been travelling for 107. Our new guide, Shikou, was proving painful. Garrulous and unwilling or unable to listen, he caused endless
problems as I tried to manoeuvre the camels into a position near the
lake for Carsten to take pictures. It was impossible to accommodate
tired camels, the demands of choosing a good campsite, a garrulous
and unthinking guide and the wishes of a professional photographer
at the same time. The camel carrying the wooden kitchen boxes was
a magnificent animal who carted his tremendous burden up and
down over the steepest dunes without complaint. I continued to
agonize whether I was leading these heroic creatures to their ultimate slaughter.

Next day I decided to head straight for Wunserik and not to
branch west to take in Lake Trona, which Vischer and Denham
visited. This upset Carsten, who said that he still hadn't taken the
pictures that he felt were good enough. But he had had his day and,
frankly, the camels had struggled enough. The dunes were putting a
tremendous strain on them. We clambered over some of the steepest
that we had yet encountered, the camels stumbling and sometimes
falling, before reaching a tiny oasis where there was grass and,
although it was early, I did not want to push on as we might not
come to another place as good before sunset. This further frustrated
Carsten who, of course, wanted to take pictures of camels on the

march in an evening light. He put his head in his hands and said. 'What a pity. What a shame. What a waste.' He should reflect for a moment that it would be an even greater shame, pity and waste if we ended up with dead camels.

As if to reinforce my point, that evening one of the camels seized up. The back legs of one of the skewbald camels were very stiff and it was becoming increasingly difficult for it to keep up with the caravan. Stiff with cold? I had no idea, but Asalik seemed to understand exactly what the problem was. His explanation was, to say the least, unorthodox.

'The blood between the camel's skin and its muscle has stopped moving around its body. This is caused because the camel is cold and exhausted.'

The recommended cure was drastic.

'We will have to make cuts down its forelegs and under its tail. This will cause the blood to move. If we don't do this, the camel will be dead in two days.'

I couldn't believe this diagnosis, but with no Japper on hand, I had no one to call on for advice. There was nothing to do but to acquiesce. The sick camel was immobilized with ropes. Another rope secured its lower jaw. The veterinarian butchery began.

Eight deep parallel six-inch cuts about four inches apart were made from the shoulder to the knee joint on both forelegs. Five parallel four-inch cuts about one inch apart, were made under the tail. The camel struggled and bellowed and the blood did indeed move – in torrents. It poured down the poor animal's forelegs. Salt was then rubbed into the wounds to staunch the flow and to act as an antiseptic. By this time I was feeling mildly sick.

Not unnaturally, the camel was in agony. To assuage this, a tin of cooking oil was poured down his throat. By this time he was too weakened to resist. Libyan cooking oil is sold in cylindrical tins about twelve inches long, so a great deal of oil went into the camel's stomach. This gruesome operation had been performed with the

utmost efficiency by Ehom, Argali and Asalik and the whole pro-
cedure had not taken more than twenty minutes.

The camel struggled heroically to its feet and staggered off, to my
great surprise, to eat grass. I cannot comment either on the diagnosis or on the prescribed remedy. All I can record is that the camel
managed to keep up with the caravan over the remainder of the
dunescape, crossed the formidable Hamada el Homra and, before
we reached Misda on 1 February, was once again carrying loads. The
operation was a complete success.

Carsten, hitched up to Argali, had set off independently to take
photographs, but rejoined the caravan looking somewhat shaken.

'We were coming up the side of a dune when an explosion took
place. It was louder than a crack of thunder and I thought that a land
mine had been detonated underneath us. I expected to disappear
down a great big hole but amazingly, the sand didn't move.'

There are many tales of thunderous noises in the sands. When
Marco Polo passed near the Kum Tagh mountains that border Tibet
he recorded that 'desert sand-hills emitted a sound like distant
thunder.' Tales from travellers in the deserts of Arabia described
similar noises, when certain sand-hills were battered by prevailing
winds. Arab desert dwellers, too, were familiar with a sound which
reminded them of the bellow of an angry bull camel. In this case,
Argali knew the answer.

'Jinns live in the sand dunes,' he opined. 'They resented us
coming too near their home.'

Carsten left us at Wunserik, still muttering about lost opportun-
ities and only having a thirty per cent chance of having his pictures
accepted. However, he was being unnecessarily tough on himself
and on me. Three weeks later he learnt that his photographs had
been accepted by *National Geographic*. In spite of his gloomy prog-
nosis, his visit had been a great success. He had been a good companion, and although he became frustrated at not being able to take
his photos when and where he wanted, he was well liked and had
turned out to be an excellent member of the team.

In 1906, Wunserik was the home of Sheikh Ahmed el Kwaidi, the head of the Kwaida people and, eventually, a great friend of Hanns Vischer who had first met him when he attached his caravan to the sheikh's for security when travelling across the Hamada el Homra.

> Till late into the night we sat in the tent of Sheikh Ahmed, drinking tea with him. I began more and more to understand and appreciate the old man's personality. Not long before he had complained of the evil smell of that Christian who insisted on travelling with his caravan, much against his wish. His dislike for Europeans was very pronounced and not without reason, but he was a gentleman to the backbone, fanatical undoubtedly, but courteous and straight as a die. He was the sheikh of the Kwaida tribe, who now live at Wunserik in the Wadi Shiati, and he was also head of his family, who can trace their ancestors to the dim times before the Prophet. His forefathers had come to North Africa from Yemen with the earliest Mohammedan conquerors. Having settled first on the north coast and later in the Fezzan, they grew rich in trade with Borno and the Sudan. [This refers to northern Nigeria.]
>
> The interior of his tent, an ordinary bell-shaped one of white cloth, was as comfortable as, and certainly more artistic than, most drawing-rooms. The cases containing his personal belongings and valuables were disposed in a circle; the ground was covered with carpets and cushions, the place being discreetly lit up by a quaint Arab lantern, such as the Jews make at Tripoli. The sheikh, surrounded by some of his Arabs, looked most dignified and absolutely independent of the surrounding world. Never did I hear the old man speak a hasty word or depart in the slightest from his solemn manner on that long and weary journey.

The dinner that Vischer was later invited to in the sheikh's house at Wunserik was clearly memorable, as he tells his friend Ruxton:

> This home of Sheikh Ahmed looked delightfully cool and peaceful, with its palm-trees and gardens on all sides, and to get once

more into touch with humanity was indeed comforting after the wilderness that we had left behind us.

The Kwaidas love their own oasis more than any tribe in the desert. It is no wonder, for, in order to reach it, they must go through such awful abodes of Shaitan that their pretty village appears to them like a veritable paradise.

A shady palm-grove with a well of its own was given us for a camping-place. The tents went up amidst general hilarity and enthusiasm. Presently a message from the sheikh bade Djamy and myself come to his house. The good old man had prepared a meal, and would not hear of any delay, and, dirty and tired as we were, we readily acquiesced.

Sheikh Ahmed's house stands in the centre of the village, the latter being the first prosperous Arab settlement I saw. It is a one-storied, whitewashed building with thick walls, and green shutters to the little windows. In the courtyard a large well bubbles up continually, forming a big pool where women draw water, and camels, goats, horses, and ducks disport themselves. This is at once the fountain and village pond of the place, most pleasant to look at, but – not clean! And how should it be clean? The water is such as Allah gives it, 'good and plenty of it,' say the people, and they never think of walling it in or looking after it.

The sheikh received us in a large square room, such as one finds in every Arab dwelling, with a low bench running round the walls, and small windows which are never closed. Carpets of the most delicate shades, mats from Kano, with some leopard-skins and soft leather pillows from the Hausa States, were disposed on the floor. The benches were covered in trade goods – large silver stirrups and saddles from Tripoli, Manchester goods, French candles and gay Italian silks, all lay about in profusion. In the centre sat our host, dignified as ever; he welcomed us politely to his house, and when we were comfortably seated among the cushions a number of black servants brought covered dishes, trays for the meal, and scented water.

The banquet began with fresh grapes, dates, and melons, followed by a bowl of bazin, fowls, roast lamb, and many spiced sweets. All this had been prepared for the returning chief by some painstaking wife or daughter. The old sheikh, as though he was turning over the leaves of a wonderful book, gave us glimpses of his travels and fights in the desert. He told us of his experiences in the negro countries to the south, of strange happenings in the towns of the northern coast and Egypt, and of his pilgrimages to Mecca. The hopes and yearnings of a straight and unbending spirit, and an unshaken faith in Allah shone through his narrative.

It was a pretty sight to watch the people coming in to welcome their sheikh on his return. They passed through continually, Arabs and negroes alike, grasping their master's hand or greeting from the door, and for each of them the old man had a kind word.

We were camped among gentle sand dunes surrounded by a clump of palm trees which provided dates to eat and dried date palm fronds to burn. On our second day at Wunserik, the owner of these date palms, Ibrahim Kwaidi, appeared on the edge of our campsite. He was light-skinned and softly spoken, full of charm, with gentle manners and a ready smile. He was clearly a strict Muslim. Imagine my surprise and delight when I discovered that he was a Kwaida Arab and that Sheikh Ahmed el Kwaidi was his grandfather.

Wunserik had not escaped the clearances of the seventies, but the old town which Vischer found so prosperous is remarkably well preserved. Among the ruined houses is a former lock-up for truculent slaves and a large rectangular mud-built school, where children were instructed in the teachings of the once powerful Senussi sect. Ibrahim Kwaidi grasped my arm and led me enthusiastically to the house where his grandfather had lived and where he himself had been born. The room where Vischer had banqueted with Sheikh Ahmed, was now full of sand, but it was not difficult to picture the leopard skins and the leather cushions, the French candles and the Italian silks. Outside in the courtyard, exactly as Vischer describes, the old well still bubbles up, but in the intervening years it had been walled in and covered over and the camels and donkeys have disappeared. I knelt down and drank some of the water which was clean, pure and sweet and silently toasted Hanns Vischer. I had never felt closer to him.

Ibrahim once again took my arm and pointed to some trees which lined an open space about 400 yards from the well.

'The people of Wunserik still remember my grandfather. Once a year they gather in that open space over there to feast and to pray for him and to ask for his blessing on the Kwaida people.'

The sheikh's authority and the institution itself may have been abolished under Qadhafi but it was wonderful to witness how the former sheikh of the Kwaida people, who was so greatly admired by Vischer, is still remembered.

In the same unpublished letter to his friend Ruxton, it is apparent how attached Vischer was to his desert and his northern Nigerian friends and why he acquired, from the latter, the complimentary nickname, *Dan Hausa*, the son of the Hausa people.

> The 'Young Turks' in Murzuk , poor exiles who had formed a sort of Club in my house and who all wept when I departed. The Murzuk people themselves who accompanied me into the desert. The wild, untamed Tubbus who saved my life by telling me, at the risk of their own lives, that the Tuareg were to attack my camp at night. The Tubbu boy with whom I attacked and defeated singlehanded the Tuaregs. The pilgrims I brought back to this land, the Kanuri who wept with joy when I finally crossed over the Yo river. These are my pals, these are my companions and for their love I give them my life, what I have and what I possess. It is no good hiding all this. I love them.
>
> I dare say all this will tone down a little, but you see I have looked into forbidden lands, forbidden to us 'civilised', corrected, sceptic Westerners and my head is a little turned!

When Vischer wrote this, he had not yet received the letter from his boss Hewby, stating that if he undertook a return crossing of the

Sahara he would have to forfeit his government job. The motivation to make the return journey and his unsettled state of mind are quite clearly expressed.

> I will stick it [the job as a Colonial administrator] as long as possible, but some morning you will read the inevitable news that 3d Resident Vischer has 'against orders and without official sanction' and to the great and righteous redtapedom's disgust, crossed into French territory to take the route to the North without ever having been relieved!! You will know that my soul could not bear it any longer. Freedom is a forbidden fruit and I have tasted it.

*   *   *

Abdulsalam was a Hotman, an Arab clan that lives in proximity to the Kwaida, but when I met him he was cool with me and did his level best to depress my spirits.

'The Hamada el Homra is a terrible place. It will take you twenty-one days to reach Misda, don't mind what anyone else tells you. There is no food for the camels and it will be extremely cold. If you think that you have experienced cold weather, you haven't seen anything yet. Only last year a truck broke down in the middle of the desert and twenty-three people froze to death, including the driver.'

This prophet of doom, a friend of Argali was tall, lugubrious and dressed in a white turban and a bottle-green gown. I had moved away from our fire where flames were flickering among fast-burning palm fronds and in the dusk Abdulsalam's face was so dark that I couldn't make out his features. The darkness matched his gloom. I couldn't understand why he had bothered to seek me out and burden me with these forebodings. What was in it for him? The reason soon became apparent.

'Your camels are weak and tired and so are you. They are bound to die [and by implication so was I]. Why don't you sell them to me and take a bus to Tripoli. Finish your journey at Wunserik. You have travelled far enough.'

Now I understood. Abdulsalam was a camel dealer who wanted to buy our camels.

'I'm sorry, Abdulsalam, my mind is made up. We will cross the Hamada el Homra and travel on with the camels until we reach Misda.'

'Allah be with you, you will surely need his help.'

He left me, melting into the darkness whence he had emerged. Later, Argali came up to me and whispered that Abdulsalam would give me a good price for the camels.

'Tell your friend, Argali, that the camels are already sold.'

The further north we travelled with guide Shikou, the more exasperated we all became. It soon became glaringly apparent that Hadira's choice had been a rare mistake. Day and night, his incessant and meaningless chatter became a source of increasing irritation. Asalik pronounced him to be mad. Argali stated that his conversation was on a level with a five-year-old child and Ehom said, in amazement, that he didn't even know how to ride a camel.

All these failings could be overlooked if he knew the route, but three days after leaving Wunserik, it was clear to all of us that he didn't. When he attempted to lead us over a rocky outcrop Argali responded, in true Argali style, by taking off and following his own line. The rest of us, relying on Shikou, were led over a terrible track. For hour after painful hour, the camels grunted, groaned and stumbled over sharp rocks and boulders. When, tired and exhausted, we finally arrived at a potential campsite where there were tufts of edible grass, Argali was sitting with his camel waiting for us. A fierce argument with Shikou ensued.

'Why did you lead them over that track? I followed a route where there were only a few stones and which was much quicker.'

'I know what I'm doing. This is my country.'

'He is mad,' muttered Asalik. '*Ya zama kayan banza*' (he is a useless burden).

I had a dilemma. The Hamada el Homra was a formidable obstacle. Once up on the plateau, we had to cross it as quickly as possible. Not one of our Tuaregs knew the route and we were in the hands of a man who appeared to be a 'madam.'

The defects of guide Abba, overweening conceit and a quick temper, and of guide Sidi, religious fervour and sloth, were minimal in comparison. They seemed to be paragons compared to the current incumbent because, for all their defects, they knew the route. It was apparent that we were to be led over the most formidable obstacle in the whole of the Sahara by an unstable character who did not know where he was going.

Meanwhile I had a more personal problem to face. I hadn't realized how attached I was to my green desert bush hat until it disappeared. It had protected me on five expeditions into the Chinese and Mongolian Gobi deserts and has followed me into the Sahara. Sweat-stained and worn, tied up with amateur stitches, slowly disintegrating but still serviceable, it was an old friend and a great comfort. How strange it is that in the desert little things like a battered old hat become so important. I suffered an hour of desolation as we packed up in a very cold north-east wind while I scrambled about searching for it. I trekked off into the desert, to no avail, to see if the wind had wafted it across the flat stony surface. So I tied on my Tuareg turban and reconciled myself to having been parted from my old friend for ever. That evening, while worming my way into my sleeping bag, I discovered it snuggling up to my toes. What a relief!

Pasha was now addicted to bread. We had bought a sack of loaves in Wunserik and they are now quite stale. But Pasha crunched them up with relish. Spiced with a date or two he found them delicious.

Fortunately, the wind dropped and it turned into a warm afternoon. At four o'clock we came to a shallow valley with ample acacia trees and grass. We only had six bales of hay left to get us across the Hamada el Homra, so the opportunity to graze the camels was worth stopping early for. They much preferred the acacia (and the sharp thorns) to tufts of wiry grass, which continued to amaze me. I watched in wonder as they ripped off branches festooned with thorns, crunched them up and swallowed them.

Pasha's wither wound was still somewhat raw but it was not being aggravated by the saddle. It is approximately 300 miles from Wunserik to Misda and we calculated that it would take us twenty days. On this calculation, seventeen remained. We were clearly following the old caravan road because loosely piled up cairns of stones indicated numerous graves. I hoped that I wouldn't be the occasion for building another one.

Next morning we set off at 9.30 a.m. This had been a good campsite and the camels had grazed happily for most of the night. We crossed stony plains and then a series of rocky hills, following the Wadi Haeran for a considerable distance. At midday we reached the grave and hut of an old Muslim sherif who died many years ago. He was considered to be a holy man and something of a hermit. Today the hut has become a shrine. A car had passed us earlier and the ever alert Argali had hitched a lift to the grave so that he could make the necessary obeisance. Vischer's route took him to a well called El Weina, the last water source before the Hamada crossing. Argali said that he knew a different route that would lead us to a pumped water supply. Shikou insisted that we go to Weina and another fierce argument ensued. Because we were trying to follow Vischer's route, I decided to go to Weina, as we had originally planned as Argali's wrath simmered near the surface. We reached a good campsite looking directly at the cliffs and the escarpment of the Hamada el Homra plateau. Vischer had sketched the scene from almost the same spot and the sketch is totally accurate. As dusk closed in, lights twinkled from the direction of Weina well. There was a police post there and no doubt we would have to check in.

The following morning, as we took on water at El Weina well for our last great physical test, I looked at the track which snaked up to the Bab el Hamada, the southern gateway of the Hamada. I thought of the many graves that Vischer had passed and of the gloomy sentiments of Abdulsalam at Wunserik. I knew that the next fortnight was going to provide a supreme test for us all – both man and beast.

11

This abode of death, where shouts and laughter cease.

Hanns Vischer

Once on the top of the Hamada el Homra, the pebble-strewn plateau stretched out bleakly in all directions. The seemingly unending disc of rock over which camel caravans slowly progress is closed in by the arch of a steel-blue sky, that extends to the very edge of the horizon. The stark beauty of the rising and setting sun, the clarity of the stars and the moon, are set against a backdrop of total desolation that turns man and his puny strivings into something of utter insignificance.

The climb up to the plateau is surprisingly steep. The natural cutting that forms the 'gate', has been widened to take a vehicle but, having reached the uppermost level, it is difficult to detect just where this '*bab*', or gate, lies. Vischer, describes how the track he was following abruptly vanished and how he was brought to a halt at the edge of a cliff that looked down upon a sombre valley lying far below.

As I trudged up the winding track, my mind laden with forebodings and Abdulsalam's gloom-laden prophecies, I had a strange sensation that Vischer was close to me. A voice seemed to be telling me that if I remained calm everything would be all right. Moreover, his sons, Peter and John, had sent me a note before I set out from Kukawa saying that they were confident that the spirit of their father would be with me all the way. Vischer had already become a constant travelling companion. But I felt that the sentiment expressed in that note had suddenly become a reality. For a few precious seconds, I was acutely aware of Vischer's presence.

Vischer felt, with good reason, that the plateau was the bleakest and most dangerous of all the Saharan deserts. It is particularly unnerving because one's eye is constantly scanning a limitless horizon. Where the line of the desert merges with the sky, mirages delude the eye with semblances of floating hills and mountain peaks. In reality, there is no undulation, hill or mountain of any substance, no point on which to take a bearing. A GPS will provide a grid reference, but whether one is on the correct track is quite another matter.

For the first few days there was mercifully no wind and the atmosphere, to our great relief, was cold but crystal clear. Later on the journey our old enemy, the bitter north-east wind, began to blow and our surroundings became uncompromisingly threatening and hostile, as gusting sand obscured the sun and blotted out the far horizon. Then it felt as though one was trudging to the uttermost ends of the earth, as if the pebbles, sand and freezing wind would continue on forever and that our journey through this sterile wilderness would never, never end.

Denham and Clapperton had not crossed the Hamada el Homra. Possibly fearing for their safety, they skirted round the huge plateau and followed a route which lengthened their travel. Only Vischer and Barth appear to have attempted the crossing. Vischer wrote that he felt as though they were: 'a little speck on the endless plain,' and that 'the caravan advances, pressing forward in anxiety to leave this abode of death, where shouts and laughter cease and the human voice is drowned in the heavy stillness. Such was the Hamada which we were gaily preparing to cross in the ignorance of children.'

However, the more prosaic Heinrich Barth who, like me, 'slept the night without a tent and felt the cold very sensibly', discovered truffles in the middle of the Hamada which, in the evening, 'afforded a delicious truffle soup'. I did not read these words until after our crossing was completed, otherwise I am certain that we would all have turned into truffle-hunters and kept a sharp look-out for that peculiar delicacy during the monotonous daily march.

At night, when the wind dropped, it was not just the stars that began to twinkle but also the multi-coloured lights of three distant oil refineries; for the Hamada el Homra is one of the sources of Libya's oil wealth. We had made a detour to avoid them and the unstable Shikou became angry when the professor pointed his camera at the glittering horizon, threatening to report him to the authorities for endangering Libyan secrets.

The professor was perplexed and trotted out his well rehearsed retort that China was a good friend of Libya and that Shikou shouldn't concern himself with a harmless photograph. On hearing this, Shikou became even more garrulous and offensive at which point the professor shook his head and observed that Shikou was a 'madam' and there was absolutely nothing that could be done about it. Shikou retreated, muttering to himself.

For the next night we were lucky to find a slight depression with two emaciated acacia trees and quite a good stretch of tufted grass. When crushed or cut, this grass gives out a pungent smell not dissimilar to lavender. Some of the camels had very sore feet, and Pasha stumbled frequently on rocks, especially at the end of the day. I continually feared for my camels and prayed that this good weather would hold until we had completed the crossing. One of the camels who was beginning to stiffen up, was dosed with cooking oil and crushed dates as a 'medicine against the cold'. I heard a bird's song which sounded just like a lark, and stared unsuccessfully skywards in a vain attempt to spot my favourite songster. In the evening, after we had pitched camp near the fragrant grass, a very tame plump little grey and black bird, with a striking black fringe over its eyes, hopped about the camp feeding on grass seeds, quite oblivious of both humans and camels. That evening, the sky partially clouded over and the setting sun created a spectacular overhead panorama as its deep red rays illuminated delicately feathered clouds. But when the sun had set it became very cold.

We left at 9.30 on 22 January after a cold but mercifully windless night. Argali had been constantly warning me just how cold this desert can get, and I fully realized how lucky we had been so far. We set off at a steady pace and about midday, spot two nodding donkey oil-extractors on the western horizon. I could not take my eyes of their rhythmically bobbing heads. Shortly after four o'clock we came to another small patch of grass. There were no acacia trees here, but how fortunate we were. Quite by chance, we had come across grass that the camels would eat. Although camels are amazingly catholic in their eating habits, there are certain desert grasses that they will not touch. Someone was clearly keeping a benevolent eye on us. Was it Allah or Vischer? Maybe it was both of them!

The camel previously ridden by Carsten Peter in the sand dunes was very lame and its two front feet were swollen and split open on the rocks. It was a horrible sight and, in an attempt to protect them, we cut up a sheepskin left behind by Japper and fashioned the pieces into camel boots, hoping that we could get the poor animal to Misda or at least off the plateau and to the well at Tabonia.

Supper was delayed by the arrival of four men in a battered pick-up truck with one headlight. They were apparently out hunting duiker which surprised me very much. Duiker? In this barren wilderness?'

The sheepskin camel boots did not last long and were ripped to pieces next day on the sharp stones and rocks. However, the camel continued to limp along and thankfully made it to our campsite and the first tufts of edible grass that we had come across all day. In stark contrast to our camel caravan, toiling under nineteenth-century conditions, we passed an overground oil pipeline, electricity pylons and on the horizon to the west the shimmering glare of another large oil refinery. The professor mercifully resisted an impulse to further impede Chinese/Libyan relations by taking another photograph. Johnny spotted and picked up a virtually pristine inner tube from a truck tyre. It could make a stout pair of superior camel boots and Argali and Asalik immediately set about cutting it up. Ehom, for the first time on the whole trip, seemed to be in low spirits, which I put down to the incessant nonsensical chatter of the garrulous Shikou, who was keeping a wary bloodshot eye on the professor and his camera.

However, the next day, in spite of the stout rubber boots, we were forced to stop early to rest the lame camel. On 25 January, it turned extremely cold and the night was bitter.

On 26 January the north-east wind started to blow. This was something that I had been dreading. We were compelled to abandon the exhausted foot-sore camel. It was dragging on the tail-end rope of the caravan and slowing the pace of the other camels to a crawl. An hour after we had abandoned it, we came across a group of camels grazing on grass. Had I known of the existence of this grass in advance, we would have left our lame camel with them in the hope that, in the company of others, it might just recover its strength. According to Argali, these ten or so camels had been brought up on to the Hamada to graze here for two or three months. They did not appear to have any water, but somehow must have been able to survive without it. I wondered whether they might be stolen camels, abandoned on the plateau, but Argali didn't think so. They were much smaller than our Niger camels from the Air mountains and had quite thick woolly coats. I learnt many years ago in northern Nigeria that a horse, when taken up to cooler, higher ground, will quickly grow a protective coat. Likewise camels.

One increasingly worrying thing was that Shikou was no longer guiding us, as he had lost his way. I believe that he didn't know where he was going from the moment we entered the Hamada el Homra. Argali had taken over his duties but there was an element of chance in all this as Argali had never been here before. The GPS fixed our position, but we had no large scale map of the Hamada as it was impossible to get hold of one for security reasons. In the morning, we met another pick-up truck and I managed to reach an agreement with the driver to fetch us thirty bales of hay and to take Shikou off our hands.

The pick-up returned at four o'clock with the thirty bales of freshly baled alfalfa grass and I paid off Shikou and gave the driver money to take him to the nearest village. Everyone without exception, Tuareg and foreigner alike, supports this action, and there was a general feeling of relief as the pick-up disappeared over the horizon. Shikou had depressed our spirits and up on the Hamada el Homra one can certainly do without that. It was a very cloudy day and during the night, which again was bitterly cold, there was a light shower of rain. The water which was left in our kettle froze overnight.

Next day the cold and the journey exhausted another camel and I was forced to abandon it. This was the camel that Argali had been riding when he went with Carsten over the dunes to the lakes. My instinct warning me not to overtax the camels in the dunes had been right. Camels should not be sacrificed for the sake of a magazine article. With our Hamada crossing nearly completed I had been praying that this second exhausted camel might reach Tabonia well.

But it was not to be. I willed the other camels to complete the journey. We had now lost three of these magnificent creatures and that was quite enough.

We discovered from the driver of the pick-up that we were much too far to the west of the route that leads to Tabonia. Shikou had cost us dearly and not only in money. Had we stayed on the correct track we might have got the exhausted camel to the safety of the well by now. Last night the camels had virtually a bale of hay each and there were piles of grass left behind on the ground the next morning. This was not waste. It might help another caravan to survive. Argali tried to correct our route by heading north-east. We crossed a tarmac road, which seems to carry infrequent traffic, and then quite suddenly we found ourselves entering a deep gully, the first substantial natural feature that we had come across since we set out to cross the Hamada. Argali was not completely certain but thought that this gully could lead to Tabonia well. At half-past-five in the evening, we progressed down into an open valley running from north to south which contained large and healthy tamarisk and acacia bushes and was bounded on both sides by towering flat-topped hills.

We had done it! We had crossed the Hamada el Homra! The steep sides of the valley protected us from the wind and the atmosphere at this reduced elevation was mild and balmy. There were flies and mosquitoes everywhere, but life in whatever form is preferable to sterility. This place seemed like paradise and my relief was indescribable. After seven days, we had at long last parted from that howling sterile wilderness.

Since the days of the Romans, this was the valley where caravans had rested to prepare for the great desert crossing that lay ahead of them. Our arrival here is, for me, one of the most memorable moments of the whole expedition.

Tabonia well water was what Vischer set off with at the start of his Hamada crossing and he did not give it a great recommendation:

In passing it should be mentioned that Tabonia water is not exactly lemonade! It has a very high sulphur content, which, after several days in the skins and the heat, helps it to mature into a rich brew, smelling powerfully of rotten eggs, dead goats and other unmentionables, making it altogether quite unsuitable for delicate palates. Nevertheless it is water. Ahead in every direction, we were confronted by a limitless, empty horizon, shimmering in the heat, on which appeared every now and then ghostly clumps of palm trees or lakes. In the shimmering haze a distant rock or even a camel, silhouetted on the horizon, would assume the proportions of a mountain, whilst a mirage of blue water or clump of palm trees would appear so close that one could clearly see beyond them. Not a plant or the vestige of any living thing was to be seen, just stones and more stones! And so we marched on until the sun dipped below the horizon in a spectacular blaze of marvellous colours, which would have gladdened the heart of a Titian or a Turner!

His jubilation at reaching our crossing's starting point was equal to mine on reaching the Tabonia valley:

A weak moon faintly illuminated the hilly and boulder strewn landscape, as we dismounted and led our tired horses through the rocks. Hardly had we taken stock of our surroundings, when the track came to an abrupt end and we found ourselves standing on the edge of a dark ravine. 'Hatha Bab el Hamada' exclaimed the Arab – 'This is the gateway of the Hamada, the waterless stone, desert!' There, in the hidden depths of the dark ravine, lay the longed for source of fresh water! Then and there Hanns let out such a yell of sheer jubilation as would have scared the wits out of all the girls in Christendom – YIPEEE.E.E.E.E.E.E.E!!! A steep descent took us rapidly down and in a short while we had reached the oasis with the pretty name of El Weina, meaning the little eye. The relief and delight of finding fresh water again was indescribable.

Tabonia well did not disappoint us. It has been built up and renovated and the circular concrete well was linked to a cement trough into which water could be poured for stock to drink. As our camels were now eating good fodder, they were allowed to drink their fill. On our arrival, a herd of young healthy camels, some of whom were very tame, were frolicking with their handler near the well. Both they and the handler belonged to a portly, middle-aged herdsman dressed in a spotlessly white cap and gown with an open friendly face called Abubakar. It was sunny, wind-free and blissfully warm as I scrambled over the surrounding sandstone rocks with Abubakar in an attempt to find the Roman inscriptions that had been revealed to the world by Heinrich Barth.

Wind and weather had clearly taken its toll in the last 150 years and, although we found a number of ancient incisions that had been carved deep into the stone, it was impossible to tell whether or not they had been inscribed in Latin. Barth had discovered a great number of Latin tags, so I was somewhat disappointed to find that nothing appeared to be legible today.

However, there was one monument, standing in a prominent position on the cliffs which form the western escarpment of the valley, which I did recognize. It had been a landmark for us as we descended down from the Hamada el Homra and also for Barth who observed: 'Its workmanship would excite the interest of travellers, even if it were situated in a fertile and well-inhabited country, and not in a desolate wilderness like this, where a splendid building is of course an object of far greater curiosity. It is a sepulchre about twenty-five feet high, and rising in three stories.'

Vischer took in the historical context.

> Since the columns of the Roman Empire rested there, Tabonia must have seen many caravans, either marching through to the south or arriving from Fezzan with thirsty camels and empty water-skins.

Large well-cut sandstones prevent the well from falling in and a low wall surrounds the open top to keep the sand from drifting into it. Other stones which lie around seem once to have belonged to a huge trough used probably for watering the camels.

A little way to the west on the higher plateau there are the remains of a small square temple or tomb, a landmark for travellers indicating the direction of the road and the position of the well. There are carved figures and ornaments on many of the stones; genii with wreaths; an eagle tearing up a gazelle, or a huntsman on horseback following game.

. . . Even now in their ruins, these remains of Rome, which have defied centuries of desert climate and generations of destroying brigands, look proudly over the wild plateaux and broad sheets of glowing, red rock, which stretch far away to the southern horizon.

Vischer had been right about the taste of Tabonia water. Lemonade it wasn't. As we left the well and headed north towards the vast dried river-bed of the Wadi Zemzem, my mind teemed with fantasies of Roman soldiers, Arab slave raiders, European explorers and other more mundane adventurers. This motley selection of travellers over the centuries would all have known that the sulphurous fluid of Tabonia was the last water they would be able to obtain until they had made the crossing of the Hamada el Homra. It was a place where countless people of all races, the old and the young alike, must have tightened their girths and screwed up their courage.

28 January, the day that we left Tabonia well, was at first an interesting but finally a very frustrating day. We began by walking through a landscape that was lush and soft, and immediately passed a strange conical hill. It was called the Slave's Haircut in Barth's day, on account of it having a boulder on top that resembled a topknot or coiled piece of hair and it is still known by that name today.

On leaving the Wadi Zemzem plain we entered as rocky and as

tiring a tract of country as any that we had encountered on the whole journey. The route leads over a high stony plateau and Argali had managed to get clear directions from Abubakar at Tabonia. However, the old camel track is hidden beneath broken rocks and stones and is now in general ruin, forcing our camels once again to pick their way over spherical rocks clustered like expended cannon-balls. Narrow gullies with precipitous sides pierce the level plateau and intersect the road from east to west. Fragments of the main plateau, detached by these gullies, form separate hills and, during one loss of direction, Argali led us over a rugged hilltop which had me wondering whether we would ever get safely to the bottom without a broken limb. Some of the hills still support the remains of an old tableland. Others have been worn down into conical shapes. Amidst the broad valleys or the little rounded hills one expects to meet rivers and villages, but there is nothing but acre after acre of rock and stone.

Eventually we descended into a grassy valley which seemed to provide good grazing and a rock-free campsite. There were, how-ever, other occupants, a wild-looking fellow with his wife and four children whose demeanour seemed to fit in well with the surround-ing desolation. He was standing outside his tent and Argali rode up to him to ask if we might camp alongside for the night.

'Certainly not,' came the reply. 'I was here first. My animals are grazing. I don't want your camels anywhere near me. Clear off. Leave me in peace.'

There is an unwritten, but meticulously observed, Libyan custom of first come first served and the newly arrived traveller has to ask permission, no matter how remote the area, if he wants to camp near someone who has selected an earlier pitch. There appeared to be ample grazing for all of us. Maybe the occupier thought we were a murderous gang of thieves and robbers. Whatever the reason for his uncompromising attitude, we had no alternative but to press on. The road retreated once more into rocks and boulders and we thanked Allah that there was a bright moon to enable us to see where we were going. It was a moon with a face to the sun; that is a moon that rose at precisely the same moment that the sun set. The professor became very excited.

'In China, we consider it a very lucky omen to see this. According to Chinese thinking, the rest of our journey will be blessed.'

He jumped off his camel, bounded up a nearby hill and set up his tripod to video the phenomenon. However, we weren't travelling in China and, sadly, a small slice of the professor's good fortune was to slip away just before we reached Misda.

It wasn't until eight o'clock that we arrived at an uninhabited, grassy, rocky valley and set up camp hastily and somewhat inefficiently in the dark. We were tired, very hungry but in good spirits. The moonlight trek had enlivened us. But our macaroni, garlic and tomato puree was unavoidably late that night.

It was in this valley, the Wadi Wuzik, where we were now camped, that Vischer experienced a similar incident to the one that we had witnessed in Mestuta, when our camels slipped under the control of desert jinns.

> Marching one pitch-dark night over endless stone fields in to the Wadi Wuzik one of our camels suddenly went mad without any apparent reason. From the midst of the sleepy caravan, the animal started up with a snort and a howl, gave one frightened look backwards and charged at a mad gallop into the disconcerted column, flung his loads right and left like stones from a catapult, and disappeared into the darkness. Other camels, scared by this sudden onslaught, ran off in all directions and a general panic ensued. The frightened yells of my escort told me that a 'ghool,' a wicked demon of the desert, had seized the camel; the flintlocks came down and several shots were fired to chase away the evil spirit. Long prayers were rattled off with a noise as of machine-guns and gradually confidence returned to their frightened hearts. The camels were brought back and loaded again, and

while the caravan re-formed I was told how these evil spirits sometimes took a fancy to mount a camel; the camel would then look to see who was digging it in the ribs and, perceiving no one, fear would grip its heart, for then he knew that the devil was on his back.

In spite of the full moon, our camels grazed quietly and contentedly. There was no interference from a 'ghool'.

The next day, as we trekked once more over tortuous rocks and boulders, that left poor Pasha wincing with pain, a blue helicopter circled overhead. We took little notice of it but the thought did cross my mind that the occupants might be looking for us. We pushed on. We were making laboriously slow progress but the thought with all of us, was, that yard by painful yard, we were nearing our journey's end.

Then, as we entered yet another boulder-strewn valley, I heard the noise of a vehicle. Minutes later, a blue police Land Rover careered erratically towards us. It screeched to a stop and a middle-aged Arab policeman accompanied by a young, jet-black assistant, armed with an automatic weapon, jumped out.

They both looked officious and very serious.

'Where are you from? Where are you going? We want to see your papers.' I was peppered with questions and the mood was tense. They had been looking for us for two days and it showed. Documents and passports were duly produced.

'From Nigeria? That's not possible. How did you manage to enter Libya?'

I explained the nature of our journey and dropped the name of the man in the Security Bureau who had helped us when we reached Tummo.

This had a sobering effect, but the intense scrutiny of our papers continued.

The older man pointed at the professor. 'This man. What is his nationality? Where is he from?'

'China. He's a very senior and important government official.'

The officer was not so easily persuaded.

'A senior Chinese government official who is riding a camel across Libya?' He stared at me in disbelief. 'We have received a report from a Tuareg that you abandoned him in the Hamada el Homra. He was concerned for your welfare as he said that you had no guide.'

The truth was out. We had been struck by the Curse of Shikou.

'He was concerned for our welfare?'

'Yes, he said that you'd hired him as a guide and that he felt responsible for your safety.'

'Well, that was very thoughtful of him,' I replied, 'but actually, it was the Tuareg who was endangering our safety, because he had no idea of the route. He saw to it that we took two days more than necessary to cross the Hamada el Homra.'

The middle-aged Arab relaxed, laughed and held out his hand. His assistant lowered the weapon that had been pointed consistently at my stomach.

'Don't worry. Your papers are all in order. You can continue on your way, but I think that you're quite crazy.'

'Thanks, officer.'

We shook hands and they sped off. I realized that Shikou had been covering himself with the police in case we had got into difficulty, so that blame wouldn't be attached to him. Maybe he wasn't quite so crazy as I had thought.

At about three o' clock, as we were moving slowly uphill over a particularly rocky area, Argali called out to the professor.

'Look, professor. Photo, photo.'

Argali pointed excitedly at a large boulder, shaped like a female torso, which the weather had worn into something that resembled a Henry Moore sculpture, with a see-through hole in the middle.

The professor grabbed his camera from his camel bag, swung his leg over the side of the baggage camel, and jumped. He had acquired this habit of leaping from a moving camel and although we had watched past performances somewhat anxiously, we were confident of his ability to perform the exercise without mishap. Not this time though. In spite of the good omens of the previous night's simultaneously rising moon and setting sun, he caught his foot in a camel rope and, clutching his precious video camera tightly to his chest, fell heavily to the ground and right on top of two sharp stones. Clearly winded and hurt, he struggled gamely to his feet and spread-eagling himself flat on his stomach behind the hollowed rock, took a photo of our moving caravan silhouetted in the hole. But that night, after we had set up camp in a valley full of lush vegetation, we discovered that he had cracked or broken two of his ribs and, in spite of stout strapping, he was in great discomfort for the rest of the journey.

That evening we were serenaded among the tamarisk bushes by a twelve-year-old Tuareg herdsboy who played a two-stringed guitar fashioned from a disused Libyan oil tin. Even though the tin was rusty and covered in dents, it made a melodious, if repetitive, sound. The boy had come from Mali to look for work and was stuck with an Arab livestock-owner who paid him a pittance. Still he seemed happy enough and was delighted to be speaking Tuareg once again.

We followed the old camel road which petered out when we came up against a new tarmac road to Misda, below a prominent Roman obelisk standing bleak and upright on a hill. The morning of 30 January had started grey and misty, but in the afternoon the weather brightened and it became quite warm. The professor's rib-cage was very sore but he bravely didn't complain. The previous night's traffic on the road between Misda and Sabha had kept me awake for hours after three and a half months of camel travel and I was reminded of the behaviour of the elders of the Cham tribe in northern Nigeria. During the years that I worked in Cham, a road was put through their village. They so hated the new-fangled noise of traffic, which maybe amounted to no more than ten vehicles a day, that they retreated high up into the surrounding hills. There they built a new settlement to escape from the whirligig of 'progress.' My feelings matched those of Cham's former tribal elders as I looked wistfully up from my sleeping bag at the surrounding hills.

We spent two days following the line of the main road. Some speeding cars stopped when they saw us and shouted offers to buy our camels, others with generous-hearted drivers, slowed to throw freshly baked loaves of bread onto the tarmac so that we could retrieve them. After weeks of a monotonous diet, we hungered for these fresh warm French loaves and this was a novel way of obtaining them.

At last on 1 February, we reach the town of Misda, set in the metropolitan municipality of Tripoli, and the end of our three and a half-month trek which had lasted exactly 100 days and covered 1,462 miles. We camped in a stony gully shaded with mature acacia trees which provided ample forage for the camels, and for the very last time unpacked our loads and spread them on the ground. We then, rather self-consciously, all shook each other's hand. It seemed unreal and scarcely believable, that our journey had finally ended. I wandered about in a daze, not knowing quite what to do or even what to say.

Vischer was not enamoured with Misda. He has painted a water-colour of the village which is incomplete and has scribbled on the bottom a note to the effect that he had to cut short his artistic endeavour because he was being stoned by villagers. However, there was another more compelling reason why Misda filled him with gloom and it carries a lesson for us today:

> Away to the south at the end of the valley the first rays of the sun lit up the palm-trees and houses of Misda.

As we descended, the valley gradually broadened, some round towers and flat-roofed houses showed through the green date-palms of the oasis. The whole group stood out from the reddish side of the mountains, and in the bright morning sun it was indeed a cheerful sight after the wilderness of the preceding days.

So far so good.

But as we neared the village the several details rose out of the picture and marred the general impression. We were at once struck by the general ruin of the oasis. The gardens were neglected, the palm-trees looked sickly and miserable; the small houses were rough and dirty and were crumbling away among the rubbish-heap. The round towers, which from afar appeared like part of some hidden castle, leaned wearily over the ruins below; everywhere there was poverty and decay. A crowd of ill-kempt urchins followed us shyly at a distance, and an evil-looking negro, the only grown-up inhabitant we could find, had no words for us in answer to our greeting. From behind their walls, the people viewed us with distrust as if resenting our intrusion.

And this was Misda, where Barth in 1850 had found a pleasant community cultivating large fields of corn and living happily amidst beautiful gardens and palm-groves. The barren stone field which extended right up to the little village was the Wadi Sofejin known throughout North Africa, the glorious valley celebrated by the ancient Arab poets for its beauty and riches.

Here the desert and its desolation have triumphed. Man, who in his own blind wickedness had played with destruction, pillaging and preaching new creeds with fire and sword, had himself opened the door and the desert had stepped in, gradually destroying the walls and the terraces and taking away all the fertile soil; it had laid the watercourses deep below the surface and covered former gardens and cornfields with thick layers of rock from mountains. Then the rain ceased, one well dried up after another, and now at Misda, even the palm-trees die because they cannot reach water-level. It had not rained at Misda for twelve years. The few wells that remain scarcely suffice to support the hundred people and their small gardens.

Vischer's description of Misda reads as though it were written by an angry, young Greenpeace activist. He would not, in his day, have encountered the ugly modern word 'desertification' which describes how fertile drylands are encroached by and then succumb to the advancing desert. Yet, the process of desertification is exactly what he is describing. Today, as in Vischer's day, the Sofejin valley in which Misda is set, which was famous throughout southern Europe for its luxurious fertility, lies barren, bare and covered in sand. No one would guess the extent of its former fertility. For me, it provided a stark lesson. How many other fertile valleys have succumbed to desert encroachment in the last hundred years due to the stupidity and greed of man? Possibly thousands. Although modern Misda now boasts more than one hundred inhabitants, the concrete township that has replaced the old mud-walled village still feels unkempt and run-down. But at least the inhabitants are uncompromisingly cheerful and they didn't try to stone me when I attempted to take photographs. They just laughed.

My mind was full of baleful thoughts about leaving the world geared to the pace of the camel and entering a world of restlessness and unnatural haste. I stared at the cars speeding along the trunk road and thought, why are they hurrying like that? What is the urgency? It all seemed so strange. I count it a rare privilege to have been able to slip back into a time and pace that our forebears would have accepted as quite normal. Only when you have experienced the true rhythm of life's natural tenor over a prolonged period of time can you fully appreciate what has been lost.

Our time capsule finally burst when Mukhtar's men arrived to pick up the camels that I had sold to Fezzan Tours. They told me that they were going to take them back to Wunserik to rest, before they turned them into a tourist attraction. I fervently hoped that what they said was true. Once I was whisked away to Tripoli, there was nothing that I could do. Two large trucks arrived and I could hardly watch as our faithful team of camels was loaded on board. No longer were they in the hands of people with whom they shared *amana* or trust. Hard-faced driven men pulled and prodded our loyal companions on to the trucks to the accompaniment of oaths and rough shouts.

The rush of traffic, the frenzied negotiations with unsmiling business men, the plaintive, mystified look of our uncomplaining camels, our emotional farewells to the Tuaregs, all forced on me the realization that our retreat into the unhurried world of the camel was finally broken. Our Tuaregs, cynical about the Libyans' attitude towards camels and unwilling to assist, turned their backs on the whole scene and their minds to home, family, warmth and clear blue skies. Johnny seemed ready to return to friends and family, and the professor ached for China and the chance to speak his own language. My feelings were very mixed – exhilaration at what we had achieved, but intense regret that our epic journey was finally over.

I looked up at the stark flat-topped mountains that surround Mizda and mused that they would survive whatever unwanted change man inflicted on the desert. With their wind-scoured black caps of rock, they exuded the bleak monotony of the everlasting. Every inch of the land that surrounded us seemed to belong to another geological age. I pondered that even today the road that we had just travelled was intact. Neither war nor blackmail nor colonial imperialism had forced the toiling caravans permanently to forsake it. It has endured through the ages as a camel road and, in spite of the internal combustion engine and man's seemingly insatiable quest for speed, it endures, like the surrounding landscape, to this day.

Vischer shared similar thoughts, and although he expressed himself differently, I know exactly how he felt.

I can't write coherent letters yet and am still a little dazed for you see – the desert is Hell and Dead and it objects to little man disturbing the great stillness. But it is a Sphinx and I long to be back on the sand, lying alongside my camel, gazing up at the stars and looking out for Tuaregs. I have learnt some things worth knowing. I can sit on the ground eating without a spoon the Arab Baseen and wash it down with sour camel milk. I can drink water which even my horse would not touch. I can keep going on some coffee and a cigarette for a day and a half and I can sleep on my camel. I have done all this without a chair or a bed, happy with my wild desert friends.

After one night in which we shared out our travel kit among the Tuaregs, we clambered aboard a Fezzan Tours minibus to be taken to Tripoli. I soon realized that it would have been impossible to take the camels further up the Tripoli road. There was intensive farming which was securely fenced and prosperous concrete suburbs, full of noisy thrusting traffic, sprawled endlessly southwards. We had travelled as far north as we possibly could with the camels. And we had reached Tripoli's metropolitan domain.

Richard Dalton, the British ambassador and his wife, laid on a generous reception to welcome our safe arrival in Tripoli. The Chinese ambassador was there and made a great fuss of the professor, treating him as a true hero of China, which, of course, he was. The Libyan Foreign Ministry and the Environment Ministry were represented at a high level and were eager to know how we found Libya and the Libyans. The Nigerian and Niger ambassadors were there and plied me with questions about security in their respective countries along the camel road. I found an opportunity to thank Bridget Brind who had helped, more than once, to extricate us from a tight spot.

Travel-stained and travel-worn, we sipped, in teetotal Libya, vintage champagne and lunched off dainty fish cutlets from delicate gold-rimmed china, embossed with Her Majesty's Government crest. I felt suddenly awkward and cack-handed, after the countless unvaried meals I had eaten of macaroni ladled onto a chipped tin plate washed down by sugared tea drunk from a rusting metal mug.

At the reception, I looked at the earnest, friendly faces of the Libyan government officials and reflected that while we were trekking along the ancient camel road, oblivious to outside events and affected only by immediate problems, the kaleidoscope of international politics had shifted. Before we set out it was impossible to predict that Britain would be undergoing a rapprochement with Qadhafi a few months later. Yet in under a year since the tragedy in New York and Washington which nearly disrupted our expedition, the unpredictable has occurred. It was salutary to recall that we had not encountered a single hostile act or individual in Libya.

Ehom and Argali had come with me to Tripoli to collect their final pay. Later in the day, the modern world impinged on them, too. Neither of them had been in an hotel lift before and as we were swept up to my room on the seventh floor to count cash, they sweated profusely in a state of high nervous tension. We shook hands and parted in totally alien surroundings. They left to go back to their world and I to mine.

Richard Burton, that eminent Victorian explorer and much else besides, succinctly expressed feelings that both Vischer and I shared, although we were separated in our travels by almost a century. In his book, *A Pilgrimage to Meccah and Medina*, Burton describes how parting from camels and desert travel affected him:

> There is a keen enjoyment in mere animal existence. The sharp appetite disposes of the most indigestible food; the sand is softer than a bed of down, and the purity of the air puts to flight a dire cohort of diseases. Hence it is that both sexes and every age, the most material as well as the most imaginative of minds, the tamest citizen, the parson, the old maid, the peaceful student, the spoilt child of civilisation, all feel their hearts dilate and their

pulses beat strong as they look down from their dromedaries upon the glorious Desert. And believe me when once your tastes have conformed to the tranquillity of such travel, you will suffer real pain in returning to the turmoil of civilisation. You will anticipate the bustle and the confusion of artificial life, its luxury and its false pleasures with repugnance. Depressed in spirits, you will feel incapable of mental or bodily exertion. The air of cities will suffocate you, and the careworn and cadaverous countenances of its citizens will haunt you like a vision of judgement.

And that was written before the invention of the internal combustion engine.

Two days later I touched down at Heathrow and was met by faithful taxi-driver, John Clarke, who makes daily journeys to Heathrow and Gatwick to pick up travellers who live in our village of Benenden.

'Hello,' he said nonchalantly. 'How are you? Had a nice trip, then? I see you've had a haircut. I expect you needed one in the Sahara. Listen, the M25 is blocked at Junction 12. We're going to have a hell of a journey home. I expect that we'll crawl along at forty. When will they do something about the twenty-five?'

I was back.

Afterword – The Wild Bactrian Camel: A Critically Endangered Species

One of the most important events in the history of North Africa was the introduction of the dromedary camel. This seems to belong to the period of Roman occupation, prior to which the animal did not exist in Africa. Pliny, who had travelled in Africa, states quite firmly that the camel belonged to Asia and it was evidently not found in Africa during early Roman times.

The camel is first referred to in Africa in 46 BC, at the battle of Thapsus, when the booty captured by Caesar included twenty-two dromedaries. For a long time they remained scarce and not until the middle of the fourth century do we learn of them in any numbers. In AD 363, Romanus demanded 4,000 camels from Leptis Magna in Libya and they were duly rounded up and delivered.

There are, however, other theories on the camels' appearance in North Africa and some will remain speculative theories. In the Hoggar mountains, in the heart of the central Sahara, there is a ruin which belongs to the Roman period and is linked with the Mediterranean, although there appears to be nothing Roman about it. Near the oasis of Abalessa stand the ruins of a small fortress or a large fortified house, a multi-chambered building constructed in a manner unknown to the modern Tuareg. Traditionally it was the home of a woman named Tin Hinan who, mounted on a magnificent white camel (like Pasha), mysteriously arrived in Hoggar from the far-away oasis of Tafilet in southern Morocco and from whom the local Tuareg aristocracy claim descent. Excavation has revealed the bones of a woman of an Egyptian, not Moroccan, type. On the arms of the skeleton were bracelets of silver and gold, on the breast a gold pendant and various beads. Beside a coin of Emperor Constantine, was discovered Roman glass and together they indicate a fourth-century date. The story of Tin Hinan and her camel, where she came from and how she reached such a remote place to live in, presents one of the desert's more elusive mysteries.

Whether the Romans were directly responsible for introducing the camel is therefore uncertain. It is possible that during their administration of North Africa they found themselves confronted by transport difficulties which in Asia they had solved by using camels. They may have grasped how quickly the economic development of Africa would be accelerated by the camels' introduction. Either or both of these considerations could have prompted their importation from Asia.

However it came about, the arrival of the camel in the Sahara was an event of such far reaching consequence that it marked an entirely new era in the development of northern Africa. Man could now use the most remote pastures of the desert and exploit the fertility of the most distant oases. Desert travel lost a great deal of its terror. There was now an animal that could cross huge mountains of sand and that could travel without water for many days. New roads, including the one that we had followed, were rapidly opened up for trade. With all these changes, there also appeared a new type of desert man, the camel-owning nomad. The camel was directly responsible for his wonderful mobility.

It was desperate need that compelled the newly mobile people of the desert to prey on one another. Anarchy, such as the nomads in

their long and troubled history had never known, became general.
The raiding of sedentary agriculturists like the Tubbu, reached proportions which none could stem. As we found, and as Vischer and
Denham had found before us, the desert oases continue to shrink,
wells have fallen in and water holes have dried up. Through human
neglect and through the former mobility of predatory nomads on
their camels, the desert has become more sterile than ever. Rob-
beries are committed today to capture four-wheel-drive vehicles
instead of camels. The perpetrators mount their attacks in vehicles.
But the motivation is just the same. Vischer's comments about Misda
bear testimony to the effects of desertification. Ehom, Argali, Asalik
and Adam are direct heirs to this Saharan desert legacy.

*   *   *

But what of the double-humped camel, the Bactrian, the animal that
also opened up other new horizons for mankind by its ability to
cross the Gobi Desert, a desert which is even more hostile and
extreme than the Sahara? How is it that these pioneers of the Silk
Roads came to be discovered and domesticated?

I hope that it has now become clear why I undertook this journey.
For the romance, certainly; to emulate Sir Hanns Vischer, after
having been mesmerized by his wonderful book, most definitely;
but there is another and equally compelling reason which may not
have been made evident. That is to raise awareness and funding for
an ongoing crusade to save the critically endangered wild Bactrian
camel (*Camelus bactrianus ferus*) from extinction.

A former nuclear test area seems an unlikely safe haven for a
critically endangered species, even more so when it is surrounded
by a vast inhospitable part of China's Gobi desert. Yet such an area is
being transformed into what we hope will be a secure survival area,
the Arjin Shan Lop Nur Nature Reserve, for the last remaining herds
of a rare breed of camel. The wild Bactrian camel is one of nature's
most astonishing survivors, descendant of a breed dating back three

or four million years, of whom only 800–1,000 are thought to have survived, 600 in China and 300 in Mongolia.

The wild Bactrian camel was 'discovered' relatively recently. In 1873, N.M. Przewalski, the great Russian explorer, was the first foreigner to see, obtain and describe the wild Bactrian camel. He took the skin and skull of a wild camel to St Petersburg where it created a sensation among scientists in Russia, and no little controversy. He outlined the range of this little known animal and collected data on its habits. Przewalski showed that the wild camel was clearly distinct from its domestic counterpart. It is more lightly built and slender; its legs are longer with narrow soles to its feet and nails that extend forward much more prominently. There are no horny pads on its knees. The humps of the wild Bactrian camel are smaller than those of the domestic Bactrian. They are conical in shape and set more widely apart. The muzzle is narrower and the head is thinner. The structure of the skull and skeleton of the two species is also different. As a result, a majority of scientists agree that the Central Asian wild Bactrian camel is an original wild form and should not be considered to be a derivative of the domestic camel.

Recently concluded DNA tests by Chinese and American scientists point to major genetic differences between the dromedary and domestic Bactrian camels and their double-humped wild Bactrian cousins. This difference is as much as three per cent which doesn't appear to be significant until one learns that mankind has a five per cent genetic difference from the chimpanzee. Indeed, the difference is so great that one day it could be conclusively proved that the wild Bactrian is a separate species. This is important because, since the discovery of the wild Bactrian camel, many critics have alleged that they are only feral animals, runaway domestics from the rigours of the Silk Road, like the feral dromedaries in Australia that have reverted from a domestic to a wild state. The wild Bactrian camel now only survives in the wild in the Gashun Gobi, the Arjin mountain foothills and the Taklamakan desert in China and in an isolated pocket of south-western Mongolia. Since the cessation of atmospheric nuclear testing, they are under new and very real threats from man. The wild Bactrian camels are shot for food by speculators illegally hunting for gold and other minerals, whose mining operations can involve the use of potassium cyanide which poisons the land. At one salt-water spring, we found home-made land mines which had been constructed from gelignite to blow up wild camels when they ventured out of the desert to seek out salt-water slush. The meat would have been picked up for food.

In addition, there is great emphasis placed by the Chinese government on developing Xinjiang Province, the north-western part of China, an area which includes the last remaining habitat of the wild Bactrian camel in the newly created nature sanctuary. This economic activity, fuelled by rich and powerful businessmen in Hong Kong and mainland China, will apply further pressures on the last remnant herds of wild camels and on the nature sanctuary that has been established to protect them. The west-east gas pipeline running from the Taklamakan desert to Shanghai will also impinge on their habitat, forcing them further and further into the unsustainable heartland of the Gashun Gobi. Subjected to all this unwarranted activity, they appear, paradoxically, to have been far safer and under greater protection from man's interference during the period of nuclear activity, especially as they appear to be well equipped to withstand nuclear fall-out.

The key factor which has caused the rapid decline in the numbers and range of the wild Bactrian camel in both China and Mongolia has been the development and settlement of their desert habitat during the last eighty years, in particular the penetration of man and his domestic flocks into hitherto uninhabited oases. When temporary or permanent settlements are established, the wild camel rapidly moves away. Their present day range occupies only those parts of the desert which for some reason or other are still sparsely populated or

totally uninhabited. Wild camels are extremely shy and cannot toler-
ate the presence of humans. This behaviour is the result of unceasing
hunting, which has been the practice in Central Asia since time
immemorial.

Man, like the wild animal, is prone to increase and outgrow his
immediate resources. This is strikingly true in China. Hunger leads
to inter-tribal feuds, then to war and eventually to mass movements
of people such as have repeatedly changed the course of history in
Asia. But the first victims of human privation, before hunger drives
man to war with his neighbours, are the beasts of the field. Today,
the greatest threat to the wild Bactrian camel is the increase in the
human population accompanied by a vast extension in tillage and an
insistent demand for more grazing. This, of course, is strikingly
obvious in Africa. In China, it is only because the wild Bactrian
inhabits a largely waterless wasteland that it is still just holding its
own. But if oil or some other precious mineral is discovered in
commercial quantities, who then will care about the future of the
wild Bactrian camel?

In Mongolia, a designated protected area for the wild Bactrian
camels is contiguous with the international border between
Mongolia and China. But wild camels pay scant regard to international borders. They wander across this border and into China, an
area plagued with illegal mining. Most of these miners are seeking
gold and it is here that potassium cyanide is poisoning the soil. It is
said that if twenty-five camels leave Mongolia, ten are fortunate if
they return.

However, the appeal of the wild Bactrian camel to conservation-
ists goes beyond genetics and curiosity value. We have a mammal
which survives under conditions where man cannot, which is why
the Chinese opted for the desolate Gashun Gobi that surrounds the
dried-up lake bed of Lop Nur as an atmospheric nuclear test site.
The Gashun Gobi has no fresh water, only the saline variety which
bubbles up to the surface from underground springs and on which

the Bactrian survives. No other living thing, not even the domestic camel, can drink it. How has this amazing animal survived on salt water? With a world water shortage looming in this century, and dire forecasts of future wars being fought over water, this is a fertile field for urgent scientific study.

The wild Bactrian camels' elusiveness gives them some protection against hunters, but may actually put the survival of the species even more at risk. Only about fifteen wild Bactrian camels are in captivity in the world, all of them in China and Mongolia. With so few captive animals, the whole species could be wiped out if their natural habitats in China and Mongolia are destroyed. It is therefore important to breed enough animals in captivity to insure against this possible disaster. As each female camel can have young at most once every two years, relying on natural methods would permit the numbers to rise very slowly. When the Przewalski horse (*Equus przewalskii*), the Asian wild horse, died out in the wild in 1969, there were hundreds of captive horses in zoos around the world. This is not the case with the wild Bactrian camel. This is why the Wild Camel Protection Foundation, after much thought and careful consultation with scientists, decided that a captive wild Bactrian camel-breeding programme is vital. It will make it possible to increase the numbers of wild offspring each year by using surrogate domestic Bactrian camels to carry the embryos of the wild camel.

For the wild Bactrian camel, an animal not yet fully studied or understood by scientists, the proposed programme provides a unique opportunity to ensure its survival into the future. The wild camel might, in its turn, yield secrets which enable man to survive on a planet where fresh water supplies are decreasing rapidly.

If one looks at the week-old embryo of a dromedary camel, one can see the remains of a second hump. So it is quite possible that the dromedary single-humped camel of the Sahara, Africa and the Middle East, is a mutant from the double-humped Bactrian, which could make the wild Bactrian the ancestor of all camels, whether single of double-humped.

How did this mutation come about? Camels are thought to have originated in North America from a species of *camelidae*. The earliest known remains of camelids have been found in the Arizona desert and they are displayed in the Natural History Museum in New York. Some of these camels wandered southwards and over the millennia developed into the llamas and alpacas of South America. Others crossed over the Bering Strait which in those days joined America to Asia. They entered a cold region and developed humps (some scientists say one and others two) to store fat for food. The camel also developed the ability to go for long periods without drinking water. During a further development period they changed into the double-humped camel that we know today. Some of these camels remained in this cold, hostile region and developed long shaggy coats to keep them warm. Others continued to wander south and entered the warmer parts of the world in Arabia and Africa. They no longer needed shaggy coats or even two humps to store their fat so some people believe they gradually mutated into the dromedary or single-humped camel. One hump for fat storage was more efficient in a much warmer climate.

At some stage, this wild ancestor from North America separated from a similar double-humped species. About 4,000 years ago man caught the wild camel and taught it to carry his loads and to carry him. But we believe that the other double-humped species remained in the wild and it is this species that we now call the wild Bactrian camel.

Their behaviour in the wild is in striking contrast to camels kept in captivity. A male wild Bactrian, or bull camel, usually controls a group of up to twelve females and their young. In 1999, while on an expedition to survey the camels near the Arjin mountains in China, we were amazed to encounter a herd of seventeen females and sixteen calves, under the control of one powerful bull. This was most unusual. The males fight each other to control these females and the loser will sometimes run up to one hundred miles to find another mate. This could be a herdsman's domestic camel and if a calf is born, it is a hybrid. Neither the Chinese nor the Mongolians like these hybrids which become very difficult to handle when they grow up. So they are usually killed.

After the mating season from December to February, the wild bull camel keeps away from the herd. In March and April one can see a number of solitary wild camels prowling about on their own. But they are not too far away from their family and will protect the females and the young camels if they are threatened. When, after thirteen months, the female is ready to give birth, she too goes off on her own to have her calf. In 1995 we were fortunate to see a female that had just given birth near the Kum Tagh sand dunes. The calf was under twenty-four hours old.

The wild Bactrian camel migrates along tracks which have been followed for centuries. In the Gashun Gobi the desert is criss-crossed with wild camel roads, usually leading from one salt-water spring to another. When the vegetation around the salt spring has been eaten, they move on. What is so interesting is that the wild Bactrian camels follow these tracks in single file. They don't spread out as one would expect and so the constant walking in single file makes deep ruts in the desert surface. In one area, a deeply scoured path leads over the Kum Tagh sand dunes to the Arjin mountains. Every year, some of the Gashun Gobi camels follow this route. In the cool valleys, watered by melting mountain snows, they escape from the high temperatures of the desert summer. In winter, they go back to their desert heartland. Unsympathetic development can cut through these migration routes and disrupt the migratory patterns that wild camels have established over the centuries.

In the spring, the temperature is milder and not too extreme. However, this is the season of sand storms and they can blow up without warning. The Uighur and Kazakh herdsmen, who keep domestic flocks on the fringe of the Gobi, describe them as either yellow or black sand storms. The yellow sand storm blots out the sun until everything has a deep yellow glow. The more powerful and much more terrifying black sand storm totally obscures the sun's light and seemingly turns day into night. In the case of a black sand storm not only sand but pebbles and small rocks are hurled through the air. The wild camel can only lie down, stretch out its long neck and trust that the storm will not last for more than two or three hours.

I hope that, through the detailed description of our trans-Saharan camel expedition, I have done something to redress the bad press the camel received from an ignorant world. Camels are stoics. They are patient, hard-working and uncomplaining and they will continue to work for man until they drop. Most of their bad habits are acquired through bad handling, when they are at a young and impressionable age. Camels are not stupid. Pasha was an outstanding animal, intelligent, responsive and spirited. Like all the other camels, he had a dual nature, but more often than not he raised himself up from his bed on the ground on the right side. My sorrow when we parted was heartfelt. He had earned care and sympathy for performing so outstandingly. All our camels, even the deaf, blue-eyed skewbalds, were a wonderful team.

In the Sahara, they were literally our life-line. If it were not for these outstanding animals, equipped so wonderfully for their environment, this book would never have been written.

Acknowledgements

Without Mallam Mamman Daura's unstinting help, support and generosity in Nigeria I would have had far greater difficulty in organizing the expedition. Mohammed Guri, the African International Bank Manager in Maiduguri was particularly kind and helpful to us, as was Alhaji Masta from Kukawa and Professor Kari Tijjani and Gisela Seidensticker-Brikay of the Trans-Saharan Centre, University of Maiduguri. Dr Suleimanu Kumo looked after me so well in Kano and my long-standing and good friend Olu Anulopo bothered to come down from Ibadan to see us safely through Lagos airport.

In Kenya, both Naomi Poulton and Barney Gaston put us up and generously put up with us. Ol Maisor ranch provided lavish hospitality and Martin Evans kindly flew us to Nairobi to obtain the professor's Libyan visa.

In Niger, Sidi Mohammed Illes took on the responsibility of finding our camels, equipping the expedition and providing reliable Tuareg herdsmen. All these things he did with consummate efficiency and skill. His brother Hadira gave me wise counsel and advice on various sections of the journey and Agi Marda Taher, the Sous-Prefet of Bilma was a very generous host. I am also most grateful to Salem Ali Mugber, the Libyan consul general in Niamey for his crucial support. Encouragement and advice also came from François Gordon, the British ambassador concerned with Niger affairs who was based in Abidjan. We would never have reached Tripoli without our faithful Tuareg team: Ehom, Argali, Asalik and Adam, and how can I forget Pasha and the other twenty-four camels.

In Libya, Richard Dalton, the British ambassador, was able to get permissions from the Libyan government that I could never have obtained on my own and Bridget Brind of the embassy staff gave invaluable support at critical times, as did the Nigerian ambassador to Libya, Lawan Gana Gubi, Dr Mo Shelly of Cydamos Ltd, and Mukhtar Ansari and Hassan B. Hassan of Fezzan Tours were also most helpful in various ways. Mike Buck and Mike Keene of LASMO, Libya provided me with invaluable maps through an introduction made by Alastair Woodrow.

The British Embassy in Beijing, in particular Ben Fender, helped to smooth the way for Professor Yuan to obtain his visa. Adam Williams, also in Beijing, has been a constant and consistent supporter of all things camel.

At the National Geographic Society, Washington, Oliver Payne of the magazine was a tireless helper during difficult times, as was Rebecca Martin of the Expeditions Council, whose efforts on our behalf made both the expedition and the inclusion of an NGS photographer possible. Silva, Sweden AB provided binoculars and North Face of America valuable camping equipment.

The Explorers Club, New York honoured me by allowing the expedition to carry their flag and Barry Moss of the British Chapter gave generous financial support. Those who gave financial support or official recognition of the expedition include HRH The Duke of Edinburgh, The National Geographic Society, The Royal Geographical Society, The Bradshaw Foundation (John Robinson, Jean Clottes and Damon de Laszlo), The Brownington Foundation (Anne Savage), The Society for Libyan Studies (Professor David Mattingley and Tim Taylor) and The Grocers' Livery Company. Hugo Berch found funding in Sweden for Jasper Evans and Fortnum & Mason of

London provided the much appreciated Christmas hamper. To all of them I am most grateful.

In England, Dr Sonia Parkinson, Tony Kirk-Green, James Douglas-Henry, Mike Davies, Christopher Neve (over the billiard table), Gail Thomson, Ann Evans, Pam Dunn and Elizabeth Mills gave me much needed support and encouragement at various times and in different ways. A very special thanks to Chris Moat who orchestrated a keen and enthusiastic supporters' club from her two geography classes at Benenden School and a special event which helped pay for Professor Yuan Guoying's airline ticket. Caroline Richardson most generously allowed me to use her former nursery as a writing bolt-hole.

I would particularly like to thank the late Sir Hanns Vischer's family, especially his sons Peter and John who have been so very generous both in their support and in making available their father's archive for research. Unknown to them at the time, his grand-daughter, Annabel ignited the spark in Benenden that set me off on the Saharan journey.

I am greatly indebted to the many supporters and members of the Wild Camel Protection Foundation, in particular Matthew Parris and also to Johnny Paterson's very generous team of sponsors.

Special thanks to Roddy Dunnett who came with me on the recce trip, did detailed and painstaking research of the route and generously contributed to the expedition funds, and to Doreen Montgomery of Rupert Crew Ltd, who has been much more to me than just a sharp-eyed literary agent. Additional special thanks to Pippa, my wife, who gave me both rare understanding and very generous financial support.

Lastly, Kate Rae, was the rock from which we launched ourselves into the Sahara. Her steadfastness, practical common-sense and help at all times and in all circumstances, made everything possible.

JH

Glossary

Alhaji (Arabic)	A man who has completed the Haj or pilgrimage to Mecca
amana (Hausa)	Trust
balta-balta (Kanuri)	The uniform worn by the Shehu of Borno's retainers
baseen or bazin	Traditional Libyan food
bore-hole	A well that has been bored out with a mechanical digger
Borno/Bornu	Borno is the modern spelling of a former Kanuri empire and now a State in northern Nigeria. The Shehu of Borno is its traditional ruler. Bornu is the old spelling
castrati (Italian)	A castrated male. Formerly castrated to obtain a high-pitched sound while singing ecclesiastical plain-song
dendal (Arabic)	The main street of old Murzuk
Fulani	A West African people some of whom are nomadic cattle owners
Gidan dan Hausa (Hausa)	The name of Hanns Vischer's house in Kano
hamada (Arabic)	A desert
Hausa	A West African Muslim people who live predominantly in northern Nigeria
Hotman	A Libyan Arab clan that lives near Wunserik
jinn (Arabic)	A desert 'spirit'. Sometimes good, sometimes evil

Kanuri	A West African Muslim people who live mainly in north-east Nigeria
kantu (Hausa)	The Hausa name given to Bilma rock salt that is shaped like a cone
kunkuru (Hausa)	The Hausa name given to Bilma rock salt that is shaped like a tortoise
Kwaida (Arabic)	A Libyan Arab clan that lives near Wunserik
mao tai (Chinese)	A Chinese liquor
muzungu (Swahili)	A white man
panga (Swahili)	A long, flat-bladed knife
rhazzia (Arabic)	A raid
salga (Hausa)	A water container made from a goat skin
Shehu	The traditional Kanuri ruler of Borno
Sherif (Arabic)	A Muslim holy man
tarhalamt (Tuareg)	A salt-bearing camel caravan
teresum (Tuareg)	A plaited leather camel rein
Tuareg	A nomadic Muslim people that live in the Sahara
Tubbu	A Muslim people that lives in the north-east of Niger
yardangs (Uighur)	Ancient land formations or 'mesas' which have been whittled away over millions of years by desert storms

Journey Stages

25 October 2001	Kukawa (Nigeria) – bush	14 miles
26 October	bush – Agege	24 miles
27 October	Agege – Bisagama	17 miles
28 October	Bisagama – Bosso (Nigerian border)	15 miles
29 October	bush – Kabelau	20 miles
30 October	Kabelau – Ngigimi	23 miles
31 October	at Ngigimi	–
1 November	at Ngigimi	–
2 November	Ngigimi – bush	15 miles
3 November	bush – Fizin wells	19.5 miles
4 November	Fizin wells – bush	13.5 miles
5 November	bush – Karediyanga well	19 miles
6 November	Karediyanga well – Ngurti – bush	16.5 miles
7 November	bush – Bedouaram well	20 miles
8 November	Bedouaram – Abba's well	8.5 miles
9 November	Abba's well	
10 November	Abba's well – Bela Berim – tintumma	21 miles
11 November	tintumma via Kofar Annabi	17 miles
12 November	tintumma	16 miles
13 November	tintumma – Agadem	9 miles
14 November	sand dunes	24 miles
15 November	sand dunes – Emi Goudonia	20 miles
16 November	Emi Goudonia – Emi Toukoye	24 miles
17 November	Emi Toukoye – sand dunes	20 miles
18 November	sand dunes – Zoo Baba	20 miles
19 November	Zoo Baba – Tinga Tinga Rock	18 miles
20 November	Tinga Tinga Rock – Bilma	11 miles

21 November	Bilma	—
22 Novenber	Bilma	—
23 November	Bilma	—
24 November	Bilma – Dirkou	21 miles
25 November	Dirkou	—
26 November	Dirkou – Emi Tchouma	23 miles
27 November	Emi Tchouma – Doumba	12 miles
28 November	Doumba – Yegguba	25 miles
29 November	Yegguba – Pic Zoumi	24 miles
30 November	Pic Zoumi – Sequedine	7 miles
1 December	Sequedine – desert	22 miles
2 December	desert – Yat	12 miles
3 December	Yat – sand dunes	16 miles
4 December	sand dunes – desert	23 miles
5 December	desert – Mabrous Tefidinga	21 miles
6 December	Mabrous Tefidinga – desert	23 miles
7 December	desert	25 miles
8 December	desert – Madama (Niger border)	8 miles
9 December	Madama – Bariga	18 miles
10 December	Bariga – desert	22 miles
11 December	desert	15 miles
12 December	desert – Tummo (Libyan border)	9 miles
13 December	Tummo	—
14 December	Tummo – desert	25 miles
15 December	desert	22 miles
16 December	desert	20 miles
17 December	desert	24 miles
18 December	desert	16 miles
19 December	desert – Tejerri	18 miles
20 December	Tejerri – desert	17 miles
21 December	desert – Gatrun	8 miles
22 December	Gatrun	—
23 December	Gatrun	—
24 December	Gatrun	—
25 December	Gatrun	—
26 December	Gatrun – desert	10 miles
27 December	desert	2 miles
28 December	desert	—

29 December	desert	—
30 December	desert	22 miles
31 December	desert – Mestuta	16 miles
1 January 2002	Mestuta – sand dunes	20 miles
2 January	sand dunes – desert	17 miles
3 January	desert – Murzuk	7 miles
4 January	Murzuk – desert	18 miles
5 January	desert	18 miles
6 January	desert	16 miles
7 January	desert –Tekertiba	15 miles
8 January	Tekertiba – Lake Mandara	12 miles
9 January	Lake Mandara – Lake Gabron	15 miles
10 January	Lake Gabron – sand dunes	14 miles
11 January	sand dunes	15 miles
12 January	desert	19 miles
13 January	Wunserik	18 miles
14 January	Wunserik	—
15 January	Wunserik	—
16 January	Wunserik – desert	20 miles
17 January	desert	21 miles
18 January	desert – Hamada el Homra	16 miles
19 January	Hamada el Homra	17 miles
20 January	Hamada el Homra	18 miles
21 January	Hamada el Homra	19 miles
22 January	Hamada el Homra	18 miles
23 January	Hamada el Homra	22 miles
24 January	Hamada el Homra	15 miles
25 January	Hamada el Homra	17 miles
26 January	Hamada el Homra	15 miles
27 January	Hamada el Homra –Tabonia well	16 miles
28 January	Tabonia well – desert	23 miles
29 January	desert	19 miles
30 January	desert	18 miles
31 January	desert	19 miles
1 February	Misda	6 miles
TOTAL	**100 days**	**1,462 miles**

Bibliography

Abraham, R.C., *Dictionary of the Hausa Language*, University of London Press, London, 1946

Alexander, Boyd, *From the Niger to the Nile*, Volumes 1–2, Edward Arnold, London, 1907

Barth, Heinrich, *Travels and Discoveries in North and Central Africa*, Volumes 1–3, Harper and Brothers, NewYork, 1857

Bovill, EdwardWilliam, *Caravans of the Old Sahara: an introduction to the History of theWestern Sudan*, Oxford University Press, London, 1933

Bovill, Edward William, *The Golden Trade of the Moors*, Oxford University Press, Oxford, 1958

Bovill, EdwardWilliam, *Missions to the Niger*, Volume 2, The Hakluyt Society, Cambridge University Press, Cambridge, 1966

Cary, Joyce, *Mister Johnson*, Michael Joseph, London, 1939

Clapperton, Hugh, *Difficult and Dangerous Roads*, Sickle Moon Books & The Society for Libyan Studies, London, 2000

Denham, Dixon and Clapperton, Hugh, *Travels and Discoveries in North and Central Africa*, Volumes 1 and 2, John Murray, London, 1826

Hallam, W.K.R., *The Life and Times of Rabih Fadl Allah*, Arthur Stockwell, Ilfracombe, 1977

Hastings, A.C.G., *Nigerian Days*, John Lane, The Bodley Head, London, 1925

Illustrated London News, London, 20 January 1909

Leonard, Major Glyn, *The Camel, Its Uses and Management*, Longman Green, London, 1894

Parkinson, Dr Sonia, *HannsVischer, 1876–1945: a Literary Portrait*, Education

Research and Perspectives, Volume 25, Number 1, the University of Western Australia, June 1998

Przewalski (Prejevalsky), Colonel N., *From Kula Across the Tien Shan to Lob-Nur*, Sampson, Low, Marston, Searle, & Rivington, London, 1879

Segal, Ronald, *Islam's Black Slaves*, Atlantic Books, London, 2001

Seidensticker-Brikay, Gisela, *Hanns Vischer Expedition 1906*, Borno Museum Society, University of Maiduguri, Borno State, Nigeria, Newsletter 48 and 49 July–December, 2001

Taylor, F.W. and Webb, A.G.G., *Al'adun Hausawa*, Oxford Univerisity Press, London, 1932

Vischer, Hanns, *Across the Sahara*, Edward Arnold, London, 1907, Darf Publishers, London, 1995

Zhirnov, L.V. and Ilyinsky V.O., *The Great Gobi National Park – A Refuge for Rare Animals of the Central Asian Deserts*, Center for International Projects, Moscow, 1986

Index